The Ghosts of Modernity

Crosscurrents: Comparative Studies in European Literature and Philosophy
Edited by S. E. Gontarski

Improvisations on Michel Butor: Transformation of Writing, by Michel Butor; edited, annotated, and with an introduction by Lois Oppenheim; translated by Elinor S. Miller (1996).

The French New Autobiographies: Duras, Sarraute, Robbe-Grillet Rewriting History, Story, Gender, by Raylene L. Ramsay (1996).

The Ghosts of Modernity, by Jean-Michel Rabaté (1996).

THE GHOSTS OF MODERNITY

Jean-Michel Rabaté

UNIVERSITY PRESS OF FLORIDA

GAINESVILLE

TALLAHASSEE

TAMPA

BOCA RATON

PENSACOLA

ORLANDO

MIAMI

JACKSONVILLE

Copyright 1996 by the Board of Regents of the State of Florida
Printed in the United States of America on acid-free paper
All rights reserved

01 00 99 98 97 96   6 5 4 3 2 1

Library of Congress Cataloging-in-Publication Data
Rabaté, Jean-Michel, 1949-
The ghosts of modernity/Jean-Michel Rabaté.
p.   cm.—(Crosscurrents)
Includes index.
Contents: The master of colors that know—André Breton's ghostly stance—
Roland Barthes, ghostwriter of modernity—Mallarmé's crypts—Verlaine and
Mallarmé between the angels and the ghosts of languages—Modernity as crime
(Broch), or, The sleepwalking of theory—Beckett and the ghosts of departed
quantities—Shades of the color gray—Uncoupling modernism—Conclusion,
The "moderns" and their ghosts.
    ISBN 0-8130-1440-9
    1. Modernism (Literature). 2. Criticism. I. Title. II. Series: Crosscurrents
(Gainesville, Fla.).
PN56.M54R33   1996
809'.91—dc20   95-46064

The University Press of Florida is the scholarly publishing agency for the State
University System of Florida, comprised of Florida A & M University, Florida
Atlantic University, Florida International University, Florida State University,
University of Central Florida, University of Florida, University of North Florida,
University of South Florida, and University of West Florida.

University Press of Florida
15 Northwest 15th Street
Gainesville, FL 32611

Contents

Foreword

The Crosscurrents series is designed to foreground comparative studies in Europe art and thought, particularly the intersections of literature and philosophy, aesthetics and culture. Without abandoning traditional comparative methodology, the series is receptive to the latest currents in critical, comparative, and performative theory, especially that generated by the renewed intellectual energy in post-Marxist Europe. It will as well take full cognizance of the cultural and political realignments of what for the better part of the twentieth century have been two separated and isolated Europes.

While Western Europe is moving aggressively toward unification in the European Community, with the breakup of the last twentieth-century colonial empire and the collapse of communist hegemony — the former Soviet Union — Eastern Europe is subdividing into nationalistic and religious enclaves. The intellectual, cultural, and literary significance of such profound restructuring, how history will finally rewrite itself, is difficult to anticipate. Having had a fertile period of modernism snuffed out in an ideological coup not long after the 1917 revolution, the nations of the former Soviet bloc have, for instance, been denied (or spared) the age of Freud, most modernist experiments, and postmodern fragmentation. While Western Europe continues to reach beyond modernism, Eastern Europe may be struggling to reclaim it. Whether a new art can emerge in the absence — or from the absence — of such forces as shaped modernism is one of the intriguing questions of post–cold war aesthetics, philosophy, and critical theory.

In the *Ghosts of Modernity*, Jean-Michel Rabaté returns to and rereads the modernist enterprise through its own hauntings, "textual or historical specters that have not been properly laid to rest." Rabaté revisits those shapers of poetic high modernism, such as Eliot, Pound, and Mallarmé, in whom ghostings testify to the failure of mourning, which is an act of integration: "The main point I would like to make is that [Eliot and Pound] help us understand how modernism is 'haunted' by voices from the past and how this shows in an exemplary way the ineluctability of spectral returns. What returns is, in a classically Freudian fashion, what has not been processed, accommodated, incorporated into the self by mourning: the shadow of the lost object is still being projected onto the subject." What returns then in its spectral guise is history, and so through that shadowy return Rabaté rescues modernism from the charge "of a systematic repudiation of history." He argues that in the modernists' attempt to "make it new," the historical trace, what Frank Kermode in the *Sense of an Ending* has called a "complementarity with the past," persists. Although Rabaté invokes Harold Bloom's figure of "apophrades," the "'return of the dead' among the living," he finally moves beyond Bloom's paradigm of the "anxiety of influence": "I shall try to apply Freud's ideas to the study of literary texts by arguing that, if 'ghost' names some repressed material that could not be mourned, the mourning process cannot be reduced to an author's struggle with literary predecessors."

More apposite is Walter Benjamin's theory of "auras" in "The Work of Art in the Age of Mechanical Reproduction," which leads Rabaté from ghosts to colors. Since the "auras" of works of art generally appear in "a variety of colors, then there may be some point in linking the experience of aesthetic enjoyment, theories of color perception, and the generalization of the problematics of haunting." Amid the theory Rabaté offers a series of brilliant rereadings of Joyce, Barthes, Mallarmé, Breton, Beckett, and Broch, as well as Eliot and Pound. Rabaté's modernity is, as for Habermas, an "unfinished project": "Such modernity resists any attempt to supersede it or any effort to declare it obsolete, even if these efforts come from a so-called postmodernity."

S. E. Gontarski
Florida State University

Preface

We are come not only past the century's closing, he thought, the millenium's turning, but to the end of something else. Era? Paradigm? Everywhere, the signs of closure.
Modernity was ending.
Here, on the bridge, it long since had.

WILLIAM GIBSON, *Virtual Light*

When he reached the other side of the bridge, the ghosts came to meet him.

ANDRÉ BRETON, quoting the film *Nosferatu*

This book is something more than an English translation of a collection of essays already published in French.[1] The necessary revision required by any rewriting in a second language has forced me to stress a number of points differently and at times to change the focus completely. Thus, the first ghost I face when presenting the issue of a spectral modernity is the ghost of another book, whose distant and foreign voice mutters half-forgotten names. My strategy aims at combining psychoanalytical and philosophical concepts in order to reread the history of modernity. But this definition would miss an important element, for, to a certain degree, the concepts I use resist a straightforward logical or theoretical definition. They seem to lead toward a darker zone of criticism, an area in which theory is obliged to question its metalinguistic assumptions. By "theory" I mean, essentially, the combination of discourses borrowed from Blanchot, Lacan, Barthes, Derrida, Althusser, and Foucault, a string of names not chosen entirely at random, since one feature common to these French thinkers is that they have been snugly pigeonholed in the category of "poststructuralism" in Anglo-Saxon countries. A labeling that insists on the "pre-" or "post-" has often presupposed a history into which these thinkers have had to be forcibly integrated.

Indeed, the reproach often voiced against poststructuralism, of moral nihilism or alleged political indifference, is generally made in the name of a "return" to previous categories which these theories had sought to discard or eliminate completely. Poststructuralism presented itself in the early 1960s partly as an apocalyptic discourse heralding the death of various entities called "man," the "self," "subjectivity," the "author," the "novel," "grand historical narratives"— in brief, announcing the demise of any term that could be used to uphold a transcendental signified and could play the role of a center from which to exclude or marginalize alterity, a value that would dominate in a series of binary oppositions. The term "structure," which had served for a time to mount the radical criticism, was itself not immune to the forays of this generalized deconstruction, as Derrida has shown in a much publicized article.[2] What was attacked was the way any discourse could appear to be slyly duplicating a theological model even though its doctrine would outwardly claim to be "materialist" or "scientific." This critique radicalized a gesture initiated when Nietzsche had announced the death of God, when Heidegger started rereading the history of metaphysics from the point of its closure, or when Kojève's idiosyncratic and novelistic translation of the *Phenomenology of Spirit* had to postulate a concept of the "end of history" to make good contemporary sense of Hegelian speculative idealism.[3] In the wake of such wholesale acts of demolition, the "classical novel" defined by "readerly" realism had to be thrown overboard along with the full subject of idealist philosophy, and the new paradigm of writerly activity—the reader taking over the privileges that had been granted to the author in Barthes's famous essay[4]—seemed defined by *Finnegans Wake* more than, say, *War and Peace*, or found a more audible echo in Artaud's or Bataille's atheological writings than in romantic meditations on time and nature.

The oversimplifications such a picture no doubt contains are nevertheless useful in that they account for a growing resistance to theory in academic and literary circles, followed by a desire to return to categories such as agency, subjectivity (often rephrased, it is true, as intersubjectivity), or history. In the name of a heightened politicization of all discourses and practices, the return to a historically given "real" seemed to relegate poststructuralism and deconstruction to heady "textualism," to mere "theories" too far from urgent pragmatic issues defined by the intersection of race, class, and gender. It is my contention that the current trend advertising itself variously as a "return to history" or a "new pragmatism" should not blind itself, on the one hand, to the actual if perhaps never clearly limitable activity of reading (since reading has to deal with the illimitation of texts), or, on the other, to the fact that such a history has to be constructed as and by a discourse—a discourse that is inhabited by all the ghosts of displaced, discarded, or sublated ("abolished") prior concepts, by all the textual or historical specters that have not been properly laid to rest.

In fact, the very notion of a "return to"—as we have learned from Lacan's trumpeted "return to Freud," followed by Althusser's "return to Marx"—embodies the supplementary logic of the "ghost," creating at least two texts instead of one, linked together by a more cunning efficacy than that of an ostensibly direct and unmediated historical correspondence. Contemporary literary criticism often falls prey to a regressive urge that welcomes—with what joy and relief—the restoration of "full" meanings often in the name of a pre- or post-Bakhtinian "dialogic" intersubjectivity. Thus, political reductionism can begin meting out praise or denunciation based on the assumption that texts merely imitate a reality "out there," easily described and verified. The paradoxical consequence of the useful battle cry of "Always historicize!" associated with Jameson's intelligent neo-Marxism, has been an expansion of the field of textuality, the creation of a sort of historical hypertextuality that has collapsed the ancient division between "texts" and "documents."

We may say that it belongs to the general program of "modernity," defined in Habermas's sense as a "philosophical discourse," to attempt such an erasure of all ghostly doublings and returns. It will be useful to understand how Kant's criticism, which can be taken as paradigmatic of an enlightened modernity, implies or presupposes a refutation of ghosts and supernatural visions. However, the current return of the hitherto forbidden "transcendental signified" has branded modernism—in the restricted sense of Anglo-Saxon "high modernism"—as guilty of a systematic repudiation of history.

To counter or qualify this accusation, I would like to reexamine briefly Eliot's famous formulation of the "historical sense." In "Tradition and the Individual Talent," Eliot defines the "historical sense" as "a perception, not only of the pastness of the past, but of its presence,"[5] by which he manages to establish a synthesis between terms that had been opposed by Nietzsche in his second "Untimely Meditation" on history.[6] For Nietzsche, modern man is encumbered by a dusty historical lore that hides the intensity of the present moment. We must learn to forget and live in the present the way animals do, so as to be able to affirm "life" in all its vivacity. Paul de Man has shown the inconsistency of such a position, which he equates with "modernism," understood as a desire to be radically new, to erase all traces of secondarity.[7]

Eliot offers a concept that is probably fraught with dangers but which mediates between the antiquarian approach to historical knowledge and the juvenile romanticism of a lyrical poet who imagines that he can start from scratch.

Writing for someone who wants to contrive being a poet after age twenty-five, Eliot has to stress both the weight of the predecessors whose work will survive in the younger author ("the most individual parts of his works may be those in which the dead poets, his ancestors, assert their immortality most vigorously" [SW, 48]) and the added responsibility of the present writer, who will not only be influenced by the dead but also "influence" them ("what happens when a new work of art is created is something that happens simultaneously to all the works which preceded it" [SW, 49–50]). This is the logical consequence of Eliot's idea of an "ideal order" of all works of art, in which all the proportions, relations, and values are readjusted as soon as a new masterpiece is added. Thus, Joyce's *Ulysses* will actively modify Homer's *Odyssey* insofar as no one will read the *Odyssey* in the same way after Joyce has written his epic novel, precisely because it is a rewriting of the older epic. The double paradox generated by this situation is that not only can "the past be altered by the present" (SW, 50) but also the whole realm of literature is seen as a thanatomachia, in which dead authors struggle among themselves through the living and strongly assert their rights on those who know more than they did only because the dead "are that which we know" (SW, 52). In this sense, literature can be described as the working through of the figure of "apophrades," Harold Bloom's coining for the "return of the dead" among the living.[8]

In spite of their familiarity, I have quoted these passages because it is my belief that Eliot's theses continue to shape our most basic assumptions about literature and to determine our sense of the link between contemporary critical issues and an historical culture. We may indeed want to question the use of "ideal" in Eliot's concept of an "ideal order": it betrays the influence of a neo-Hegelian speculative spirit, yet hesitates between the disclosure of an objective *Geist*, hidden behind the idea that cultural "monuments" keep reordering themselves in an autonomous way, and a subjective or speculative reappropriation referring to the aspiring writer. We may wish to attack the simultaneity, unity, and hierarchy we must presuppose in order to imagine a single "order." We may attempt to extend Eliot's canon to see whether or not it will fall apart as soon as it covers not just the Western world but African myths, Confucian wisdom, and pre-Socratic philosophers—which was after all Pound's desire in his monumental synthesis of comparative literature. Eliot's concept nevertheless offers the only workable basis for a revisionist agenda. For, indeed, a revisionist agenda wishes not merely to add to the traditional canon new works from excluded eras or minority writers but aims more fundamentally at altering the values of the whole by the insertion of the new. Even if we become more aware of all the ideological, political, and economic determinations that create certain "values" at a given moment in a particular society, no description of the system constituted by literature as a global entity can avoid considering the relative place and importance of all authors, from Homer to Pynchon, from Sappho to Toni Morrison, from Confucius to Kenzaburo Oe.

Eliot's system nonetheless poses a great problem: how do the dead writers arrange themselves within the huge nebula formed by all their works? Do they fight, negotiate, or peacefully sleep? Harold Bloom thought he had found a solution by imagining that each new writer would have to struggle against an immediate predecessor whom he would then "kill," in a Freudian way, more often than not by misreading him. My use of masculine pronouns has already spelled out part of the problem: most of the poets examined by Bloom are male, and they keep castrating each other in a way that structurally excludes a female intervention, as Annette Kolodny has cogently argued.[9] The strictly patriarchal application of an oedipal pattern simplifies the issue of intertextuality by reconstructing imaginary filiations and lineages: Pound will thus directly beget Williams, as Stevens will indubitably beget Ashbery. The work of mourning is reduced to a sort of psychic wrestling match between males, erecting a series of paternal figures on a pedestal, most of whom can then be knocked down by cunning aggressors.

Bloom seems to posit a different sort of grandeur or sublimity in the case of "apophrades." With the figure of the "return of the dead," the secondary work's very openness to parallels and echoes from its predecessor appears to enact Eliot's paradox with a vengeance, since "the uncanny effect is that the new poem's achievement makes it seem to us, not as though the precursor were writing it, but as though the later poet himself has written the precursor's characteristic work" (*AI*, 16). Thus, in this trope it is as if all contemporary writers were so many Pierre Menards claiming authority over *Don Quixote*.[10] In fact, to the brilliance of the critic's mind and the ingenuity needed to implement such a reading program, we may prefer a more open network of intertextual relations while deploring the fact that Eliot's "ideal order" never allows for such duels between stronger and weaker writers. His choreography of the ghost dance performed among the dead is most confusing and confused, precisely because the dead can never die. The "ideality" of the order supposed by Eliot implies an automatic reshuffling of works whenever a new "monument" is produced, which would dispense with the series of dual agonistic relationships envisaged by Bloom.

We can conclude that mourning is nearly impossible in Eliot's order: the dead are always there and insist upon haunting the living. As Gerontion expresses it, thinking of a "knowledge" that encompasses all the dead writers we are forced to "know" even if we have never read them and of the perversity of a feminized and hystericized history: "After such knowledge, what forgiveness?"[11] The figure of the poet who would wish to continue writing after his twenty-fifth birthday will therefore be equivalent to that of Harry in the *Family Reunion*, a survivor "wounded in a war of phantoms" who will find peace only when he expiates a collective guilt and wanders in exile under the "judicial sun" of the desert.[12]

This is, after all, more or less the way we see Pound today, as a wounded and half-crazy survivor of a War against Usury in which, despite his anticapitalist heroism, he succumbed to the worst sirens. Pound's nemesis would be history. He who could reproach the dadaists and surrealists for their lack of historical sense had to survive himself, living as a silent witness within the inescapable testimony to the perverse nature of the values he had embraced. However, Pound's dramatic transformation into a living ghost in the 1960s had its roots in the very beginnings of his imagist poetics. Pound himself dated his birth as a truly modern poet from the moment he wrote the famous haiku-like "In a Station of the Metro," which I quote in its original version:

> The apparition   of these faces   in the crowd   :
> Petals   on a wet, black   bough   .[13]

The striking metaphor linking faces and petals blends the pastoral qualities of a Japanese spring with a glimpse of contemporary modernity. The Parisian subway provides an apt ground for this magical transformation, not devoid of mystical overtones (as "station" and "apparition" skillfully build an internal rhyme).

These elements constitute another irrevocable break or radical departure, when we consider Pound's inversion of the order of his first Cantos and his use of his translation from Homer's *Nekuia* to launch his odyssey not only in medias res but also *in medias animas ex Erebro cadaverum mortuorum* (to quote Andreas Divus's Latin translation of Odysseus's journey into the kingdom of the Dead).[14] Pound's gesture is typical of high modernism in that he shows how the new poet must duplicate the sacrificial rites by which the dead Tiresias will be able to show the way to Odysseus. The heroic return to Ithaca is made possible by another spectral return of the dead, accompanied by the even stranger apparition of a man who has just died, Elpenor. It is not enough for the hero to bring "blood for the ghosts"—a phrase that aptly describes Pound's and Divus's efforts as translators, both miming the rites "aforesaid by Circe"—and to fend off less important shades with a sword curiously wielded "to keep off the impetu-

ous impotent dead" (for there is a hierarchy even in hell); Odysseus has also to
be surprised by the return of one companion he thought still alive:

> . . . And I cried in hurried speech:
> "Elpenor, how art thou come to this dark coast?
> 'Cam'st thou afoot, outstripping seamen?'"[15]

Odysseus's misunderstanding adds something terribly funny to this unexpected
meeting in hell. The scene of general haste ("hurried speech") can have only
one equivalent among the dead: Tiresias asks, "A second time? why? man of ill
star," because Odysseus's unexpected arrival duplicates Elpenor's fate so precisely. He has just mistaken Odysseus for Elpenor, who has arrived almost at
the same time and thus becomes a comical figure, similar to Madame Sosostris,
the clairvoyante who has a bad cold in the *Waste Land*.

From the beginning, then, Odysseus appears not only as a precursor of Dante
touring the circles of hell but also as a strange hero who can be thought of as
having died twice. This is why Elpenor's injunction to Odysseus culminates in
a prayer for rites and memory that involves some writing:

> But thou, O King, I bid remember me, unwept, unburied,
> Heap up mine arms, be tomb by sea-bord, and inscribed:
> "*A man of no fortune, and with a name to come.*" (*Cantos*, 8)

Pound takes the liberty of adding the word "inscribed" when the Latin text
says only "*Sepulchrumque mihi accumulia cani litore maris*" (LE, 261). He also
adds the colon and the italics which turn the last line into a written quotation.
And by transforming the *fama* ("*viri infelicis, et cuius apud posteros fama sit*")
in Divus's Latin translation into the more ominous and vague term "name"—
he could have written "fame" if he did not want to use "reputation"—Pound
allows for his later identification with Elpenor's fate. If, in the first Canto,
Elpenor pays an elegiac homage to Gaudier-Brzeska, at the time of Pisa, Pound
depicts himself as an "unfortunate" No-man, closer to anonymity than to posthumous celebrity.

The interaction between live men and dead shades shows how a dead "writing" always already has been incorporated into the living act of (re)creation—
which corresponds to the effect of what Derrida has called "arche-writing."
The living hero's ruse, which makes him famous for being *polumetis* and
polumekhan, is being replaced by a mechanical cunning, the "polymechanics"
of writing. Writing deploys itself as an automatic apparatus linked with death
or the crossing of the boundaries separating life from death, in a plurality whose

excess counterbalances the suggested sterility of a purely technical reproduction. The encounter between living heroes (although they may actually be
dead) and ghosts or living dead provides the *Cantos* with a general pattern that
develops as a spiral of fugal returns and counterpointed motifs, according to
Pound's musical analogy with a fugue: "A. Live man goes down into world of
Dead. // B. The 'repeat in history.' // C. The 'magic moment' or moment of
metamorphosis."[16]

The idea of a repetition of what never took place triggers a series of spectral
associations. The poet gives voice to various ghosts or shades who write their
fate or fame through him. In the opening lines of the *Pisan Cantos*, when
Pound contemplates Mussolini's corpse, a dead leader identified with Dionysos,
the post-Nietzschean collapsing of "Dionysos or the Crucified" into one single,
composite, suffering body is suggested by the name "Diogenes," punned as
"digenes" or "digonos," meaning twice-born. Made up of such ghostly doublings,
Pound's mythical fascism provides a deeper insight into the nature of our
century's politics.

The two examples of Pound and Eliot could be developed at greater length.[17]
The main point I would like to make is that they help us understand how
modernism is systematically "haunted" by voices from the past and how this
shows in an exemplary way the ineluctability of spectral returns] What returns
is, in a classically Freudian fashion, what has not been processed, accommodated, incorporated into the self by mourning: the shadow of the lost object is
still being projected onto the subject. Modernism postulates both the necessity and the impossibility of mourning—and my contention is that this applies
not only to high modernism but also to a wider history that begins with the
Enlightenment, reaches its heights with Mallarmé, and finally informs the
history of postmodernity, from Beckett to contemporary writers such as Blanchot
and Derrida.

Freud's entire work could also be described as a meditation on mourning:
he places mourning at the origins of all thinking and sees in the "work of mourning" (*Trauerarbeit*) an equivalent to psychoanalysis itself. Freud also quotes
Homer's *Nekuia* in the second part of his "Thoughts for the Times on War and
Death," alluding to Achilles's famous praise of life: when Odysseus celebrates
the dead hero's fame, Achilles answers ruefully that one should not "speak
smoothly of death" and that he would prefer to live a lowly life on earth rather
than "reign sole king among the realm of the bodiless phantoms."[18] Freud also
refers to the theory previously developed in *Totem and Taboo* that, like "primitive" people, we still fear the possible revenge of the bloodthirsty souls of the
dead. The paradox he develops in this short wartime essay is that if, on the one

hand, we lose interest in life when a loved person has died, "dying" in some way with the other (like the Arabic people who "die-with" (*mitsterben*) when dear persons disappear), in a process that stems from the proximity of mourning to melancholy, then, on the other hand, we fear the return of the dead person as a stranger, an enemy, a foreign body ready to invade our soul.

This is why, according to Freud, literature is so useful: it enables us to "die" with a hero with whom we identify, thus fulfilling the principal unconscious fantasy that sees each of us as immortal. But in times of real and massive death, no fiction can avail: loss is overwhelmingly present and must be resolved by a theory. Philosophy has also attempted to solve the enigma. Freud complements it with his own concept of the ambivalence of affects in the face of death, which triggers intellectual *Forschung*, research, or investigation: "What released the spirit of inquiry in man was not the intellectual enigma, and not every death, but the conflict of feeling at the death of the loved yet alien and hated persons" (*SE*, 14:293).

The whole of psychology and indeed of rational thinking finds its source in love and hate of the dead, in compromise formations, symptomatic abreactions, and the outward projection of spirits, born out of the corpses of the dead loved ones. Thought both celebrates and mourns the destruction of the dead body, projecting its qualities into *Geister*—spirits—who embody the ambivalence we feel. Thus, mourning becomes an endless process by which we can learn to bear life by preparing ourselves to die: "*Si vis vitam, para mortem.*"[19]

I shall try to apply Freud's ideas to the study of literary texts by arguing that, if the "ghost" names some repressed material that could not be mourned, the mourning process cannot be reduced to an author's struggle with literary predecessors. The ghosts Dante sees in hell are real enough to hide historical figures, then endowed with symbolical or allegorical meanings; the "familiar compound ghost" Eliot meets in *Little Gidding* may well be made up of Yeats, Pound, and Dante; the ghost remains "both intimate and unidentifiable."[20] The specters I shall address here are both textual and personal. They emerge from an inner crypt well hidden within my chosen authors' works. They generally come from the authors' pasts, combining personal traumas, as in the case of Mallarmé's mourning for his dead son, Anatole, and sexual encounters, as with the strange attractors generated by the couplings and uncouplings of a few key modernist writers. I shall have recourse to the neo-Freudian concepts elaborated by Nicolas Abraham and Maria Torok who have jointly systematized a theory of the phantom as a transpersonal secret inscribing itself in a textual crypt.

In his influential "Notes on the Phantom: A Complement to Freud's

Metapsychology," Abraham demonstrates how the belief that the spirits of the dead return to haunt the living finds a direct equivalent in unconscious formations when a repressed secret somehow actualizes itself in symptoms produced by the following generation. The "phantom" cannot be reduced to the effect of an unsuccessful mourning since it migrates from one generation to another: "It is the children's or descendants' lot to objectify these buried tombs through diverse species of ghosts."[21] The phantom appears when the work of mourning has failed in the earlier generation, for it "bears witness to the existence of the dead buried within the other" (SK, 175). The phantom's nature is essentially linguistic, sustained as it is by "secreted words" that give rise to "endless repetitions," thus "eluding rationalization" (ibid). This phantom works like a ventriloquist within the subject's unconscious discourse and often stems from an unspeakable family secret. Thus, when Abraham creatively rereads Hamlet from the phantom's point of view, he supposes that the elder Hamlet had been guilty of a horrible murder and that Hamlet the son's hesitation in the face of his father's injunction comes from an unconscious awareness that his father is not such an idealized model as he wishes to believe.[22] This is how Abraham is able to add a last scene to the famous play! I shall try to show how a similar "cryptonymia" is at work in Mallarmé's endless deferral of the great "Book" and in Beckett's nihilistic humor.

In Abraham's and Torok's definition of the phantom, it is crucial that the concept should resist rationalization, both in the subjective sense of "having a theory" of, and in the philosophical sense of being "irrational." Even if everybody knows that ghosts, phantoms, and spirits belong to the realm of the irrational, their very locus must be described more precisely. In a sense, we might say that "modern" philosophy has always attempted to bury this irrational Other in some neat crypt, forgetting that it would thereby lead to further ghostly reapparitions.

Modernity, which for Habermas remains an "unfinished project" yet to be implemented, can be defined in the terms of Hegel's philosophy of history, Baudelaire's aesthetic theory, and finally Benjamin's theses on the philosophy of history. In a long and critical review, when Habermas surveys Heidegger, Bataille, Derrida, Foucault, and Lyotard, he criticizes them for rejecting the positive sides of the rationalist program known as Enlightenment.[23] I would like to throw a different light on the issue of modernity by examining briefly the text in which Kant criticizes Swedenborg for his "irrational" or pre-rational belief in spirits, and Schopenhauer's neo-Kantian rectification of this critique.

For Kant, who in 1766 published his Träume eines Geistersehers, erläutert durch die Träume der Metaphysik (literally, Dreams of a seer of spirits, explained through the dreams of metaphysics), the main illusion to destroy was that man consists of two substances, the body and the soul. Just as Eliot's essay on "Tradition" aimed at attacking the belief in "the metaphysical theory of the substantial unity of the soul" (SW, 56), Kant's critique refuses to believe that the soul, conceived as an immaterial entity, can continue to be perceived after death has separated it from the body. Kant demonstrates that the soul cannot have the properties of a body, that is to say, cannot move in space and be seen as a more or less translucent ectoplasm. This essay, one of the first "critical" statements of Kantian philosophy, fifteen years before the publication of the "First Critique," mounts an amusing and polemical attack against Swedenborg's visions in that it derides his credulity and his unfounded reputation.

Kant does not negate the existence of the soul, but rather that it could be subjected to the a priori conditions of perception in space and time. He begins his critical examination by saying that he does not even know what the word *Geist* means,[24] then accepts that man's soul be called *Geist*, only on the condition that it be located in all the parts of the body that it animates. When Kant summarizes Swedenborg's philosophy as the "ecstatic journey of an Enthusiast into the world of Spirits"[25] (in a debunking mode that seems to anticipate Marx's demolition of neo-Hegelian metaphysics in the *German Ideology*), he points to the difference between a metaphysical dream, defining in the process traditional metaphysics as nothing but a dream, and his own rational attempt at a strict delimitation between what can and what cannot be known, a move that entails a rigorous investigation of the conditions of possibility of knowledge.

When dealing with the "vision of spirits," Schopenhauer's starting point is different: he accepts the premises of Kantian philosophy but interprets the "thing in itself," which Kant had always left unknowable and undecidable, as the unconscious will underlying all aspects of life. He thus admits that if a spiritualist view of all these *Geister* is fallacious, an idealist conception may nonetheless be legitimated. Schopenhauer's "Essay on Spirit Seeing and Everything Connected Therewith" must be seen as a development of his major theses in his *World as Will and Representation*. In this essay, Schopenhauer grants factual weight to the lore of ghostly apparitions, spectral hallucinations, animal magnetism, and premonitory dream visions, all of which Kant had disqualified. Always intent upon going beyond the subject of representation to reach this universal will that is connected with the body, Schopenhauer examines the physiological evidence provided first by dreams, then by sleepwalking. He concludes that in these two states, the brain is capable of purely internal perceptions and speaks its own language.[26]

Schopenhauer quotes the English term "second sight," judging it a "second faculty of intuitive perception" that does not need the senses. This faculty, evinced by the "dream-organ," covers the whole range of intuitive knowledge. In the case of sleepwalking, Schopenhauer even goes so far as to admit some perception of reality without the intervention of actual vision: this he calls "sleepwaking" (*Schlafwachen*), which half-dreams and half-sees the truth of reality in a "*Wahrträumen*" (literally, a true dreaming or dreaming the truth).[27] The evidence of clairvoyance is discussed in anatomical terms and reinforced by the testimony of one of the author's servants, who had dreamed beforehand that she would scrub a floor that had just been stained by spilled ink (*ESS*, 254). Dreams and magnetism show how the body can become totally identical with the will at an unconscious level of perception, for which the usual categories of time and space do not apply. Thus, Schopenhauer admits of premonitory dreams and visions of the future: these somnambulistic prophetic soothsayings consist in freeing knowledge from its phenomenological limits.

Schopenhauer grants the "truth" of all these extrasensory phenomena but not their empirical "reality": the ghosts of departed persons are mental images, creations of the dream organ, and all the details provided by accounts of these visions confirm that they are not bodies or pseudo-bodies but internal impressions produced by the brain (*ESS*, 274). This explains why ghosts and specters are generally seen at night or in darkness: they are like a phosphorescence of the brain whose inner eye sees its proper objects and not external representations. This unconscious activity opens a new realm for investigation, an opening that Freud would take seriously, resisting only the idea that *will*, which defines the link between the thing-in-itself and man's inner being, lies outside the principle of individuation whereby individuals are separated (*ESS*, 303). Freud's translation of the will into libido or desire will in fact reestablish an uneasy cohabitation of materialism with metapsychological entities—such as the unconscious itself. Schopenhauer's idealist reconciliation of the world and the unconscious has the merit of philosophical consistency. By squarely admitting as philosophical objects that which a purely rationalist mind would term "hallucinations," he bridges the gap between bodily phenomena and a universal unconscious.

Schopenhauer's position represents a rare exception in philosophical discourse, and I shall show later how, from Spinoza to Marx, a constant distrust of irrational phenomena seems to haunt rationalist critiques and any discourse that is not ready to pay the price Schopenhauer had to pay, namely, the loss of the materiality of the "real world." When Hegel demonstrates that everything can be rational in the world because history is only the deployment in time of a *Geist* that has masterminded everything, is he not placing the entirety of the knowable under the domination of a ghostly—haunted and haunting, cunning and mystified—absolute reason? This is the point of Stirner's critique and of Marx's critique of Stirner in the *German Ideology*. Derrida has recently shown how Marx's materialism is itself haunted by a series of specters, from that of the revolution to that of a time that is "out of joint."[28]

Moreover, Derrida's essay on the Heideggerian *Geist*[29] also suggests that one way of avoiding the return of sinister specters, of being haunted by one type of "burning Spirit," will be by translating the concept into various languages or, in other words, to speak several languages simultaneously: no nationalist reappropriation will be possible because no single language will be allowed to present itself as the only path to the disclosure of truth. From the Greek *pneuma* or *psyche*, from the Hebrew *ruah*, all suggesting "breath" and "wind," to the Latin *spiritus* or the German *Geist*—a term that is never far, as Mallarmé and Beckett knew, from ghost on the one hand and *gaz* on the other hand (as we shall see in chapters 5 and 7), a whole prehistory of our spectral delusions remains possible, even urgent and necessary.

Can we speak of "ghosts" without transforming the whole word and ourselves, too, into phantoms? Such a question and the worry within it sustains the opening of Breton's *Nadja*, since it lies at the very heart of modernity. This question returns with a great acuity in Walter Benjamin's theory of history, a history that produces the loss of the "aura" and the increasing mechanization of all art forms.[30] For Benjamin's concept of "aura" to retain validity, it cannot avoid its religious or mystical connotations. For "aura" is both presence *and* distance, distance in presence, the uniqueness less of an object than of a privileged moment giving access to the object's essence—its "epiphany," as Joyce would have said. But the "epiphany," like the "aura," sends us back to the trauma of disappearance more than to the halo circling a figure in its "full" apparition. In other words, the "aura" functions like the halo of a trace that manages to survive through history. A neo-Marxist program analyzing the commodification of all art productions could hardly accommodate an investigation of "auratic fields"; yet if we accept the theosophic definition of the "aura" as an "electromagnetic field surrounding the human body," generally appearing in a variety of colors, then there may be some point in linking the experience of aesthetic enjoyment, theories of color perception, and the generalization of the problematics of haunting. Consequently, the concept of aesthetic experience presupposed by both Joyce and Benjamin falls into the category of haunting, which is produced less by the loss of an object than by the awareness that it was always, in its ravishing uniqueness, destined to have been lost.

I shall try to follow some of the ramifications of such ghostly tensions and shall often have to pun on "specters" and "spectrum" in order to deal with this frail, fading, fragile quality of the half-visible ghost. Mallarmé, Freud, Barthes, and Breton will be the first guides who will teach us to see the colors of the whole "spectrum." Or, to expand the image, their writings help us see the world in all its "spectral emanations"—a term I borrow from a poem by John Hollander. I shall quote a passage from his poem entitled "Yellow," in which one submerged pun relates "mourning" with "morning," so as to conclude on a brighter note an all too long preface:

> And all that matters in the end
> Is of the moment of late, fine morning
> When the world's yellow is of burning sands
> Leading down to the penultimate blue
> Of, say, the Ionian Sea whose waves
> Gave light that had to have been their own[31]

"The Penultimate ... is dead"

It was probably Roland Barthes who most accurately and honestly evoked the sense of doubt and apprehension an individual may experience on occasion when confronting the musical, artistic, or literary productions of our contemporary avant-garde. In his journal he relates how he forces himself to read current novels and see new art works, out of a sense of purely professional obligation, then returns with real delight to pieces by Schubert and Schumann, or to his familiar frequent reading of the works of Chateaubriand and Proust. When Barthes surprisingly describes Chateaubriand's *Memoirs* as his "one and only book," he adds: "Always this thought: what if the Moderns were wrong? If they had no talent?"[1] Even while lavishing praise on experimental writers and promoting artistic pioneers of his time (praising Robbe-Grillet in the sixties and Sollers in the seventies), Barthes admits to a lifelong fascination with Michelet and Balzac. Proust's masterpiece remained the sole model he envisaged for the forthcoming autobiographical novel he kept announcing until his death.

This uneasiness about the real "talent" or worth of the "moderns" can serve as a starting point for an investigation into the value and value systems of what is often called in a broad way modernism or postmodernism. What seems telling in this respect is the fact that Barthes's interrogation only evolves in the space of his private diary or of pages that he knows will be published posthumously. The positioning of an eschatological truth beyond the grave is needed to articulate the real questions of value and enjoyment. In the same vein, Chateaubriand could present his *Memoirs* (*Mémoires d'outre-tombe*, that is, from beyond the grave) as a posthumous tribunal that would preside over his past life and a whole century: "I have been urged to publish portions of these Memoirs during my life; I prefer to speak from the depths of my grave: my narrative will then be accompanied by those voices which are in a measure consecrated, because they issue from the tomb."[2] Such is the curious figure I would like to offer as being allegorical of our postmodernity: an author writing from the grave who imagines himself correcting his own proofs in a surreal afterlife:

These Memoirs have been the object of my predilection. St. Bonaventure obtained from Heaven permission to continue his after death; I hope for no such favour, but I would wish to rise at the ghostly hour at least to correct the proofs. However, when Eternity shall have with its two hands stopped my ears, in the dusty family of the deaf, I shall hear nobody. (*Memoirs*, 1:xxx)

Chateaubriand's presence is not incongruous here, for aside from his masterful use of rhetoric he is often invoked for having coined the term *modernité*, although in a negative sense, when he employs it in the same *Memoirs* to describe an ugly building.[3] Chateaubriand narrates his voyage from Paris to Prague in 1833, where Charles X lived in exile. He arrives at the Würtemberg border and opposes in a rather romantic fashion the grandeur of nature to the ugliness of a customhouse: "The vulgarity, the modernity of the custom-house and the passport formed a contrast with the storm, the Gothic gate, the sound of the horn and the noise of the torrent" (*Memoirs*, 5:330). There is nothing surprising here in view of Chateaubriand's alleged cult of the past. A few pages later, however, a different customhouse situated in Bohemia, only fifty miles from Prague, serves as a setting for a different scene of distress. There, the validity of his passport is questioned, and Chateaubriand has to retrace his steps and wait for additional official letters. The forced stay in Waldmünchen allows for an outburst of descriptive frenzy; Chateaubriand depicts his room in detail, not forgetting the hue of the fillets adorning the ceiling or the framed engravings, and, obviously satisfied with himself, he adds with a hint of irony: "I describe, for the benefit of travelers, the excellent room in which I am writing this inventory. . . . This page of my Memoirs will give pleasure to the modern literary school" (*Memoirs*, 345).

The "modern" mode, no longer identified with ugliness, results from a mimetic superposition of the act of writing and the context of that act. The stylistic exercise that seems to announce the experimental fiction launched by the "Nouveau Roman" a century later is nevertheless dedicated to Chateaubriand's "grandnephews" while declaring itself to be a parodic imitation of August Lafontaine's descriptive novels, which provided the Biedermeyer atmosphere with its real cachet. Since the descriptive passage must come to an end after having exhausted the intricacies of an almost bare and empty room, Chateaubriand proceeds to recount his walks in the village and his observations of the peasants' daily routines. The tone then becomes mock-epic, for he views himself as a modern Odysseus:

I perceive, in fact, that this part of my Memoirs is nothing less than an Odyssey: Waldmünchen is Ithaca; the shepherd is the faithful Eumaeus with his

swine; I am the son of Laertes, returning after wandering on land and sea. I
should, perhaps, have done better to intoxicate myself with the nectar of
Evanthes, to eat the flower of the moly-plant, to linger in the land of the
Lotus-eaters, to remain with Circe, or to obey the song of the Syrens saying:
"Approach, come to us!" (*Memoirs*, 347)

Most of these allusions will be familiar to readers of *Ulysses,* and we can see
how these few pages seem to presage those modes of writing between which
most twentieth-century writers have hesitated: a "mythical method" that T. S.
Eliot saw as Joyce's crucial scientific discovery, and the neutral and scientific
tone of a bland inventory, a mere list of a world of things.

At a midpoint between these two extremes, there stands a writer who is also
a public figure engaged in the recuperation of past values, intent upon paying
homage to the "real king" of France while feeling acutely that history has chosen other alternatives. From such a vantage point, Chateaubriand can appear
both as denigrating the "modernity" of the present—a present summoned by a
few customhouses that institutionalize its degradation—and extolling a modernity to come, which will be bequeathed to selected literary and familial
heirs.

Thus, in order to go beyond the limitations of a purely philological investigation into the uses of "modern" and "modernism," I wish to conjure up the
figure of a ghostly writer who imagines himself posthumous so as to mediate
between his past and future and to judge the present. The writers I examine in
the following essays—Joyce, Barthes, Mallarmé, Breton, Beckett, and Broch—
should, in connection with this historical problematic, serve to map in this
way the dim contours of a haunted modernity revisited by "spectrographic"
analysis, a modernity that is by definition never contemporaneous with itself,
since it constantly projects, anticipates, and returns to mythical origins, but
that also teaches us more about the "present," which it historicizes. As we will
see, such a modernity resists any attempt to supersede it and any effort to declare it obsolete, even if these efforts come from a so-called postmodernity.

These essays are united by a common theme or perhaps by a variation around
one central metaphor: the transformation of the writer into a specter, because
his own past returns whenever he imagines that he can predict, arrange, or
control the future. In most recently produced histories of the concept of modernity,[4] the return of the past is too often overlooked because the declaration
of the "new" is taken at face value. If indeed the main thrust of high modernism—as launched by Yeats, Hulme, Wyndham Lewis, Pound, and Eliot in the
frantic London years just before World War I—has been to link the wish to

"make it new" with an awareness of the primitive nature of ritual, then their
√modernity can no more escape the return of the repressed than preempt its
unforeseeable effects.

Although these essays sketch a symptomatic history of modernity, they are
not arranged in strict chronological order, but articulate a thematic link between aesthetics (with a survey of broad genres such as modernism, postmodernism, surrealism, and Hegelianism in the discourse of the avant-garde) and
ethics, if by this term one agrees to place, on the one hand, art's social and
political relevance and, on the other, the tension I wish to introduce between
the cult of forms and that sense of loss or mourning that I see as crucial to an
understanding of modernity.

In this respect, the two great inventors are Rimbaud and Mallarmé, because both exemplify the fascination for a lost object that they see as constitutive of their writing. Joyce and Beckett then amplify this concern in two widely
divergent ways, so that I shall need to look for a general theoretical problema-
tization when the issue of the belief in ghosts develops into a questioning of
rationality itself. Marx's criticism of ideology had been anticipated by Spinoza's
prudence and irony, but their belief in rationality nevertheless needs to be
complemented by a meditation on loss such as can be found in Freud's considerations on mourning. The first "object" I adopt as a pretext for such a spectrography of Joyce and Freud's works is "color," a strategic object because its
very universality leads to an analysis of the unpresentable or the unthinkable.
The lost object has to be mourned, for otherwise it reappears as a ghost; these
considerations find their logical conclusion in the suggestion of an "ethics of
mourning" whereby the eternal repetition of the same could be overcome.

I have referred to Mallarmé as the champion of a haunted modernity not
only because several of his early poems revolve around the problematics of
haunting ("I am haunted"),[5] but also because he paves the way, through rever-
ent references to Baudelaire and Poe, to subsequent avant-gardists when he
pictures himself balancing between the futility of everyday life and an absolute that takes several names: the azure, the ideal, the "Book," or even the
complex interaction between poet and crowd in the ceremony of the great
"Book"'s serial recitals.[6] To haunt signifies to "frequent" a place, to inhabit
it frequently, but to do so in the mode of an obsessive absence, of nameless
remorse, and the haunted poet struggles against the commonplaces of a "quotidian" that appears all the more evanescent as it expects the return of the
anguishing spirit. As we shall see, this spirit cannot be reduced to the absence
of God nor to a Hegelian idea—both more powerful since the time of their

disappearance—but takes on a poignant quality when it is embodied by the poet's dead son, Anatole.

This is why Mallarmé's work can also herald a postmodernism that predates the birth of modernism, in keeping with Lyotard's thesis that the postmodern occurs before rather than after the "mode" of the modern.[7] His literary career begins under the sign of derision and parody when he single-handedly writes the women's magazine the *Latest Fashion* or *La Dernière Mode*, whose title already suggests the inversion of "post" and "modo" on which Lyotard's paradox is based. In Mallarmé's famous letter to Paul Verlaine where he reviews his own intellectual development, he stresses the opposition between the absolute and unique great "Book" (*Le "Livre"*) and the rest of his literary endeavors: "What work? It is hard to explain. I mean a book, simply; a book in many volumes; a book which *is* a book, architectural and premeditated, and not a miscellany of chance inspirations, however marvelous they may be. I will even go further and say: the Book, for I am convinced that there is only One, and that it has been attempted by every writer, even by Geniuses."[8] But he explains that in 1874–75, having despaired of composing the "Book" ("At one time, though, I did give up in desperation on that tyrannical book of my dreams; and after I had peddled a few articles here and there, I tried to get out a review by myself called *The Latest Fashion*, and write about dresses, jewels, furniture, even theater programs and dinner menus"),[9] he had written under several female pseudonyms this collection of articles on fashion, jewelry, upholstery, food, entertainment, and education. Written as a systematic exercise in futility for want of the absolute and despotic great "Book," these pages continue to sustain their author's fantasies and dreams. I have developed elsewhere the idea that Mallarmé's *Latest Fashion* exemplifies precisely Lyotard's notion of a postmodernism that precedes actual modernity.[10] The glossy magazine, full of illustrations of vapid and iridescent prose, is a hymn to trinkets, *bibelots* meant to tinkle gaily in the void; thus, as I shall demonstrate in chapter 6, the insight into sheen covering a fundamental nihilism would be as relevant for Mallarmé's Paris as it is for Hermann Broch's Vienna.

Yet we cannot apply the same moral or political diagnosis to both types of writing, since with Mallarmé everything takes "place" in the suspension introduced by language. For him, the word never aims at designation but at evocation, suggesting a false presence while the thing and even the world are bracketed off. An early formula describes this phenomenon in temporal terms with the word "penultimate." Let me quote from Mallarmé's relatively well-known prose poem, "The Demon of Analogy":

I left my apartment with the particular feeling of a wing, gliding over the strings of an instrument, languid and light, which was replaced by a voice pronouncing with a descending intonation the words: "The Penultimate is dead," so that

The Penultimate

ended the line and

Is dead

detached itself from the fateful suspension more uselessly in the void of meaning. I took some steps in the street and recognized in the sound *nul* the taut string of the musical instrument which had been forgotten and which glorious Memory had certainly just touched with its wing or a palm branch and, my finger on the mystery's artifice, I smiled and implored a different speculation with intellectual wishes. The phrase, virtual, released from a previous fall of a feather or a branch came back henceforth heard through the voice, until finally it articulated itself alone, living through its own personality (no longer satisfied with a perception), reading it at the end of a line of verse, and, once, as though testing it, adapting it to my speech; soon pronouncing it with a silence after "Penultimate" in which I found a painful pleasure: "The Penultimate" then the instrument's string, so stretched in forgetfulness over the sound *nul*, probably broke and I added in the style of a prayer: "Is dead."[11]

This text describes a peculiar type of aural obsession and links it with the reasons that may push an individual to write. Poetry, or indeed literature allied with music, holds in reserve this great stock of phrases one is free to quote or let resound silently within oneself. When they "return" in hallucinatory fashion, as a sentence heard in a waking dream, these phrases come back as so many refrains that together constitute an aural horizon. Here this horizon is blurred and mysterious by the detour of a chance encounter with a meaningless sentence—"The Penultimate is dead": one comes into contact with the mystery itself which opens onto a scene of death and mourning.

The French term is in the feminine (*la pénultième*): first interpreted as a banal symptom of intolerance to the "remains of linguistic labors," the word evokes the ordinary drudgery Mallarmé knew as an English teacher in a French high school (as he writes in the prose poem: "on account of which my noble poetic faculty daily weeps to be broken off"). Indeed, the word "penultimate" is generally used in the context of the rules of stress distribution in English, rules that have to be conveyed to deaf French ears, but here, this inexplicable penultimate somehow evokes the sense of mourning for a deceased woman, the most poetic of subjects according to Poe's poetic principle.[12] We are not too far from the protruding "horny feet" of a female corpse laid down on a kitchen table as if to bemoan nature's demise:

> If her horny feet protrude, they come
> To show how cold she is, and dumb.
> Let the lamp affix its beam.
> The only emperor is the emperor of ice-cream.[13]

The submerged pathos culminates in a renewed expression of condolence when the narrator describes himself walking and murmuring, "The Penultimate is dead, she [is] dead, dead indeed, the desperate Penultimate," in an effort to "bury it in the chant's amplification." But this attempt fails because of the very nature of this auditory hallucination; heard again, the stubborn repetition testifies to an afterlife: "When, horror!—by an easily deductible and nervous magic—I felt that I had, my hands being reflected by a shop window there making the gesture of a caress coming down on something, the very voice (the first, which had undoubtedly been the only one)" (MPP, 7). As Robert Greer Cohn writes in his excellent commentary, this text owes a lot to Poe not only because it exposes a "mystery" (which, uncharacteristically, remains open and unsolved) but also because the tone betrays an agitation that the assumed rationalizing discourse cannot hide, as in so many of Poe's masterful tales in which the narrator slowly exposes his madness. There is no real lunacy here, however, but a deep anxiety that starts from purely linguistic considerations and centers around the root of *nul*, a "nul" that confirms the promise of general annulment. Thus, after the return of the *only one* and same voice fails to bring any relief to the narrator, the piece has to conclude with an interminable labor of mourning for an undefinable object:

> But the moment at which the irrefutable intervention of the supernatural sets in, and the beginning of the anguish, under which my mind, not long ago lord and master, agonizes, that was when I saw, raising my eyes, in the street of the antique dealers which I had instinctively taken, that I was in front of a lute maker's shop, a vendor of old musical instruments hung on the wall, and, on the ground, some yellow palms and ancient birds, their wings hidden in shadow. I fled, a queer person probably condemned to wear mourning for the inexplicable Penultimate. (7)

The multiplication of levels remains tantalizing, yet does not offer a real clue; the visual realm duplicates the aural hallucination, offers a glimpse of instruments that may or may not have produced the fatal sound of broken strings. The narrator flees from an all too real emblem, a blazon of his fears allegorized in the shop's walls and floor. His mounting anxiety also comes from the fact that the sentence he hears contains in itself the principle of its disappearance: if one listens to *nul* in *pénultième*, one cannot miss the placement of this annulling instance in the penultimate syllable (provided that *tième* is pronounced in one vocal utterance, without the dieresis always possible in French). This is why the narrator has to explain how the string breaks precisely on *nul*, since the "string is so stretched in forgetfulness"; the syllable *tième* is thus the "ultimate" that spells out the death confirmed by the poet's own conclusion: "Is dead."

In that fateful syllable, the overly taut string of an unconscious lamentation is revealed to consciousness as it snaps. Such a break, or discordant chord, contains in nucleo the entire Mallarméan machinery of abolition and quasi-Hegelian *Aufhebung* that I shall attempt to describe in chapter 4. The mourning scene presided over by a "demon of analogy," which recalls Poe's "Imp of the Perverse" (translated by Baudelaire as *"Démon de la Perversité"*), gives rise to a system of analogies without a referent, deprived of any object other than the universe of poetic correspondences as their horizon. The analogies are apparently apprehended linguistically and musically before being rationalized into a consistent explanatory whole. The lack of an object is strategic, for it allows a constant return of the haunting phrase by which the subject is both shaken out of the banal everyday world and rendered capable of hearing himself express his suffering on a strange vocal "lute." However, this lute still bequeaths the technical power to write, since the "pen" (*plume*) silently inhabits the letters of *PénULtièME*—or, in English, one might say that the pen gives the key or the cue to the penultimate.

The writing and surviving subject becomes a "penultimate," less a center of consciousness than a decentered agency of writing, never quite able to stress either primarity or secondarity, never either the first or the last, but always waiting for a repetition of the almost same. Joyce provides a more cynical and relaxed version of this secondarity or sequentiality when he describes how Leopold Bloom could have smiled when he entered a bed in which, just a few hours before, his now sleeping wife Molly had entertained her lover, Boylan:

If he had smiled why would he have smiled?

To reflect that each one who enters imagines himself to be the first to enter whereas he is always the last term of a preceding series even if the first term of a succeeding one, each imagining himself to be first, last, only and alone whereas he is neither first nor last nor only nor alone in a series originating in and repeated to infinity.[14]

This excellent example of that "objective humor," so dear to Hegel and Breton alike, displaces the anxiety of a solitary consciousness toward the cosmic laughter of interstellar spaces. Infinity figures as the last remedy against the angst of early belatedness so typical of a postmodern sensibility.

Joyce and Mallarmé occupy two opposed poles in the refraction of Hegelian aesthetics, Mallarmé on the side of a poetic impossibility, Joyce on the side of a prosaic admission of dissatisfaction. It would be tempting to elaborate upon the libidinal structures underlying these positions, Mallarmé being closer to an obsessional pattern, while Joyce appears closer to the hysteric mode, if we could apply Jacques Lacan's all too neat distinction.[15] Joyce, however, had the advantage of a superior belatedness, as it were, and could benefit from the controversy between two of the thinkers who aided him in the construction of an aesthetics—an aesthetics that owes a lot to Mallarmé in the first place.[16]

Joyce's earliest program was probably due to the influence of Henrik Ibsen: like the Norwegian master, Joyce was able to mediate subtly between naturalism and symbolism, while retaining a distinctive sense of being haunted by something that resisted language. Such a program might be described as Anglo-Irish translations of Ibsen's major plays, *Ghosts* and *When We Dead Awaken*. They could evoke Joyce's trajectory, from the early naturalism of *Dubliners*, so attentive to the proliferation of symptoms of death and paralysis, to the linguistic and metahistorical allegorism of *Finnegans Wake*. In between, *Ulysses* would figure as a Dublinized *Peer Gynt*, as Joyce once suggested. Joyce felt the need to ground his theory of literature not only in Aristotelian poetics but also in the work of more contemporary thinkers whose debt he never acknowledged, using for instance Bernard Bosanquet's neo-Hegelian aesthetics to move from Aquinas to Hegel, then to Vico and Croce. Benedetto Croce, the Italian philosopher who was most instrumental in restoring Giambattista Vico to his proper place on the map of modern culture, will serve as a rather unexpected link between Joyce and Breton, especially when Croce replies to Bosanquet on the question of the end of history.[17]

Croce radically questions the Hegelian postulate of the overcoming of art by philosophy and links this with a refusal to accept the concept of the "end of history" in which neo-Hegelians such as Alexandre Kojève and Francis Fukuyama thought they had found the cornerstone of Hegelian phenomenology.[18] Implicitly identifying the *Geist* with a ghost, Croce repudiates "what is dead" in Hegel's system in order to assert his belief in art's positivity and endless creativity.

André Breton will in his turn embrace an art that can integrate a positive infinity, thanks to its close connection with the unconscious and an erotics of language. Although less haunted by the pure idea than Mallarmé, and refusing the domination of a ghostly philosophy that arrives at dusk like the owl of Minerva and asserts its rights over everything in sight, Breton nevertheless chooses to see art and himself as haunted, because he wishes, in the wake of Rimbaud, to perceive life as directly visited by real or imaginary phantoms. These half-real, half-imaginary figures will contribute toward drawing language out of the circle of reflexivity and self-referentiality, opening it to otherness and exteriority. Just as Baudelaire saw in Paris a city teeming with specters ("Ant-seething city, city full of dreams, / Where ghosts by daylight tug the passer's sleeve"),[19] in the same way, Eliot can hail a certain Stetson—a specter who has just returned from the battle of Mylae to wander in the streets—in the London City, and Breton can make out famous historical characters under the disguise of bistro patrons or find in the half-crazed Nadja, who hallucinates a mystical network of coincidences, his muse of love and poetry.

Of all who have believed in the possibility of a total work of art that would not be subsumed by philosophy but would constitute the equivalent of the Hegelian spiral tending toward absolute knowledge, all who have forged these huge synthetic masterpieces, Proust, Joyce, and Broch have acted upon the belief in the possibility of a radical overcoming: Proust and Joyce do indeed write "novels to end all novels," just as the Great War was supposed to be a war to end all wars—a prediction that history would quickly contradict. Hence neither Proust nor Joyce nor even Broch see themselves as "modernists"; the closest they can get to such a historicized periodization is to call themselves "modern."

Joyce repeatedly stressed the link between Proust's efforts and his own, despite a certain reluctance to deal with the complexities of the social world depicted in the *Recherche*. In several talks with Arthur Power, Joyce spoke of Proust and himself as modern writers opposed to the romantics of the previous century.[20] The only "modernism" in whose cause Joyce could have enlisted himself would have been that of the Catholic rebels who, at the end of the nineteenth century, fought against the Church's antiquated values. This controversy over science and faith finally gave birth to neo-Thomism as the Catholic Church's official philosophy. For Joyce, therefore, a Hegelian Aquinas could be taken as the true arch-postmodernist philosopher, much more than Nietzsche or Freud, both of whom he felt had been anticipated by Bruno and Vico.

As for Proust, the fact that he cannot allow himself to be reduced to the category of modernism can be proved from a reading of *Time Regained*, the last part of *Remembrance of Things Past*. Proust decided to include the Great War in his work at a very late stage, and this entailed substantial modifications and readjustments: he wanted to place Combray on the frontline and therefore moved the location of the village from Normandy to northern France. Among these revisions, we find the introduction of the term "modernism" in two rather derogatory contexts. Linking literary critics and war strategists in a denunciation of modern follies, Charles says: "And this time, to make things worse, the public, after resisting the modernists of literature or art, is falling into line with the modernists of war"[21]—thus betraying his pro-German and passeist views that are, nevertheless, more profound than those of Cottard turned official journalist. Meanwhile, Saint Loup's experience of the front confirms the idea that war is fundamentally Hegelian in nature ("War," he wrote, "does not escape the laws of our friend Hegel. It is in a state of perpetual becoming" [*TR*, 774]), but this implies a general inversion or perversion of values.

In the same way, Bloch praises Rachel's "modernistic diction" (*TR*, 236) as she triumphs over the Berma—but this only stresses how the apotheosis of false values after the war transformed all social relations and brought down all noble individuals. Through these characters, Proust criticizes a purely historical or sycophantic modernism in the name of the material inscription of truth identified with a certain type of writing. The danger always lies in the many reasons one can find to defer or postpone the task, simply because one refuses to listen to one's instinct, an instinct that finally writes in minds as in a book: "This book, more laborious to decipher than any other, is also the only one which has been dictated to us by reality, the only one of which the 'impression' has been printed in us by reality itself" (*TR*, 139).

In moments of great optimism, as when he meditates on the curious thrill he experiences in reminiscing the past, the narrator may feel "freed from the order of time" and therefore liberated from any anxiety of death: "Situated outside time, why should he fear the future?" (*TR*, 134). But the order of time still encroaches upon the vocation of the budding writer; the book yet to be written by the narrator feeds on the social life and countless dinners, receptions, conversations that defer its redaction. The moment of exposure comes at the close of the Guermantes's afternoon reception, when he suddenly realizes that all the protagonists of his book in the making are actual ghosts and that time has transformed a dinner party into a spectral dance. The narrator's greeting of old friends is twice compared to Odysseus's descent into hell, more precisely to the moment when Odysseus tries to embrace his mother without holding anything more than thin air. If each guest seems to have painted his or her face in order to maintain a mere illusion of life, the allegorical embodiment of the "ravages of time" brings about a discovery that, among other things, ✓ reinforces the rejection of a modernism that would abolish the past. The subsequent decision to opt for a strategic retreat out of the social world seems to confirm the pregnancy of the submerged pun on the name of those who stand for the social values in their rapid metamorphosis, the Guermantes, who homophonically suggest that *les guerres mentent* (wars are a lie).

In the face of such a social and political lie, the temptation of a radical revolt would seem a happy antidote; but André Breton was soon to discover another lie, or another danger in the model of the tabula rasa. One way he found out of the trap of pure dadaist destruction was to discover precursors and kindred spirits and to draw up the long list of all the neo- or para-surrealists. Like Eliot in his efforts to radically rethink "tradition," Breton and the surrealists produced the interesting concept of a "tradition of the new." Breton thus takes up the torch of symbolism, thanks to Paul Valéry, and yet manages to blend poetic lyricism with social and political concerns. From a very different vantage point, as I shall try to show in chapter 9, Eliot and Pound were doing the same thing during the 1920s.

My starting point in this investigation of some major modernist ghosts is color but could just as well have been any type of perception or sensation, provided it lead to that act of reminiscence that abolishes time. Again, let me quote Proust quoting Chateaubriand's *Memoirs* in connection with the world of analogies that open the door to a pure "time regained." Chateaubriand has just noticed a scent of heliotrope coming from a batch of beans, which reminds him of his American travels: "In this perfume, not breathed by beauty, not cleansed in her bosom, not scattered where she had walked, in this perfume of a changed sky and tillage and world there was all the diverse melancholy and regret and absence and youth" (*TR*, 959).

Proust lists Chateaubriand, Baudelaire, and Gérard de Nerval as having preceded him in the route toward the full power of analogies. He could, of course, have mentioned Mallarmé or Poe. In the economy of the *Recherche*, it is clear that if one character embodies the principle of demonic analogy and of the penultimate, it is Albertine, who reappears as a ghost to haunt the narrator in the last pages of *Time Regained*. Albertine is at once dead and alive (an untranslated sentence reinserted in new editions at the penultimate page reads:

"Deep Albertine whom I could see sleeping and who was dead"). The narrator who describes himself as Scheherazade, telling his endless stories in the expectation of an imminent death, nevertheless feels jealous of a beauty that forgetfulness cannot erase, precisely because an untimely demise has prevented the cruel work of destruction that all the ghostly guests of the Guermantes had evinced:

> And it is because they contain thus between themselves the hours of the past
> that human bodies have the power to hurt so terribly those who love them,
> because they contain the memories of so many joys and desires already for
> them, who are loved, half effaced but still cruel for the lover who contem-
> plates and prolongs in the dimension of Time the beloved body of which he
> is jealous, so jealous that he may even wish for its destruction. (TR, 1106)

The ghost of Albertine survives as a perfume, a color, a birdsong, endlessly present and absent, the penultimate trace of a writing that is full of pain but ineluctably haunting and haunted.

The different writers analyzed in these pages perceive the agony of this position, and most of them posit an "ethics of mourning" identical with an acceptance of loss in order to go beyond mere repetition. A "successful" mourning is generally thought to lead to incorporation, which merely reproduces another transpersonal and translinguistic "phantom," as Abraham and Torok have argued. What occurs when mourning generates another text? Such a combination of haunting and mourning is difficult to imagine, but it could resemble the state Dante describes in canto 30 of the *Inferno* when he shows how his namesake as a character of the *Commedia* feels shame in front of Virgil. Virgil says that Dante the character, by showing his shame openly, has already excused himself, and Dante the poet compares this complex stance with the experience of waking up during a nightmare:

> Qual è colui che suo dannaggio sogna,
> che sognando desidera sognare,
> si che quel ch'è, comme fosse, agogna. (30:136–38)

> [Even as one who dreams that he is harmed
> And, dreaming, wishes he were dreaming, thus
> desiring that which is, as if it were not.][22]

We are mourners and, like these dreamers, only wake up to dream again, caught in a pain that is real and hallucinated at once, a pain such that it makes us wish that all were a dream, whereas all, because of the terrible loss, is already a dream. Like the pure and impossible "gift" introduced by Derrida in his read-ing of Baudelaire,[23] such an endless mourning can avoid a reduction to a purely melancholic posture if it trusts the unconscious and allows for a gesture that "excuses" (thus perhaps exculpating itself from the guilt that the loss of loved ones always triggers): it literally leaves the "cause," transcends any origin to which mourning could be attributed.

This tangled knot of motivated demotivations lies at the root of Dante's epic of judgment: "I wanted to excuse myself and did / excuse myself, although I knew it not" (30:140–41). The poet will have to be told by his guide, Virgil, the truth and the effectivity of this unconscious wish that comes true as soon as it is expressed.

In the same way, the mourner who accepts the agency or general "will" of the unconscious exemplifies the true Schopenhauerian "sleepwalker" *and* "sleepwaker." Will the mourner who wakes up in the middle of an unfinished dream glimpse the light of truth? At least, this hypothetical glimpse ought to reconcile a sense that freedom is merely the acceptance of fate and the notion that any utopian struggle entails a positive resistance to fate. Like all the ghostly mourners and writers I have called upon in these pages, we have to write a life that will then turn into a fate; we have to invent a fiction that will later be accepted as a "true story"—thereby learning to "desire that which is as if it were not," but still wearing mourning for the inexplicable penultimate.

The Master of Colors That Know

Like any reader, I have often felt challenged by the difficulty of important texts that seemed to beg fresh rereadings, which could never erase the memory of previous misreadings. In this respect, James Joyce's later texts are exemplary in that they generate a web of creative mistakes (for no one possesses all the references his texts mobilize) that are made to work toward the constitution of meaning. I confess that for years I have stuck to one such misreading in the opening of chapter 3 of *Ulysses*, reading too much into the text: an error in an Italian phrase, *maestro di color che sanno*, which I read all too literally as "the master of colors that know," let me dream of knowledgeable colors, and strange Renaissance masters whose unheard-of pigments occupied my imagination. Let me first quote the full context of this famous passage:

> Ineluctable modality of the visible: at least that if no more, thought through
> my eyes. Signatures of all things I am here to read, seaspawn and seawrack,
> the nearing tide, that rusty boot. Snotgreen, bluesilver, rust: coloured signs.
> Limits of the diaphane. But he adds: in bodies. Then he was aware of them
> bodies before of them coloured. How? By knocking his sconce against them,
> sure. Go easy. Bald he was and a millionaire, *maestro di color che sanno.*
> Limit of the diaphane in. Why in? Diaphane, adiaphane. If you can put
> your five fingers through it it is a gate, if not a door. Shut your eyes and see.[1]

We should not rush immediately in desperation toward a guide or annotation: this type of text is meant to let the reader participate in Stephen's experiment; we have to "shut our eyes and see." When we reach chapter 3, we do not even know that these thoughts belong to a character named Stephen Dedalus, but the style of these meditations is already familiar. Stephen's interior monologue accompanies his perambulations along the beach as he is walking from Sandymount, a southern suburb of Dublin, toward the city center. His meditations on the nature of vision lead to a general aesthetic and to a whole philosophy of creation that will be developed in the long discussion of Shakespeare in the "Scylla and Charybdis" episode.

We need to have read the entire episode, if not the whole novel, to realize that Stephen's first sentence refers to one particular object, namely, color. "Limit of the diaphane" quotes Aristotle's *De Sensu* (3:439 b): "We may define colour as the limit of the Translucent [or Diaphane, according to different translations] in determinately bounded body." Thus, "at least that" in the first sentence defines "colored bodies" seen by Stephen on the beach, and "he" of sentences four, five, seven, and nine alludes to Aristotle. How can we surmise this? The intertextual detour, though relatively long, entirely corresponds to Stephen's allusive mode of thought. He remembers the lines in Dante's *Inferno* that present Aristotle as the leader of the "philosophical family," sitting at the top and surrounded by Plato and Socrates: "*Vidi'l maestro di color che sanno / seder tra filosofica famiglia.*"[2] The literary reference is amplified by allusions to medieval gossip that paint a bald and rich Aristotle. My misreading of the relative *color* in the sentence "the master of those who (*color*) know," as a noun meaning "color" was due to insufficient knowledge of the Italian language but was nevertheless favored by a context saturated with actual colors ("snotgreen, bluesilver, rust") and with the problematics of "coloured signs."

Was Joyce punning on *color* to situate Aristotle's philosophy as primarily a phenomenology of (colored) perception? If I have been the victim of the submerged pun, it is because my past misreading tallies with Stephen's lesson: the knowledge we can derive from and about colors is never far from illusion. The truth of this knowledge is conveyed through colored lures that haunt the eye even after they have been demystified. If to see is to think, as George Berkeley said in his *Essay Towards a New Theory of Vision*, and as Stephen reiterates ("thought through my eyes"), can this thought be dissociated from knowledge? And can this knowledge avoid error when it concerns colors? This is a question I would like to pose to the "master of colors that know," a master who will lead me toward Sigmund Freud and Leonardo da Vinci after Joyce.

In order to advance a little further on this arduous path, quite similar to Dante's progression through limbo toward hell, saluting Homer, Ovid, and Lucanus before encountering all the famous philosophers of antiquity, I would like to stress the complexity of the entangled references to philosophy in Stephen's thoughts. In fact, his first sentence collapses the positions of Aristotle and of Berkeley when they both tackle the issue of our perception of colors, and we almost see the bald head of the philosophical "famillionaire" (to quote Heine's well-known joke used by Freud in his book on *Witz*) knocking against sensible appearances so as to check their solidity, just as Doctor Johnson thought he had refuted Berkeley's immaterialism by kicking at a stone. Berkeley is not called up directly in this passage but appears a little later as the "good bishop of Cloyne" (*U*, 40). The tension between Aristotle and Berkeley should not be reduced too quickly to an opposition between commonsense realism and wild immaterialism.

In fact, when walking on the beach, the texts Stephen has in mind—quite literally—are more subtle. In *De Anima* as well as in *De Sensu et sensibili*, Aristotle explains that if the object of vision is the visible, the visible appears primarily under two modes, colors and transparencies: "The object of sight is the visible, and what is visible is (a) color and (b) a certain object which can be described in words but which has no single name."[3] Indeed, as Aristotle then explains, colors are not visible without light, and this light needs a "diaphane" substance to be perceived: "Now there clearly is something which is transparent, and by 'transparent' I mean what is visible, and yet not visible in itself, but rather owing its visibility to the color *of something else*." Light traverses transparent substances such as water, air, and glass to reach colored bodies, for "light is as it were the proper color of what is transparent" (*De Anima*, 3:418 b). In *De Sensu*, Aristotle opposes the limitless nature of light in the transparent to the limited nature of colored bodies: "Color being actually either *at* the external limit, or being *itself* that limit, in bodies."[4]

This is the problem taken up by Stephen: is the limit of a body a "real thing"? Is it a quality such as color or a quantity such as a geometrical surface? Is the color just on the surface, and if so, what is the transparent that allows it to be seen? "It is therefore the Transparent, according to the degree to which it subsists in bodies . . . that causes them to partake of colour. But since the colour is at the extremity of the body, it must be at the extremity of the Translucent in the body" (*De Sensu*, 3:439 a). The proof adduced here is the fact that transparent bodies such as water exhibit their colors only at the exterior limit or surface. In fact, Stephen is right to ask whether these bodies are perceived as such before they are perceived as colors—this will be the starting point of Berkeley's dissociative analysis, which tends to leave each series of sensations to itself. For if to perceive a color means perceiving a body as such, then we are indeed interpreting nature as a language that we have learned—Berkeley will just add, from God.

Aristotle's way of avoiding the question is generally simple: he distinguishes between actuality and potentiality. If he can state that, on the one hand, "the actuality of sight is called seeing, but the actuality of color has no name," he also concludes that the pure subjectivists were wrong: "The earlier students of nature were mistaken in their view that without sight there was no white or black, without taste no savour. This statement of theirs is partly true, partly false: 'sense' and 'the sensible object' are ambiguous terms, i.e., may denote either potentialities or actualities: the statement is true of the latter, false of the former" (*De Anima*, 3:426 a).

When we reach the end of the first paragraph, Stephen seems to have opted for an Aristotelian solution and needs simply to meditate more systematically on the value of the term "diaphane." This is why he needs to continue the experiment:

> Stephen closed his eyes to hear his boots crush crackling wrack and shells. You are walking through it howsomever. I am, a stride at a time. A very short space of time through very short times of space. Five, six: the *Nacheinander*. Exactly: and that is the ineluctable modality of the audible. Open your eyes. No. Jesus! If I fell over a cliff that beetles o'er his base, fell through the *Nebeneinander* ineluctably! I am getting on nicely in the dark. (*U*, 31)

The mixture of allusions to Gotthold Ephraim Lessing's dichotomy between spatial simultaneity and temporal successivity (which explains the difference between music and the visual arts in *Laocoön*) and to Hamlet's Elsinore creates a mental landscape in which the young man of *Portrait of the Artist as a Young Man* is presented as theorizing with renewed fervor, although perhaps closer to philosophical investigation than to actual poetic creation. After having reopened his eyes and found that the real world has not disappeared ("See now. There all the time without you: and ever shall be, world without end"), Stephen seems to assert his belief in the objectivity of the natural world.

What is, however, extremely striking is that, toward the end of the episode, Stephen abandons his neo-Aristotelian position to adopt a typically Berkeleyan tone in a superb meditation on light and darkness, colors and forms. Stephen has just written a line of poetry on a slip of paper torn from Mr. Deasy's letter and he rests on a rock:

> Me sits there with his augur's rod of ash, in borrowed sandals, by day beside a livid sea, unbeheld, in violet night walking beneath a reign of uncouth stars. I throw this ended shadow from me, manshape ineluctable, call it back. Endless, would it be mine, form of my form? Who watches me here? Who ever anywhere will read these written words? Signs on a white field. Somewhere to someone in your flutiest voice. The good bishop of Cloyne took the veil of the temple out of his shovel hat: veil of space with coloured emblems hatched on its field. Hold hard. Coloured on a flat: yes, that's right. Flat I see, then think distance, near, far, flat I see, east, back. Ah, see now! Falls back suddenly, frozen in stereoscope. (*U*, 40)

As Pierre Vitoux has shown with exemplary rigor, this second experiment with vision marks Stephen's adoption of the main ideas exposed in Berkeley's *New Theory of Vision*.[5]

Berkeley's starting point is an analysis of perception which proves that distance is not perceived in itself but results from an act of judgment that abstracts a few ideas from a host of colored impressions on the retina. Stereoscopic vision is constructed through a number of similar experiments with forms, colors, and distances but in such a swift, unconscious way that we are unaware of the mental act involved. For Berkeley, the primary qualities, such as extension or motion, which John Locke distinguished from secondary qualities (such as shapes, colors, sounds, and odors), are all perceived at one and the same time and can only be dissociated from one another by an intellectual act. Indeed, primary qualities are deduced from secondary qualities by a kind of radical phenomenologism or systematic sensationalism but with a theological agenda attached to them.

This is where Berkeley's famed immaterialism takes its root: the idea of material bodies is superfluous, since bodies, like distances, are only ideas in the mind and can never be logically or experimentally proved to exist in themselves. When we see objects, we perceive only "light and colours, with their several shades and variations,"[6] which the brain sees as planes variously coloured, then interprets as solids and planes placed relative to each other. Apart from the fact that this view corresponds more adequately than the Aristotelian conception to what contemporary science teaches, this theory of perception provides Stephen with a quasi-religious or mystical metaphor for writing.

Perception has been freed from the constraints imposed upon it by commonsense realism, and the colored world deploys its riches like the "veil of the temple," described in Exodus 26:31 as the limit between the Holy of Holies and exterior space. Berkeley's theory presupposes a concept of infinity provided by a direct insight into the nature of things, much as William Blake would do later in his poems. This is why Stephen associates Berkeley and Blake in the first passage I have quoted, while musing on the possibility that his shadow embodies the "form of form," that is, his infinite soul. The point of passage between Stephen's initial Aristotelian position and his subsequent acquiescence to protean immaterialism lies in the connection he makes between the theory of the soul as "form of forms" (which may still be traced back to Aristotle) and Berkeley's belief in a sort of continuous divine creation in which humans can participate.

This conceptual amalgamation derives from the general movement of the episode, in which Stephen appears to be groping toward a unified theory of

aesthetics that would both guarantee a theoretical justification to his forthcoming texts and explain how he was led to compose them. Stephen's meditations always preserve this genetic quality which the earliest texts seem intent
upon proving.[7] This genetic and theoretical position is confirmed by the drift
of his thoughts, which bring him back to his own conception. Earlier in the
episode, Stephen sees two women walking on the beach and imagines them to
be midwives who have come there to bury a "missbirth with a trailing navelcord"
in the sand. "Wombed in sin darkness I was too, made not begotten. By them,
the man with my voice and my eyes and a ghostwoman with ashes on her
breath. They clasped and sundered, did the coupler's will. From before the
ages He willed me and now may not will me away or ever. A *lex eterna* stays
about Him" (*U*, 32).

Vitoux has pointed out in his commentary that Stephen refers here to
Aristotle's idea that generation actualizes the preeminence of form over matter, since he sees himself as "made not begotten"—in a direct contradiction of
Christ's descent. Unlike Jesus who, although of a divine nature, had been conceived according to the flesh (*genitum, non factum*), Stephen insists on the
secondary role played by his parents. Indeed, they have been the agents of his
birth, but if his soul is an eternal "form of forms" linking him to God, the
"eternal law" consists in the transmission of a likeness (same voice and eyes)
that realizes the concept of an infinite form. Stephen's existence is thus founded
on more than a chance encounter of two persons, and he finds reassurance in
the "divine substance wherein Father and Son are consubstantial." In spite of
the introduction of "consubstantiality" here, Stephen's logic brings him closer
to an Arius who spent his life teasing out the paradoxes of "contransmag-
nificandjewbangtantiality" (*U*, 32), and it is Arius who then paves the way for
Berkeley's immaterialism.

Arius stresses the likeness of forms as a way of bypassing the identity of substance; the principle of likeness or resemblance has to be applied to man's
conception of the divine. When Stephen moves from a theology of eternal
forms—although they are indeed heretical and perhaps more Sabellian and
modalist than Arianist[8]—to a phenomenology of colors, he radically shifts the
angle of perception. Just as Stephen's Arianist postulation leads him away from
Aristotle's definition of the soul as deposited "in" bodies, the awareness that
neither forms nor colors are to be found "in bodies" pushes him toward a notion of writing as the key mediating concept. Whereas Aristotle states that if
the soul can neither be a body nor be without a body and has therefore to be
"*in* a body, and a body of a definite kind" (*De Anima*, 3:414 a), Stephen con-

cludes with the power of vision (as colored vision) that can serve as an introduction to a natural semiology: "Who watches me here? Who ever anywhere
will read these written words? Signs on a white field. . . . Coloured on a flat:
yes, that's right. Flat I see, then think distance, near, far, flat I see, east, back.
Ah, see now! Falls back suddenly, frozen in stereoscope" (U, 40).

The irony of Stephen's parallactic vision is that when he imagines himself
alone and unseen, he is in fact perceived by another type of father, Bloom,
while his real father, Simon Dedalus, fails to notice him. If on the one hand,
blindness would then seem to be a precondition for real fatherhood, then on
the other hand, Joyce's Berkeleyan perspectivism would lead him to assert that
the principle of *esse est percipi* determines paternity as well and that one can
only be called a "son" when perceived by someone who can be called a "father." This will have more momentous consequences for Shakespeare than for
Bloom and far more for them than for Stephen. At about the same time, but in
a new narrative development, Leopold Bloom and Simon Dedalus, two similar "fathers," are riding together in the funeral carriage.

> Mr. Bloom at gaze saw a lithe young man, clad in mourning, a wide hat.
> —There's a friend of yours gone by, Dedalus, he said.
> —Who is that?
> —Your son and heir. (U, 73)

On the basis of the location (Watery Lane) and the suggestion that Stephen
has visited his Uncle Richie Goulding—a possibility envisaged by Stephen at
the beginning of his monologue—we reconstruct the scene of his interior
monologue and realize that the "stereoscopic" vision has always implied two
or more observers. This doubling of perspectives confirms Stephen's dialogic
aesthetics of creation, yet should normally undermine his confidence in a foun-
dational origin. Stephen bridges the gap between bodies and souls, matter and
form, substance and relation by blending a protean sense of the infinite richness of nature with a romantic belief in the power of poetic imagination.

As in *Portrait*, Stephen moves constantly from the usual meaning of aesthetics, understood as a theory of art, to a more philosophical sense gesturing
toward different modes of apprehension of art and reality.[9] In the "Proteus"
episode, his meditation on perception leads him to a theory of nature understood as a great book of signs that he is not merely to read but also to write,
cosigning the world with its author, who is also implicated in some way in his
own conception and birth. The genetic theory of perception turns into a theory
of genesis itself, although written signs do indeed contribute to the blurring of

origins. It is with the paradox of a de-origined origin that Stephen is struggling and, through this struggle, gains a deeper understanding of the problematics of paternity and self-generation.

Stephen will have to battle later with the "new Viennese school" when he takes Shakespeare not only as the paradigm of the universal artist but also as the essence of the father fathering himself. What is forgotten in the idealized reconstruction that follows (presented as Stephen's theory of art) is the materiality of the "blank page" upon which he himself—if he wants to be a real "poet"—will have to write his poems and add his signature. This implies first that he reconciles himself with his erotic drives:

> She trusts me, her hand gentle, the longlashed eyes. Now where the blue hell am I bringing her beyond the veil? Into the ineluctable modality of the ineluctable visuality. She, she, she. What she? The virgin at Hodges Figgis' window on Monday looking in for one of the alphabet books you were going to write. Keen glance you gave her. (U, 40)

A similar "glance" or "gaze" will be necessary in order to understand the material precondition for the inscription of any form: "Spouse and helpmate of Adam Kadmon: Heva, naked Eve. She had no navel. Gaze. Belly without blemish, bulging big, a buckler of taut vellum, no, whiteheaped corn, orient and immortal, standing from everlasting to everlasting. Womb of sin" (U, 32). When he remembers his youthful follies and adolescent enthusiasms, Stephen recalls his "epiphanies written on green oval leaves" (U, 34) to be sent to "all the great libraries of the world, including Alexandria" (ibid.). I shall try to account for this particular form (oval) and color (green), while moving to an examination of Freud's theses on art as sublimation. Joyce owned a copy of Freud's German essay on Leonardo da Vinci and no doubt saw many parallels between Freud's reconstruction of an ideal genesis and his own presentation of a young artist struggling with self-knowledge.

Just as Stephen is presented as engaged in a meditation on colors that provide the "ineluctable" access to a knowledge of perception, generation, and writing, Freud shows Leonardo as an artist slowly condemned to impotence and sterility by an overwhelming desire to know—a desire rooted in the perception of colored objects:

> Leonardo's researches had perhaps first begun, as Solmi believes, in the service of his art; he directed his efforts to the properties and laws of light, colours, shadows and perspective in order to ensure mastery in the imitation of nature and to point the same way to others. It is probable that at that time he

already overrated the value to the artist of these branches of knowledge. Still constantly following the lead given by the requirements of his painting he was then driven to investigate the painter's subjects, animals and plants, and the proportions of the human body, and passing from their exterior, to proceed to gain a knowledge of their internal structure and their vital functions, which indeed also find expression in their appearance and have a claim to be depicted in art. And finally the instinct, which had become overwhelming, swept him away until the connection with the demands of his art was severed.[10]

Leonardo is carried away by his *Wissensdrang*, an unquenchable thirst for knowledge that ultimately cuts him off from ordinary human contacts:

His investigations extended to practically every branch of natural science, and in every single one he was a discoverer or at least a prophet and pioneer. Yet his urge for knowledge was always directed to the external world; something kept him far away from the investigation of the human mind. In the "Academia Vinciana" [p. 128], for which he drew some cleverly intertwined emblems, there was little room for psychology. (*LVMC*, 76–77)

It seems that Freud is indirectly meditating on his own *libido sciendi*, a desire that is turned toward psychological investigation and not toward the natural sciences.

Malcolm Bowie has shown the importance of the images of conquest and discovery summoned by Freud whenever he has to account for his trajectory.[11] Freud's presentation of his interpretive method when he faces art works is surprisingly similar to his description of Leonardo's attitude. He states in the *Moses of Michelangelo* that even if he acknowledges that an art work produces an effect on him, he cannot take real pleasure in art unless he has cracked the enigma of its working: "Some rationalistic, or perhaps analytic, turn of mind in me rebels against being moved by a thing without knowing why I am thus affected and what it is that affects me."[12] This leads Freud to envisage the great art works of the past as a series of "unsolved riddles" that test the limits of psychoanalytic interpretive skills.

In Leonardo's case, the craving for knowledge may derive from different sources, but the result is almost identical:

What interested him in a picture was above all a problem; and behind the first one he saw countless other problems arising, just as he used to in his endless and inexhaustible investigation of nature. He was no longer able to limit his demands, to see the work of art in isolation and to tear it from the wide context to which he knew it belonged. After the most exhausting efforts to bring to expression in it everything which was connected with it in his thoughts, he was forced to abandon it in an unfinished state or to declare that is was incomplete. (*LVMC*, 77)

On the contrary, a few passages in Leonardo's notebooks suggest that he was aware of the inexhaustible variety and riches of nature, much as Stephen discovers writing as signs on the Sandymount beach. This is the piece of advice Leonardo gives to painters whose imagination needs to be stimulated:

If you look at any walls spotted with various stains or with a mixture of different kinds of stones, if you are about to invent some scene you will be able to see in it a resemblance to various different landscapes adorned with mountains, rivers, rocks, trees, plains, wide valleys and various groups of hills. You will also be able to see divers combats and figures in quick movement, and strange expressions of faces, and outlandish costumes, and an infinite number of things which you can then reduce into separate and well-conceived forms.[13]

This famous paragraph could indeed anticipate Max Ernst's practice of rubbing sheets of paper on old knotty boards in order to create visions of cities or forests, or the more contemporary technique of exhibiting old ragged posters taken from their street panels and treating them as collages, found objects, or even paintings in their own right.

In the same vein, Stephen can hear God as a "shout in the street" ("Hooray! Ay! Whrrwhee!" [*U*, 28]) because the children at play unwittingly perform a vocal variation on the vocalization of the tetragrammaton or find a verbal equivalent for the sound of waves ("Listen: a fourworded wavespeech: seesoo, hrss, rsseeiss, ooos" [*U*, 41]). Leonardo summarizes this nicely: "With such walls and blends of different stones it comes about as it does with the sound of bells, in whose clanging you may discover every name and word that you can imagine" (*Notebooks*, 874).

Leonardo's method is not too far from Edmund Husserl's phenomenological reduction, by which consciousness fabricates an object from the diversity of its *Abschattungen*; indeed the Italian wording lends itself to such a notion: "*le quali potrai ridurre in integra e bona forma.*"[14] The chaotic mutiplicity of an untreated surface of colors and textures allows for an endless projection of forms that will generate scenes and entire compositions. The artist's work is less that of selection than an oneiric accompaniment of the implicit logic in the given material. Shapes are products of a creative waking dream, associating a few signs in a more or less coherent whole.

Joyce's theory of aesthetics in *Portrait* could provide a general theoretical context for Leonardo's musings. It would also be tempting to link Leonardo's countless inventions (he not only invented the airplane but also the inflatable lifejacket to be used in case of shipwreck) to Bloom's various schemes by which he hopes to improve himself and modernize Dublin (e.g., a new transportation system). Leonardo's paean to water in the *Notebooks* ("And as the mirror changes with the color of its object so it changes with the nature of the place through which it passes: health-giving, noisome, laxative, astringent, sulphurous, salt, incarnadined, mournful, raging, angry, red, yellow, green, black, blue, greasy, fat, thin. Sometimes it starts a conflagration, sometimes it extinguishes one; is warm and is cold; carries away or sets down, hollows out or raises up, tears down or establishes, fills up or empties, raises itself up or burrows down, speeds or is still, is the cause at times of life or death, of increase or privation, nourishes at times and at times does the contrary, at times has a tang of salt, at times is without savour, at times submerges the wide valleys with great floods" [734]) reveals a desire that encompasses the most varied and contradictory aspects of a substance. Such a substance is always connected with an interplay of colors, for Leonardo systematically points out in his theory of colors that the color of all objects is modified by the color of the ground or of other objects. In comparison, Joyce's praise of water—through Bloom's admiration—in the "Ithaca" episode also lists "its gradation of colours in the torrid and temperate and frigid zones: its vehicular ramifications in continental lake contained streams and confluent oceanflowing rivers with their tributaries and transoceanic currents, gulfstream, north and south equatorial courses: its violence in seaquakes, waterspouts, Artesian wells, eruptions, torrents, eddies, freshets, spates, groundswells, watersheds, waterpartings, geysers, cataracts, whirlpools, maelstroms, inundations, deluges, cloudbursts" (U, 549). Indeed, this deluge of words smacks more of the encyclopedia or thesaurus than scientific investigation, but denotes the same desire to contemplate the whole world in all its diversity and to find an adequate discourse or an adequate artistic representation for it.

Freud tends to see a deep continuity in Leonardo's life, but starts by stressing the unfinished nature of most of his paintings and the painstaking slowness in his productions. The source of such a multiplication of hesitations or even technical failures (such as the destruction of the *Last Supper* at which he had worked for three years) must be found in Leonardo's strange attitude toward sexuality. Like Stephen, who hates water and would never swim in the nude as his friends are wont to do in the beach by the Martello tower, and who exists at a distance from his body, Leonardo appears strangely indifferent to moral issues or to pleasures of the senses: "In an age which saw a struggle between sensuality without restraint and gloomy asceticism, Leonardo represented the cool repudiation of sexuality—a thing that would scarcely be expected of an artist and a portrayer of feminine beauty" (*LVMC*, 69). His frigidity led him to avoid only one issue, that of Eros: "So resolutely do [his writings] shun everything sexual that it would seem as if Eros alone, the preserver of all living things, was not worthy material for the investigator in his pursuit of knowledge" (*LVMC*, 70). A footnote added in 1919 qualifies this bold statement and deals with the well-known drawing representing the act of coition.

The key to Leonardo's strangeness and inhibitions is not that he lacked creativity or passion, but that this "divine" passion had been converted into a craving for knowledge. Rather than stress the useful sublimation that this process could entail, Freud notes its paralyzing consequences: "His affects were controlled and subjected to the instinct for research; he did not love and hate, but asked himself about the origin and significance of what he was to love and hate" (*LVMC*, 74). In a compelling metaphor, Freud describes the release from long and strenuous intellectual labors as "a stream of water drawn from a river is allowed to flow away when its work is done" (74–75), which corresponds to the climax of emotion discernible in so many passages of the *Notebooks*, where Leonardo is merely praising the Creator for his bounty and magnificence. According to Freud, Leonardo's interest in all sorts of machines, from weapons to artificial wings, betrays an inability to understand the real feelings of men and women. And so, in order to reach the root—the origin—of this inhibition, Freud returns to Leonardo's earliest memory. Leonardo explains that his obsession with the flight of birds must stem from one of "the earliest recollections of my infancy": "When I was in the cradle . . . a kite came and opened my mouth with its tail, and struck me within upon the lips with its tail many times" (*Notebooks*, 1122).

By a strange misreading due to the German translation, Freud mistakes the *nibbio* (kite) mentioned by Leonardo for a vulture. This slip seems to have been caused by the rich string of mythological associations he brings to bear on the passage. The tail is interpreted as the mnesic trace of an exclusion link to the mother, which turns into a wish to suck the penis of a phallic mother. This passive homosexual fantasy is underpinned by the association of the "vulture" with androgyny and bisexuality. The vulture is a female father, and Leonardo becomes a sort of Virgin Mary, a "vulture child" (*LVMC*, 91).

Leonardo's desire to know had to take its origin in the infantile anxiety about "where babies come from"—a wish triggered by the difficult position of the illegitimate child who was taken into his father's family when he was five years old and who knew his mother to be single, a "Virgin" of some sort. Mona Lisa's blissful smile will thus be seen as an echo of the loving and luminous smile of the mother, who lavishes all her love on the boy for want of a real husband, thus triggering his infantile sexuality.

In the angelic and mysterious smiles of the Madonna and Saint Anne in the Louvre painting called *Saint Anne with Two Others* or *Santa Anna Metterza*, the doubling of Leonardo's real mother finds direct expression since the painting depicts Christ with his mother and grandmother. According to Freud, this "picture contains the synthesis of the history of his childhood. . . . In point of fact Leonardo has given the boy two mothers . . . and both are endowed with the blissful smile of the joy of motherhood" (*LVMC*, 112–13). Saint Anne appears radiant and beautiful as the mother; nothing in her face betrays the passage of time.

We can understand how a faithful disciple could have literally hallucinated, discovering a vulture on the surface of the Virgin's robe. Made in 1913, Oskar Pfister's cryptographic discovery is mentioned with a certain reserve by Freud ("a remarkable discovery has been made in the Louvre picture . . . even if one may not feel inclined to accept it without reserve" [*LVMC*, 115, note added in 1919]) because it seems to prove his theory almost too tidily. The vulture seen in the piece of "blue cloth" as a "light grey field against the darker ground of the rest of the drapery" belongs to the category of "picture puzzles," as a key to the allegorical meaning of the painting. This vulture indeed thrusts its tail toward Jesus, as the *nibbio* did to infant Leonardo in his fantasy. Even if we are not entirely convinced by Pfister's solution to the visual riddle linking the two mothers to a complex of passive homosexual attitudes embodied in the painting and the fantasy, it remains true that we cannot forget the presence of a hovering vulture-kite in the painting. The fateful bird remains as a sort of after-image, a perceptual lure called for by Leonardo's family portrait, emerging from the reduction of a curious splash of nondescript colors and turning into a single shape. Imagination can only seize upon this blob of gray, green, and blue and carve in it a gestalt that gives a meaning to the threatening confrontation between shapes and colors.

Like Freud and Pfister ("After we have studied this picture for some time, it suddenly dawns on us that only Leonardo could have painted it, just as only he could have created the phantasy of the vulture" [*LVMC*, 112]), whoever attentively considers this painting will be struck by a series of troubling details. First, the folds of the Virgin's dress, which could contain a strange bird, are dotted with irregular spots, and the coloration is uncertain, hesitating between blue and green. The suggestion of a degraded coloration is reinforced as soon as we compare this surface with the red velvet of Mary's right shoulder or with the olive green of Anne's left arm. The first impression is that the substance has not aged well and remains as a grayish curtain, a poor veil hastily daubed in order to hide a secret and also to enhance the miraculous beauty and freshness of the faces. The painting is built on the opposition between two complementary colors, red and green; the ground is reddish brown, the flesh is nacreous and pink, while the background presents a montaneous mass of bluish shapes, just separated from the blue-green sky by a thin opalescent halo. Leonardo has followed his own precepts, since he notes that blue is a color that denotes distance:

> Of the various colours other than blue, that which at a great distance will resemble blue most closely will be that which is nearest to black, and so conversely the color which least resembles black will be the one which at a great distance will most retain its natural colour.
>
> Accordingly, the green in landscapes will become more changed into blue than will the yellow or the white, and so conversely the yellow and the white will undergo less change than the green, and the red still less.
>
> The shadow of flesh should be of burnt *terra verde*" (*Notebooks*, 924).

The strange impression created by the Virgin's dress is that it creates more of a background than a foreground, even if it describes the first frontal plane met by the eye. This surface occupies almost one-fifth of the whole canvas and is described by some observers as green, by others as blue. All color reproductions evince the same alternation and confirm the principle that any mixed color is a function of all the other colors. As Leonardo repeats in his *Notebooks*: "The colour of the object illuminated partakes of the colour of that which illuminates it" (923).

My contention is that Leonardo wanted to achieve this effect of an indescribable color, a color that would hover in the air or in the spectator's vision like an invisible kite. This enigmatic blue-green separates as much as it unites the three entangled figures of the child and his two mothers. The two mothers seem to have only one body in common, while the lamb held by Jesus almost fuses with his body. The grayish blue-green of the folds thus calls up the hues of a crucified flesh (as for instance Grünewald's famous Colmar triptych described in Huysmans's *Là-bas*), more than the draperies that fascinated Leonardo: "The draperies thin, thick, new, old, with folds broken and pleated, soft lights, shadows obscure and less obscure, either with or without reflections, definite or indistinct according to the distances and the various colours . . ." (*Notebooks*, 913).

If we agree to see a return of the distant background in this greenish foreground, it is because the rocky substance has already devoured the mother's dress in order to evoke the Golgotha of a future passion. The blue-gray surface is already a Holy Shroud waiting for the inscription of a bleeding face. Its strange shape, an oblique pyramid, mirrors the construction of the whole group, while unbalancing and tilting it to the side. The Virgin's knees form two jutting angles that provide the bird with a skeleton and force one to imagine some rock or steep earthen bank by which she would be supported (besides sitting on her mother's lap), in order to account for the strange angle formed by the right leg, covered by an almost transparent fabric, and the left knee, smothered by folds with an elbow draped in the same color.

Meyer Schapiro's remarkable essay on Freud's text has shown how the indefinable quality of the color and the strange grouping of the three figures with the lamb can be interpreted in the light of various theories centering around the rehabilitation of Saint Anne.[15] The cult of Saint Anne culminated around 1485–1510, precisely when Leonardo was busy drawing the Virgin and her mother in numerous sketches and cartoons. This led to the official dogma of the Immaculate Conception adopted by the Roman Catholic Church in 1854. But as Schapiro notes, there was a divergence between one view, which tended to stress seniority and authority and would thus depict Anne as older and higher than Mary, and another, northern view, which tended to see them as equals. If Leonardo wished to present "an articulation of contrasts which could render the spontaneity and conflicting impulses of the individuals while retaining the family attachment,"[16] the aesthetic result suffers from unresolved tensions:

> In spite of Leonardo's refinement of drawing and search for graceful forms, I do not believe that the new classical ideal is perfectly realized in the *Saint Anne*. There remains an aspect of the rigid and artificial in the group, most evident in the abrupt pairing of Anne and Mary, with the sharp contrast of their profile and frontal forms. It may be explained, perhaps, by Leonardo's commitment to the traditional mediaeval type of *Anna Metterza*, in conflict with his own tendency toward variation, distinctness and movement. Throughout his life, he conceived his more iconic compositions around a

> dominant, isolated, central figure . . . and therefore found in the *Saint Anne*, with its two mothers of equal weight, an especially refractory theme.[17]

Schapiro also notes how contemporary commentators saw in this feminine trinity of two mothers and a child a new passion theme in a different key, since the painting was also understood as a foreboding of the death of Christ: the lamb with which Jesus plays presages both the sacrificial host and John who will tell of the coming Passion. Mary seems to hesitate between a desire to reclaim her child and to let him go, since his passion is, after all, to redeem all humanity. The riddle of the famous *nibbio* revolves around a strange trinity whose enigma results from a careful interplay between forms and colors.

The fascinating quality of this painting derives from a mystery, which can be variously identified as that of the Immaculate Conception (and consequently, all the theories about sexuality) or Incarnation (the link between humanity and divinity condensed in an impossible "carnation" or the color of flesh). If we look again at the painting, we see that the Virgin, almost seen in profile, has just moved to catch Jesus. Only three feet are visible for three human figures, while the lamb also shows three feet. Only three hands are visible, as if to stress the enigma of a purely feminine and sinless conception and birth— indeed, quite the reverse of what Stephen Dedalus imagines to be his direct link with a divine father. When he states that fatherhood is a mystery that relies on the unconscious, he takes pains to distinguish his own vision of an "apostolic succession, from only begetter to only begotten" from the "madonna which the cunning Italian intellect flung to the mob of Europe" (*U*, 170). The roughly triangular shape of the blue-green dress thus hides and reveals the absolute riddle of a generation that would bypass any male agency, be it divine or human. The mystery of conception adheres by a strange metonymy to the color and shape of the dress.

In its unnamable hue, the entire burden of a world of pain has been suggested. Suspended between tears and laughter, in the indecision of a fixed smile, Anne and Mary simultaneously clutch and repel the beautiful boy who has apparently found his transitional object, the lamb which metaphorizes his future role. It is not necessary to transform the smile into smirk or laughter, as when surrealist humor distorts the painting into a scene in which the Virgin spanks the child, while she herself is being beaten by her mother. The spectator will remain captivated by this blue-green drapery that can be read as a prophecy as well as the impossibility of deciphering the prophecy.

Can we congratulate Freud for having at least attempted to read behind or beyond the riddle ? No, not really, of course, since he had to atone for his boldness by heaping up misreadings that are still embarrassing today. Schapiro is probably right in seeing in Freud's book on Leonardo as a "brilliant *jeu d'esprit*" and "no real test of his theory, which here has been faultily applied."[18] It is true that Freud neglects material that would contradict his biographical speculations, such as the notes on kites made by Leonardo, which rule out any systematic association (as postulated by Freud) between these birds and loving mothers. But as K. R. Eissler's forceful defense of Freud's reading and critique of Schapiro's historicism has shown, we should not be misled by reconstructions of whole "traditions" whose very presence is perhaps as spectral as the bird seen by Pfister on the famous painting.[19] Eissler proves that Schapiro has occasionally distorted his evidence in order to prove Freud wrong: while he postulates an entire series of images in which Mary and Anne appear to be equally young and beautiful, the only painting he quotes is a painting by Luca di Tommè, which presents a Saint Anne who is nevertheless much bigger than her daughter (*LV*, 38–39, and plate 4). Another point made by Schapiro is that, contrary to what Freud wrote, Leonardo did not invent the pyramidal composition. However, what Schapiro presents as an earlier example of pyramidal composition turns out to be a stilted and squarish frame by Masaccio, which obviously has very little to do with *Saint Anne with Two Others* (*LV*, 48, and plate 6).

Eissler thus suggests conclusively that Freud would probably not have abandoned his "theory" even if he had known Schapiro's objections: Freud situates his analytic reconstructions in a realm for which the unconscious is determining. On the other hand, a Freudian axiom that remains to be questioned is his belief in a direct link between childhood fantasies and the creation of masterpieces. In such an investigation, culturalism and historicism often miss the real questions, because they presuppose a positivistic answer. Eissler thus writes: "If we could interview Leonardo himself, we probably would not get those answers that might decide whether Freud was right or wrong as to most of his conclusions, whereas most of the problems raised by Schapiro fall within the area in which the subject is in principle capable of deciding what the correct answer is" (*LV*, 43). In fact, Leonardo himself may have provided a solution to his own riddle when pointing to the real link between men and birds ("Feathers shall raise men towards heaven even as they do birds:—That is by letters written with their quills" [*Notebooks*, 1115]), a link that entails the possibility of error as a precondition to writing and flying.

If in his *Notebooks* Leonardo remarks that neither white nor black can be transparent—a point that will later recur in Ludwig Wittgenstein's *Remarks on Colors*—and that all colors turn bluer when they are distant, then we can surely see in the strange blue-green of the Virgin's robe a transversal cut that suddenly presents time on a two-dimensional surface, time with all its momentous and eschatological suggestions. Another irreverent way of defining this color would be to return to the first chapter of *Ulysses*, when Buck Mulligan attempts to force Stephen to face his mother, who had died a year ago but who still haunts his thoughts. Mulligan has just borrowed Stephen's handkerchief to wipe his razor.

> Buck Mulligan wiped the razorblade neatly. Then, gazing over the handkerchief, he said:
>   —The bard's noserag! A new art colour for our Irish poets: snotgreen. You can almost taste it, can't you? (*U*, 4)

This immediately leads Mulligan to a favorite theme, the return of the Greek world in Ireland: "God! he said quietly. Isn't the sea what Algy calls it: a great sweet mother? The snotgreen sea. The scrotumtightening sea. *Epi oinopa ponton*. Ah, Dedalus, the Greeks!" (*U*, 4).

By identifying the color of the Virgin's robe with such a "snotgreen" surface, I do not mean to be impertinent but rather to stress the connection between this lack of a "proper" definition and the mother's fundamental role symbolized by a "dirty" white that would contain all the colors, or a shadow that does not result from the privation of light but from a fleshy *terra verde*, the foil and backdrop for the idealized incarnation of the divine as well as for the suggestion of an unnamable horror.

Such a green horror resurfaces in Stephen's vision of a drowned man at the end of the "Proteus" episode I have already discussed at some length:

> Bag of corpsegas sopping in foul brine. A quiver of minnows, fat of a spongy titbit, flash through the slits of his buttoned trouserfly. God becomes man becomes fish becomes barnacle goose becomes featherbed mountain. Dead breaths I living breathe, tread dead dust, devour a urinous offal from all dead. Hauled stark over the gunwale he breathes upward the stench of his green grave, his leprous nosehole snoring to the sun. (*U*, 41–42)

It is difficult to articulate with more precision the horror of death, from the punning games involved by incarnation ("fish" refers to the symbol used for Christ in Greek and "barnacle goose" to medieval legends that supposed that the birds would be born from shellfish) to the formidable power of death that mutilates, castrates, devours, thus bringing about this awful transformation of flesh into rotting matter closer to urine, gas, and excrement. No sublimation will therefore appear possible, especially when the snotgreen substance oozes from a "leprous nosehole." The fact that the same color is used in both contexts is sufficient to remind us not only of green's nationalistic Irish associations but also of its composite and unstable nature, hesitating between transubstantiation and abjection.

Green suggests the color of all future decompositions or degradations, as Denis Diderot noted when describing the composition of a painting's ground. He defines the "background" of a painting in these terms: "It is either a boundless space in which all colors of objects blend in the distance, and end by producing the effect of a grayish white, or a vertical plane which receives a direct or oblique light, and which in both cases follows the rules of degradation."[20] Diderot attempts to find words for what resists language most stubbornly—that is, the color of flesh in the interaction between shape and ground. He quotes the seventeenth-century specialist of color theory, Roger de Piles, who had praised Giorgione for having used only the four fundamental hues in order to depict the flesh's carnation, but who also blames Leonardo for a faulty use of color.

In the English translation of the *Art of Painting and the Lives of the Painters* (1706), de Piles refers to Leonardo's idea of the contemplation of an old wall so as to excite the imagination: "Leonardo da Vinci writes, that the spots which are to be seen on an old wall, forming confus'd Ideas of different Objects, may excite Genius, and help it to produce something."[21] De Piles vindicates Leonardo against the critics who might object that it is all too easy to work from such old walls: "The more a Man has of Genius, the more things he will perceive in those sorts of Spots, or confus'd lines."[22]

But in his long catalogue of artists, de Piles devotes only a few pages to Leonardo, whose works he admits not knowing very well despite his reputation (most of his paintings were still in private collections at the time). He praises Leonardo's perfect taste in his designs, the exactness of his expression, the skill of his anatomical reproductions, and refers to a letter written by Rubens (the great model among painters for de Piles, who is an ardent advocate of colorism), but remains critical of one element, Leonardo's "colorings": "Leonardo's Carnations have too much of the *Lees*-Colour in them, and the Union in his Pictures is too much tinctured with the *Violet*, which is there Predominant: this, in my Opinion, proceeded from the Painters of his time, not *knowing well* enough the use of Oil, and from the negligence of the *Florentines* in the part of the Colouring."[23]

Such a view was not prevalent among the Italian contemporaries who unanimously praised Leonardo's colors, as Giogio Vasari noted in his *Lives*, stressing the way Mona Lisa's face imitated life itself in the exquisite rendering of flesh.

De Piles's carping comments reveal not only a different taste, formed by two centuries of debate over the prevalence of form or color, but also the simple reality of the aging process undergone by Leonardo's oils and paints, which render any evaluation doubtful as long as no proper restoration intervenes.

G. W. F. Hegel's *Aesthetik*, which borrows so freely from Diderot and Goethe (as we shall see later in connection with Breton), demonstrates that by the middle of the nineteenth century, the school of the colorists had won the day. He, too, like de Piles, takes the rendering of flesh as the ultimate criterion in the art of color. Incarnadine, or the special rosy or pink hue of the skin becomes the ultimate test for painters, who can show their skills in blending all colors so as to evoke the fair faces of blonde ladies. One full page, often quoted, lists all the primary and secondary colors needed to reproduce the human skin, with red, violet, blue, and yellow linked to the transparencies of skin texture and the network of veins, with the accompaniment of ochres, browns, and grays necessary for the cumulative effect.[24] What matters for Hegel is that this palette should create a mere shimmering effect but should produce the effect of an illumination from the inside, like the surface of a lake lit by a sunset, so that it mirrors objects but lets the glance penetrate to the depths. He then quotes a passage from Diderot's *Essay on Painting*, which follows in full, for it exemplifies the point of view that if a painting's realism derives from form, life only originates from color:

> It has been said that the most beautiful color in the world was this lovely redness which innocence, youth, health, modesty and chastity use to color a young girl's cheeks; and this was not only subtle, touching and delicate but also true: for indeed flesh is difficult to render; this unctuous white, even without being pale or mat; this mixture of red and blue which imperceptibly perspires; this is blood, and life, which create the colorist's despair. He who has acquired a feeling for flesh has progressed a lot; the rest is nothing in comparison. Thousands of painters have died without knowing flesh; thousand others will die without feeling it.[25]

Like de Piles, Diderot's moralizing art theory finds its model in the voluptuous paintings of Rubens and does not shrink from metaphors that could be applied to real-life situations. A good painter is a good lover, or at least turns his beholder into a lover, and seduces him by the suggestion of a passion hidden under the demure rosy cheeks of young women.

In the domain of passion, the painter has a great disadvantage in comparison to the writer or poet. He must not be tempted by the contagious blush of his models, otherwise he runs the risk of ruining his painting. Diderot proposes to the painter a model of aesthetic asceticism, verging on coitus inter-ruptus, for the simple reason that this art demands time to be completed.

> Does a woman keep the same color when she is waiting for pleasure, in the
> arms of pleasure, or just leaving its arms? Ah, dear friend, what art is that of
> painting? I realize in one line what a painter takes a week to sketch; and his
> sad fate is that he knows, sees and feels just as I do, and cannot render it and
> be satisfied; this is because sentiment, carrying him forward, deceives him
> about what he can do, and has him spoil a masterwork; he was, without
> being aware, on the last limit of art.[26]

Colors, which are the stuff and life of painting, are also the most dangerous lure, tempting the painter either to have sex with his model, thus deferring execution, or to endlessly modify a texture that becomes all the more complex as it strives for perfection—as would be confirmed by Leonardo's famous slow-ness and inability to finish a painting. The painter is always "on the last limit of art," above all because he plays with truth and illusion and needs to exploit illusion if he wants to produce truth.

The question of color in painting has always been associated with a moral-ized problematic linking truth and lie, knowledge and illusion, in a debate that finds its roots in Plato and Aristotle, as Jacqueline Lichtenstein has shown in her study of the debate concerning the "rhetoric of color" during the French classical age.[27] Roger de Piles will again serve as a model, for he stands as the best exponent of the school of colorists at a time when design and the art of drawing were praised as superior because they appeared closer to the simple idea or to Platonic essences, and when colors were considered too sensual or rhetorical, bent on seducing rather than on conveying truth.

De Piles distinguishes between "simple truth," that is, imitation of an ob-ject by an exact copy; "ideal truth," or the creation of ideal beauty; and "com-posite truth or perfect truth," which presents a synthesis of exact imitation and ideal perfection.

> Among all other arts, the art where truth has to be found the most sensibly is
> no doubt that of painting. Other arts only wake up ideas of absent things,
> whereas painting stands in for them [*supplée*] entirely, and makes them
> present by its essential nature which does not consist in pleasing the eyes
> but also in deceiving them.[28]

In one and the same sentence, de Piles has shifted from the presentation of truth to the art of lying, and what was seen as a disadvantage by Diderot—painting takes time, the production of substitutes entails many practical difficulties—appears here as positive: painting produces the illusion of presence and obeys the strict laws of a truthful lie. The essence of painting is to "catch the eyes by surprise and deceive them, if this is possible" (PP, 25). Color plays a fundamental role in the strategy of surprise and illusion, for de Piles distinguishes between "color" as the colors of nature and *coloris*, or "coloring" that relies on the tones and hues of painting: "Coloring is one of painting's most important parts, through which the painter imitates the appearances of colors of natural objects and distributes to artificial objects the color that is most advantageous to deceive vision" (PP, 142).

De Piles's illusionism is no vulgar naturalism, since for him the painter's aim is to assemble all the means contributing to the creation of the illusion. Painting implies a staging, a calculation of the effects on the beholder, and a consideration of certain basic truths such as that a canvas is two-dimensional, that chemical hues soon lose their vigor and freshness, and that distance has to be reckoned with (PP, 143). This system teaches in an entirely Cartesian fashion how to exaggerate shades, tone up or down lights, distances, colors, substances. If the precepts are followed, then the painting itself will speak: "Finally, the portraits must be able in this sort of attitude to talk to us by themselves and to say, for instance: Well, look at me, I am this invincible King surrounded by majesty" (PP, 132). De Piles thus lists about ten types of "speaking portraits" and uses the example of Rubens to stress the "speech" of a painting, which is more important than exact resemblance:

> We know enough that painting is only a kind of make-up, that its essence is to deceive, and that the greatest deceiver is the best painter. Nature by itself is barren, and he who would try to copy it purely and simply without any artifice would always produce a poor thing. . . . In that sense, one can say that in Rubens's paintings, art is above nature, which seems to be but the copy of the great works of this great painter. (PP, 159)

This was written at the end of the seventeenth century, thus anticipating Oscar Wilde's paradoxes by two centuries, but with Poussin and Rubens as models. De Piles's rational demonstration then comes very close to an Aristotelian terminology, since for him design and drawing correspond to the "genre" of painting, whereas color functions as the "difference" of painting. Just as objects of the natural world are differentiated above all by their colors, in the artistic realm—which follows different laws, as we have seen—coloration or *coloris* embodies "difference in painting" (PP, 145).

In fact, if we synthesize what de Piles says about genius and Leonardo's old wall, and the practice of such creative "difference," which does not aim at imitating nature but at surprising and convincing an audience, we should have no difficulty in seeing in this active painterly difference the inception of such modern techniques as monochrome painting. Yves Klein's special blue, his famous IKB, with which he covered surfaces and objects alike can now safely cover Leonardo's old spotty wall: it will excite imagination and perhaps also suggest a frenzied enjoyment of pure absence. This blue will not be the sky or the sea, but their radical vanishing and the potentiality of all other "pure" colors. The desire to radicalize difference has been pushed beyond the frontiers of illusionist representation and has led to questioning the meaning of the artistic gesture itself. But Yves Klein's magnetic blue has the Mallarméan ambition to hold all other colors in reserve, whereas the blue-green cloth I have taken as my starting point is precisely an undecidable color. Does this hesitation call for more "difference"?

The problem posed by the Virgin's dress is that it baffles interpretation, since nobody will agree on the color (most commentators call it blue, a statement which I hope I have shown to be partially untrue). If we cannot decide between green and blue, then how can we speak of a symbolism of colors? If the seduction of the painting derives from the dirty and uncertain hue, is it in order to force the viewer to hallucinate the most arbitrary shapes (as that of a vulture), or is it to help the viewer throw fresh doubts on the nature of perception? I tried to present this gray-blue-green color as a nondialectizable power, a disruptive force undoing the theological and patrological discourse of Incarnation, but, in doing so, have I not been guilty of the same sin as Freud's reading, who desired to read too much into the painting? And even if I pay attention to the multiple layers of the historical contexts, the countless artistic models and genres necessary to create the *Anna Metterza* motif, am I not obstinately reading the painting with a modern agenda in mind, inspired, say, by Derrida's *Truth in Painting?*[29]

I do not wish to discard too hastily the teachings of anthropology and history. It is crucial to realize that green was not perceived as such by the Greeks, who saw it as a variety of blue, or by most Europeans in the Middle Ages, when green was seen as a variety of black.[30] Green, which is not a primary color, has nevertheless been promoted in our electronic culture, since the triad of the three classical primary colors (red, yellow, and blue) has been replaced by the three colors used in color television, red, blue, and green—which suffice to reproduce the illusion of all the other hues by their strict combination. Green, a synthetic color, now plays a fundamental role in the coloring of all our screens, without allowing us to forget its original duplicity, its first ambivalence.

The current growth of video art, which often questions the ideological constructions of television programs, provides a way of presenting "haunting" in a concrete manner. Indeed, video art sends us back to the magical function of art as described by Freud in *Totem and Taboo* and to its obsession with the great "mysteries" of a religious past such as the Trinity, the Immaculate Conception, and even the Crucifixion in Gary Hill's famous sequence; it forces us to rethink a certain idea of the "real presence" of auratic objects that used to be connected with a sense of the sacred. As in the worst television program, but with the added dimension of conscious and systematic usage, the images shown by video artists generate fictive beings who are "there" as it were, since they inhabit the electrical pulsation of a colored light. This entails a crucial difference with the technique of the film, which obeys a logic of the colored image traversed by a flow of light. Ontologically speaking, movies belong to the category of stained-glass windows, the sun of truth being replaced by the electric bulb's white light, whereas video images vibrate in a continuous pulsation, whose incandescent flicker adorns every shape with a sort of magical halo.[31]

Films need to stress their theatricality in huge theaters that still cling to the principle of the Italian stage with its monumentality, tricks of perspective, and audio-visual depth. A television set or monitor must rely on a palpitating virtual presence that can adequately replace the portable altars of the ancients, with their attendant statuettes lit by candles or oil lamps, or the warmth of traditional winter evening gatherings by a blazing fire. The electronic image moving on the screen is closer to sculpture than to painting. This warm moving sculpture replaces absent gods while telling the tales of their high deeds, night after night, in a series of puppet plays. Cinema presents the audience with the projection of colored shadows, while television shows Balinese puppets with their painted leather faces. Following Plato's allegory of the cave, the electronic image would be situated closer to essences and presences, while its lack of a material support, such as a celluloid film, brings it closer to a sense of pure electric difference.

In its very ontological doubleness, this magical theater of the electronic image could embody what Antonin Artaud found so fascinating in the Balinese puppet shows. In order to reach back to his impassioned defense of a color that would also be flesh and life beyond the usual categories of signification, it will suffice to turn to his essay on Vincent van Gogh, a manifesto that can be read as a poem. It begins like this:

> One can speak of the good mental health of van Gogh who, in his whole life, cooked only one of his hands, and did nothing else except once to cut

off his left ear, / in a world in which everyday one eats vagina cooked in green sauce or penis of newborn child whipped and beaten to a pulp, / just as it is when plucked from the sex of its mother.[32]

Artaud's mixture of poetic insight and rhapsodical ranting aims more at bourgeois hypocrisy than at the dim flicker of our television screens whose "green sauce" is a daily menu more for the eyes than for vaginas or mouths! The creation of his poetical "exorcisms" and strident prayers brought him too far, beyond "the ultimate limit of art," and hence into madness. Madness of having seen too far and too straight, with a glance that bores a hole and does not satisfy itself with the reassuring triadic halo of greens, reds, and blues. The hole—which we shall rediscover in Beckett's own problematics of creation and writing—is a gaping emptiness left by the trauma of birth, a birth whose pain has destroyed all mnesic traces, apart from the jagged contours of a mutilation.

> The look of van Gogh is suspended, screwed in, it is glazed behind his unusual eyelids, his thin smooth eyebrows. / It is a look that penetrates immediately, it transfixes. . . . But van Gogh has caught the moment when the pupil is about to pour itself out in the void, / when this look, fired at us like the bomb of a meteor, takes on the expressionless color of the void and of the inertia that fills it. / Better than any psychiatrist in the world, this was how the great van Gogh located his illness.[33]

Even if we can say that Artaud gives a romantic portrait of the artist "suicided by society," his excess cannot be reduced to categories of aesthetic or psychiatric knowledge. His empathic identification with the suicidal rebel no doubt accounts for his own delirious texts, but also forces us to meditate on a submerged anaphoric link between "painting" and "pain." The primary colors of van Gogh's canvasses, which are thrown at our pupils, cannot be equated with Leonardo's undecidable blue-green, although they bespeak an intensity of suffering that somehow pierces through the painted surface.

A similar internal rhyme between pain and paint is heard in a written text discussing a photograph. To fully translate this poem, we should be required to hear a "yell" in the name of such a "primitive" color as yellow that, with just a touch of *blue*,[34] will produce the enigmatic green I have been obsessed with. As Jorge Luis Borges said in a lecture: "It is indubitable that physical pain exists, as indubitable as the fact that yellow exists as a color."[35] I shall thus quote a poem that evokes a yellow pain while providing a contemporary—

hieratic, simplistic, and haunting—variation on the medieval litanies of the Virgin Mary:

> Your dress is white.
>
> Of a whiteness,
> that as it were
> illuminates.
>
> The folds are graceful, above,
> at the base of the neck.
>
> A veil covers your head,
> Down to the brow.
>
> After many curves
> the veil falls
> on your shoulders.
>
> It hardly
> envelops
> your arms.
>
> Through other undulating folds
> it falls
>
> down the chest
> to the feet.
>
> A girdle clasps your loins.
> It is blue.
>
> Its intertwined
> ends (no knot)
> float in front.
>
> Your feet show
> naked.
>
> Above the last folds,
> a rose at the parting.
>
> Yellow,
> in full bloom.

The entire image
then

becomes
yellow.

There is too much pain.

The next instant,
where you were
there remains
only a hole.

The yellow (of pain).

The yellow (upon your lips).

The yellow (of pain)
on my hands.[36]

André Breton's Ghostly Stance

Ghostly Stances

I don't attach any importance to life
I don't pin life's least butterfly to importance
I'm unimportant to life
But branches of salt white branches
All the bubbles of shadow
And sea anemones
Go down and breathe deep inside my thought
They come from tears I don't shed
From steps I don't take which are steps twice over
And which sand remembers when the tide rises

One day a woman entered it
That woman grew so radiant I couldn't see her
With these eyes that have even seen me burning
I was already as old as I am now
And I watched over myself over my thoughts like a night
watchman in an immense factory
The only watchman

ANDRÉ BRETON, *Earthlight*

As early as 1949, Maurice Blanchot could remark that surrealism no longer existed as a movement, precisely because of its indisputable success, which was confirmed by the ubiquity of its manifestations: "Surrealism has vanished? This is because it is to be found neither here nor there: it is everywhere. It is a ghost, a brilliant haunting [*une brillante hantise*]. In its turn, by a well deserved metamorphosis, it has become surreal."[1] This insight seemed confirmed by the exhibition which the Centre Pompidou devoted in 1991 to "André Breton and Convulsive Beauty."[2] The retrospective synthesis of various periods clearly illustrated the difficulty of positing the unity or even the concept of a "surrealist style" or "surrealist art." As a movement, surrealism seems to have traversed all the ruptures of this century, deriving much of its energy from a dialogue with almost all the artistic avant-gardes.

Blanchot's idea that the movement should have turned into a "ghost" by the middle of the century seems to enact an insight of André Breton with a vengeance. I shall take Breton's *Nadja* as the most provocative synthesis of early surrealist values, a synthesis precisely because its author attempts to bare everything, to confess everything, thus linking his person and surrealism as a mode of expression. Because of the fictionality implied by the confessional mode, Breton begins his account by asking: "Who am I?" adding that this question cannot be dissociated from a localization: "Where am I?" Soon after, the issue of place leads to the question of "haunting": "What am I?" signifies "What am I haunting?" Here, Breton rephrases a common French saying that connects being with haunting, since "to haunt" signifies to live in a particular place with a certain regularity. The ubiquity of haunting is nevertheless constrained at the end of the novel, which concludes with a passage from a newspaper clipping that describes how an airplane has disappeared within fifty miles of Sand Island: "The operator states he can localize the plane within a radius of 50 miles around the *Ile du Sable*." It is at this point that Breton interjects his famous final sentence: "Beauty will be CONVULSIVE or will not be at all."[3]

The formulaic "or will not be at all" suggests the threat of a nonplace, a nontaking place of beauty, a menace of annihilation that would be conveyed by the bland statement of Mallarmé's *Un Coup de dés jamais n'abolira le hasard* when he confirms that "Nothing will have taken place but place" (*Rien n'aura eu lieu que le lieu*) and points to the possibility of an "esthetics of disappearance," to quote the title of an essay by Paul Virilio. It is only an airplane that mysteriously disappears in *Nadja*, but Blanchot's idea of a disappearance of surrealism as such connects the movement with the logics of German idealism, from Hegel's *Phenomenology of the Spirit* to Husserl's phenomenology as rigorous science, implying a "return to things themselves."

What disappears, according to Blanchot, is less the communal dynamics of the movement than a type of discourse limiting language to the status of instrument: "Language disappears as an instrument, only because language has become a subject."[4] There is no longer the split between a collective subject identified with a "movement" and a language of rupture; language has become the central agency and thus accomplishes the linguistic turn of the second half of this century, a "turn" that stresses the *textual* as produced by a multiple agency that is more than just a group of friends.[5] Language is not just seen as the instrument that unlocks the unconscious through various poetic practices aimed at subverting rational censorship; it becomes the very substance of what Hegel, quoted by Breton, would call "the madness of the Spirit's manifestation" (a phrase I shall discuss later). Since Blanchot points to the centrality of Hegel in surrealism, I would like to suggest that different readings of Hegel actually oppose Breton and Georges Bataille.

The split between Breton and Bataille has often been held to have caused the "death" of the surrealist movement and has had repercussions reminiscent of the split between Freud and Jung. Bernard-Henri Lévy has, for instance, contrasted their strategies, asserting that only Bataille's way was possible, since he stressed an individualist strategy and refused to take orders from "Pope" Breton. Annie Lebrun has reacted with a violent and convincing defense of Breton and the values of surrealist poetry, surmising that the "new philosopher" wished above all to endorse history's judgment. It seems more accurate to say that both Breton and Bataille have been right in the quarrel that opposed them: Bataille was right to denounce the "idealist pains in the neck" who wanted to enroll him in doomed crusades; Breton was right to attack the perverted mysticism of a man he saw as "sexually obsessed" because he himself could not grasp Bataille's mental categories. In that complex ballet, their interaction actually precludes any dialectical twist that would show how anyone could be "right" in the dialectics of avant-garde movements.

Rather than Kant or Hegel, I would suggest another pair of opposites: Bataille's fierce celebration of a metaphysical brothel in which God is embodied as a prostitute's open vagina leads us in the direction of the provocative prophecies of someone like D. H. Lawrence, who systematically questions the rational and axiologic foundations of Western civilization. Lawrence's lifelong struggle with a puritanism that nevertheless left a mark on him finds an equivalent in Bataille's struggle with God.

Breton's vaunted purity would be closer to the visionary aesthetic and dogmatic serenity of another poet, William Butler Yeats. Both Breton and Yeats, who present themselves as magi and interpreters of another world, nevertheless insist on the political relevance of their writings. They maintain a fondness for the Celtic world of spirits, goblins, and apparitions; both see ghosts in broad daylight *and* believe in the force of morals as a key to collective action. Indeed, they both consent to answering the question "Who am I?" in the same way. "Who am I? If this once I were to rely on a proverb, then perhaps everything would amount to knowing whom I 'haunt'" (N, 11).

Nadja's well-known opening can serve as an introduction to this particular aesthetic. In fact, the word "to haunt" seems to lead Breton astray and propose to him the role of a living ghost: "I must admit that this last word is misleading, tending to establish between certain beings and myself relations that are stranger, more inescapable, more disturbing than I intended. Such a word means much more than it says, makes me, still alive, play a ghostly part, evidently referring to what I must cease to be in order to be *who* I am" (N, 11). No sooner has he defined himself as a ghost than all sense of personal identity is jeopardized or insists to be produced again and again—in compliance with the etymology of "identity," which derives from *identidem*, in other words, "repeatedly," through countless returns. Indeed, Breton's self-portrayal as a ghost follows the classical paradigm and departs in mourning, lamenting the loss of some dear person, doomed to retrace his own steps. This is what accounts for the nostalgia and poignancy of these pages relating an encounter which, despite all its magic, was doomed to fail. Such is the source of a constantly doubled narration. All that follows is presented retrospectively but with a sense of urgency that comes from the "exploratory" or "excavatory" (as Beckett would say) confession in these lines:

> My image of the "ghost," including everything conventional about its appearance as well as its blind submission to certain contingencies of time and place, is particularly significant for me as the finite representation of a torment that may be eternal. Perhaps my life is nothing but an image of this kind; perhaps I am doomed to retrace my steps under the illusion that I am exploring, doomed to try and learn what I should simply recognize, learning a mere fraction of what I have forgotten. (N, 12)

Retracing his steps in this way, Breton attempts to redeem the unredeemable, to live through the work of mourning—a mourning connected with love or with a denial of love—and to find a moral justification for this act. His self-definition also implies "an idea of irreparable loss, of punishment, of a fall whose lack of moral basis is, as I see it, indisputable" (N, 12). The following sentence displays a syntax so curious that a literal translation is almost impossible, as if to reveal a conceptual difficulty or an ethical uneasiness: "Hardly distorted in this sense, the word [to 'haunt'] suggests that what I regard as the objective, more or less deliberate manifestations of my existence are merely the premises, within the limits of this existence, of an activity whose true extent is quite unknown to me" (N, 11–12). The literal translation of this last sentence would be: "What I hold to be the objective manifestations of my existence . . . is only what passes, in the limits of this life, from an activity whose true field is totally unknown to me."[6] This "passing" is indeed ambiguous, since it can express the idea of an outlet, a derivation of a supplementary production, as well as the idea of an excess that passes all understanding.

Indeed, the mere notion of the process of "haunting" suggests for Breton someone passing beyond or through all boundaries. De Chirico is named several times in *Nadja* as the model of such a passing through appearances and "objective" data. The same notion symptomatically recurs in a contemporary text devoted to painting, which offers a critical evaluation of Chirico's works. In the realm of plastic art, Breton acknowledges Chirico as a natural leader who has unfortunately been led astray. He has nevertheless shown the way to the surrealists:

> How often have we found ourselves in that square where everything seems so close to existence and yet bears so little resemblance to what really exists! It was here, more than anywhere else, that we held our invisible meetings. . . . At that time men like Chirico took on the appearance of sentries stationed along a road of perpetual challenges. Certainly, when we reached the point where he was standing guard we found it impossible to turn back, it became a point of honour to *pass*. We did pass.[7]

Breton alludes to the "period of the Porticos, period of the Ghosts, period of the Mannequins, period of the Interiors" in order to lament the fact that now — in 1928 — Chirico stands outside the magical city he has erected with and for his friends. The betrayal of Chirico is all the more poignant since he led his comrades to a new type of vision, which literally was haunted.

> Still, it was not in vain that Chirico, in his youth, completed what was for us the most extraordinary journey ever undertaken. It may not be inappropriate to apply to him the phrase that, weaving through the night of the unknown, the future and the cold, must send shivers down the spines of the spectators of that marvelous film *Nosferatu*: "*When he reached the other side of the bridge the ghosts came to meet him.*" Ghosts. . . . However reticent he may show himself to be today on this point, Chirico still admits that he has not forgotten them. (*SP*, 16–17)

Breton then recalls how Chirico was obsessed by the historical meeting of Napoléon III and Conte di Cavour in 1858, "the only time to his knowledge that two ghosts have ever had the chance to meet *officially*" (*SP*, 17). While Chirico is noted to have declared that a child selling flowers in a Pigalle café was indeed a ghost, the theme of ghosts is then turned against this painter whose spectral visions are used to condemn and damn him: "Simply fixing on canvas a nondescript sky, a cup and a bunch of sour grapes will not do the trick. Because you will still be called to account for the apparitions that have ceased, and if you fail to answer quickly enough everyone will turn his back on you contemptuously" (SP, 17).

Breton's violent denunciation concludes by remarking that Chirico has become his own ghost, especially since he had begun copying his own earlier paintings (a practice that has been confirmed by many dismayed contemporaries):

> There are people, then, who dare speak of love when they are already no longer in love. I have actually witnessed the painful scene of Chirico attempting to reproduce one of his own early paintings with his present heavy hand, not indeed because he sought some illusion or disillusion in this act which might have been touching, but because by cheating on its external appearance he could hope to sell the same picture twice. It was so far from being the same, alas! (SP, 17)

Such behavior appears especially scandalous since Chirico's paintings seemed to embody the most authentic values of surrealism. While paying homage to Picasso, whose genius and anteriority Breton acknowledges, Chirico's elegantly stylized and dreamlike landscapes corresponded more precisely to the discovery of a visionary power in art that cubism kept at some distance with its abstraction and constructivist fervor. Indeed, the first *passeur* (ferryman or boatman of dreams) was also the first who thought he could control these visions at will as well as sell them! "So much the worse for him if he suddenly imagined one day that he was the master of his dreams!" (SP, 16). Chirico's "amorality," his temporary flirtation with fascism, his return to a neoclassical style all contributed to "undermin[ing] our faith in the truth to which I and my friends all subscribe, namely that in its passage through time the human spirit must inevitably remain absolutely identical to itself!" (SP, 16). Breton's remark sounds like a curious mixture of Hegelian historicism and moralist naiveté, and we cannot help smiling at the "faith" so strangely put forward.

This faith is also quite clear in the opening of *Nadja*, when Breton describes himself as a ghost: "This sense of myself seems inadequate only insofar as it *presupposes* myself, arbitrarily preferring a completed image of my mind which need not be reconciled with time" (N, 12). The great issue becomes how to reconcile the alleged timelessness of the self with the experience of loss: this describes the entire trajectory of the mourning process that will reveal the self's mortality.

At the close of the novel, Breton confesses to a failing in his ability to give and receive love:

> But I am judging *a posteriori* and I merely speculate when I say it could not be otherwise. Whatever desire or illusion I may have had to the contrary, perhaps I have not been adequate to what she offered me. But what was she offering me? It does not matter. Only love in the sense I understand it— mysterious, improbable, unique, bewildering, and *certain* love that can only be *foolproof,* might have permitted the fulfillment of a miracle. (N, 135–36)

Breton's glib "It does not matter" hardly dismisses Nadja's obvious passion for him, coupled with her sense of deep social alienation (she would tell him in a transparent understatement: "I have no friends but you" [142]), as inferior to the "unique and bewildering" love he idealizes. The abrupt sentence beginning the next paragraph renders all the more stark and evident the reason for such a rejection: "I was told, several months ago, that Nadja was mad" (136). Even if Breton attacks the institution and the practice of psychiatry with great vehemence, his aggressive flurry cannot hide his sense of embarrassment and guilt: "My general contempt for psychiatry, its rituals and its works, is reason enough for my not yet having dared investigate what has become of Nadja" (141). Is *Nadja* only a "seducer's diary," a poetic journal of the intense attraction linking Nadja and the poet between October 4, 1926, and the time between October 12 to 13, when they spend their only night together in a Saint Germain hotel?

Would this not be ignoring the fact that Breton kept seeing her afterward, at least until February 1927, before he abandoned her and she was certified insane in March 1927? *Nadja* contains an oblique confession that is written by a man unable to respond to passion, transforming that failure into the sublimation of romantic love: "It is unforgivable of me to go on seeing her if I do not love her. Don't I love her?" he asks, mystified, in the entry for October 7 (N, 90). The ending overlaps strangely with the covert announcement of another, much more serious, love affair, as if the entanglement with Nadja had only anticipated or precipitated the possibility of a serious commitment to another woman. Is this just a flight forward, which would confirm the picture of a "master" (Nadja had told him: "You are my master" [116], in order to confess: "I am your slave"), a master who nevertheless keeps running away from the beautiful hysterical women who inspire him.

Indeed, the whole "affair" of the book results from a displaced diagnosis: Breton takes Nadja to be a free spirit, a muse, or a magical hysteric, while she demonstrates obvious signs of the psychosis that will later submerge her rea-

son. The theme of "haunting" would thus belatedly admit of the error of diagnosis. However, this description would probably be too reductive, either too
moralistic or psychiatric, and would ignore what I see as the most fascinating
element of the book: its account of a "haunted" encounter and the attempt to
take this as key for a renewal of an everyday life that should appear permeated
by a wild and bright "beauty." The reflexive nature of these terms nevertheless
makes it almost impossible to discuss the text in terms other than the ones it
provides for the reader.

The terms are those that compose a riddle consisting of a few limited elements. Life is to be *read*, deciphered as a text: "Perhaps life needs to be deciphered like a cryptogram" (N, 112). We shall see how this thesis leads to the
fundamental discovery Breton arrived at through Nadja: that the activity of
deciphering is not neutral, but, on the contrary, discloses the "madness of light"
(Blanchot's *La Folie du jour* would be the exact equivalent) or, in more Hegelian
terms, the madness of manifestation (Hegel's *Folie der Offenbarung*, a phrase
to which I shall return).

The first to start reading signs in a slightly "crazy" way is Nadja herself,
who, drawing from her many shady adventures that do not stop at prostitution
and drug peddling, narrates to Breton how she had "wandered all night long
in the Forest of Fontainebleau with an archeologist who was looking for some
remains which, certainly, there was plenty of time to find by daylight" (N, 113).
Her privileged space is, however, in the streets of Paris, "the only region of
valid experience for her," "the street, accessible to interrogation from any human being launched upon some great chimera." Nadja embodies the principle of *tuché* ("chance" as described by Aristotle in *Physics*, 2, chaps. 4 and 5),
which Lacan takes as the key to a fundamental experience of the Real, but this
Real both resists and demands interpretation—hence all the mysterious doubles,
hallucinations, chance coincidences. This Real is a gateway to a new perception of reality: "Who were we, confronting reality, that reality which I know
was lying at Nadja's feet like a lapdog?" (N, 110–11). Thus, the only time she
decided to miss a rendezvous with Breton, he runs into her earlier, and then
keeps catching glimpses of her during the week following their encounter.
Indeed, Nadja seems to embody the major tenets of surrealist doctrine (a footnote confirms this, when Breton comments on Nadja's habit of telling herself
stories: "Does this not approach the extreme limit of the surrealist aspiration,
its *furthest determinant?*" [N, 74]).

It follows from Nadja's almost magical predisposition that Breton, who thinks
he is going to educate her by giving her two of his previously published books,
has to learn from her as a reader. As we have noted, Nadja's favorite "haunt" is

the street that she "haunts" like a living ghost, especially when looking more like a prostitute than a muse. Thus, when Breton offers his book *Les Pas perdus* (whose title can be interpreted either as "lost" or "wasted steps" and is often used in the phrase "Salle des pas perdus," meaning "waiting hall"—or, conversely, as "those who are not lost") along with the *Manifesto of Surrealism*, she immediately remarks: "Lost steps? But there's no such thing!" (N, 72). And then she leafs through the book and immediately starts freely associating, hallucinating a scene with a man lost in a forest. Soon after she thinks she finds death in the lines of Jarry quoted in *Les Pas perdus*. From the start, Nadja appears as a reader, and both finds and loses herself in a poem that speaks about ghosts. A premonitory passage that Breton does not quote mentions "L'ombre des spectres d'os, que la lune apporte, / Chasse de leur acier la martre et l'hermine" (The shadow of bone-ghosts carried by the moon / Drives away from their steel the marten and the ermine) (*OC*, 1:217).

Nadja exemplifies Breton's ideal reader: someone who reads fast and intensely and makes strong connections between texts and life—the "wild" reader roaming the streets of Paris, as it were, a reader who prefers the encounter with reality to libraries or museums. In fact, this is how Breton describes himself in the opening pages of *Surrealism and Painting*, when explaining how easily he loses himself in a painting:

> A few lines, a few blobs of colour hold me in their thrall as nothing else can do. . . . In such a domain I have at my disposal a power of illusion of which I cease to perceive the limits unless I am very careful. . . . I turn the pages and, despite the almost uncomfortable heat, I do not withstand my consent in the very least from this winter landscape. I mingle with these winged children. "He saw before him a brightly lit cavern," says the caption, and indeed I see it too. (2)

No sooner has he made this confession, which entails his admission that he conceives paintings as windows looking onto a new reality that is not different from that of all the readers for whom he writes, than he has to add the following caveat about museums: "But I must confess that I have stalked furiously through the slippery-floored halls of museums. . . . The enchantments that the street outside has to offer me were a thousand times more real" (3). Like Nadja, Breton prefers the streets to cultural institutions; both know that in the street there are no "lost steps." Each step brings you closer to your ghost and sharpens the "wild eye" of the primitive, the children, and the mad.

Just as *Surrealism and Painting* or the first *Manifesto of Surrealism* question the truth of "reality," *Nadja* hesitates between a purely magical transfiguration of reality into coincidences and "signatures" and a more realistic awareness of the intolerable realities of everyday life. Indeed, as economic pressures begin to encroach on Nadja's freedom (she asks Breton to pay for her rent, not wishing to prostitute herself since meeting him made her ashamed of this act), Breton has to differentiate between the "real Nadja, this always inspired and inspiring creature who enjoyed being nowhere but in the streets, the only region of valid experience for her" (N, 113) and the trivial cliché by which commonplace morality refers to a young and beautiful woman who walks up and down the pavements. This second picture presents a half-crazed Nadja whose ramblings sound futile and sordid: "She had no hesitation, as I have said, about telling me the most unfortunate vicissitudes of her life, not omitting a single detail, occasionally succumbing to uncalled-for coquetteries, forcing me to wait, brows knit, until she felt like proceeding to other exercises" (N, 134–35). Breton's *very* knit brows (*le sourcil très froncé*) seem almost ironic, in his expectation of something more magical and substantial at the same time!

He suggests at one point that life may be compared to a wandering through secret staircases, revolving partitions, and hidden doors: "We may imagine the mind's greatest adventure as a journey of this sort to the paradise of pitfalls" (N, 112). The "paradise of pitfalls" indeed provides one with a sort of fantasy of fun, a fair in which no one is assured of escaping from a perplexing hall of mirrors. This is why Breton's ultimate and pathetic cry to Nadja echoes so emptily: "Who goes there? Is it you, Nadja? Is it true that the beyond, that everything beyond is here in this life, I can't hear you? Who goes there? Is it only me? Is it myself?" (144).

This is not, however, the conclusion of the book. *Nadja* indeed rebounds again and transforms the deadend of the affair into a general aesthetics, as if aesthetics could only be erected upon the ruins of ethics. The question opened by the "haunting," which supplies a meaning to Breton's reiterated "Who am I?" and is taken up in Nadja's hexed and possessed adventures, can never be closed off again. There is indeed in this book a constant vacillation between a derealized ontology and a failed ethics: this would point exactly to the function and place of the ghost, a being who may or may not be, who returns only because of some unknown sin or unsettled debt, such as a revenge to enact or a denunciation to convey to survivors. This operates in *Nadja*'s complex prologue, in the circuitous route taken by the narrator to introduce us to the eponymous character.

The counterpart to her bewildering simplicity and openness is the initial fantasy of a glasshouse in which Breton would like his readers to see him whole: "I shall myself continue living in my glass house where you can always see who comes to call; where everything hanging from the ceiling and on the walls stays where it is as if by magic, where I sleep nights in a glass bed, under glass sheets, where *who I am* will sooner or later appear etched by a diamond" (N, 18).

This praise of utter transparency does not preclude the promotion of a concept of color. Breton tends to negate the fictional character of the text, insists that it is not a novel—but is it a strict autobiographical account?—and attacks traditional novels that disguise reality or transform it into psychology. When Breton briefly examines a few "biographemes" (as Roland Barthes would say) taken from the lives of writers and artists (Hugo, Flaubert, Chirico, Huysmans, Lautréamont)—placed in the order of an increasing disappearance or impersonality of the artist—he selects Flaubert, the novelist par excellence, and mentions with approval his alleged ambition to produce the effect of the color yellow in *Salammbô* and to write *Madame Bovary* in order to suggest the color of moldy cornices. This colorful transparency, if we may link the two terms, should produce exactly the same effect as Chirico's notion of aesthetic revelation: through this new prism, the feeling of surprise (a variation on Baudelaire's dictum that "The beautiful is always bizarre") is coupled with a new vision of everyday reality. But a haunted reality. Breton had read Jacques Rivière's article on dadaism, in which the critic alluded to Flaubert as a great precursor who would only write in order "to give shape and body to fancies [*lubies*] which were haunting him."[8]

Breton is thus ready to enact his fancies and bring forth a mythical and real woman whose status hesitates between that of pure mythmaking, with much affabulation and hallucination, and that of a real and therefore verifiable encounter. Hence the several photographs (I shall develop this theme in the next chapter) and the numerous documents in the text. Nadja's ultimate function is then to embody the ghost, to play the role of the specter that Breton felt he himself was turning into. The return of the ghost at the time of the book's writing—in the summer of 1927—gives all its poignant quality to the figure encountered in the fall and winter of 1926. He who feels himself summoned in front of a tribunal of shadows must account for his grave failures and thus found his writing upon an absence of foundations. Such an absence nevertheless stresses the urgency of a moral law. This is Breton's negative transcendental that starts from a collapse, an erosion of values, a hollowing out of narcissism by a feeling of responsibility. The "lack of moral basis" he alludes to (N, 12) in connection with a sense of "irreparable loss" can be countered if and only if Breton manages to accept that time is not fixed in a figure of eternal grief. This finally entails a meditation on certain Hegelian motifs such as the "end of history"—and the invention of a new aesthetics of surprise. Ultimately, there should be no gap, no difference between his aesthetics and his ethics: the aesthetics of haunting can be directly translated into an ethics of haunting.

Breton repeats that he loves moralists, not only because of a personal predisposition for morality (of which Bataille could make fun, as we have seen), but also because moralists tend to write well: "The Moralists, all of them, I love them, especially Vauvenargues and Sade. Morals is the great conciliator. Even when you attack it, you keep paying homage to it. It is in morals that I have always found my main sources of exaltation."[9] The coupling of Vauvenargues and de Sade should not surprise a reader of Jacques Lacan's essay on "Kant with Sade," which exposes the deep affinity of perverse discourse and transcendental philosophy.[10] Like most ethical writers and thinkers, Breton extols the unfinished nature of action and minimizes the actual product: "I only love, of course, unaccomplished things."[11] As Hermann Broch states in numerous writings, aesthetics becomes a perverted ideology as soon as the act is negated by the value attributed to its result (a theme I shall develop in chapter 6). Breton thus finds in Nadja a kindred spirit since she walks the streets in quest of a purely transient beauty, the joy of ephemera, and the pleasure of chance occurrences.

We can understand a little more clearly how Breton blends a certain moralist dogmatism and an appeal to nonbeing with open trajectories. This provides the rhetorical impetus for sentences such as the famous concluding statement in Nadja: "Beauty will be CONVULSIVE or will not be at all" (160). The "or will not be at all" condenses all the power of negation that is needed as a counterpart to any aesthetic axiom. Ironically, the sentence is molded on political rhetoric and finds an illustrious model in Thiers's famous maxim: "The Republic will be conservative or will not be at all." The implications of all or nothing, of freedom or death, easily radicalize a program for the future. Breton had already used it in a text of 1925: "The plastic work of art . . . will thus have to be referred to a purely interior model or will not be at all."[12] But after Nadja, the formula becomes a sort of cliché of Breton's manifestos and pronouncements on art. A good example is to be found in the first chapter of L'Amour fou, published in the magazine Le Minotaure in 1934: "Convulsive beauty will be erotic-veiled, fixed-explosive, magic-circumstantial, or it will not be."[13]

The statement condenses several theses that can be formulated as Breton's complete aesthetic in the early 1930s. Three pairs of adjectives function as oxymorons in order to suggest the following ideas: (1) Beauty will at the same time eroticize and veil the body; it will disclose and hide in imitation of the hysterical gesture. (2) Beauty will be both vertiginous and static; it will radiate as Arthur Rimbaud's concept of "defining [*fixais*] vertigos." (3) Finally, beauty will keep a magical component that should never be cut off from its immediate context of production and consumption.

After the thirties, "or it will not be" recurs as a reiterated self-quotation and a constant exhortation: it is used in a text devoted to Max Ernst in 1942, in which the fourth of seven commandments states that "beauty will be convulsive or will not be at all" (*SP*, 164–65), and Breton adds that the axiom "already promulgated is still relevant." This triggers a fantasy in which Max Ernst becomes a priest in the Saint-Médard cemetery, linking him with the famous episode of the "Convulsionaries of Saint-Médard" (1731), one of the first cases of collective hysteria. The historical allusion exemplifies the panic and sexual thrill of beauty.

A modulation intervenes in 1956, in a text written on Yves Tanguy: "Criticism will be love or will not be at all."[14] In 1957, we find again the same formula with the three groups of adjectives in *L'Art magique*. What returns is the urgency of a future that poses the maxim as an exhortation. The legislator's tone is never far, indeed, as if it were necessary for Breton to be all the more moralistic and imperious as he runs the risk of seeming naively paralyzed by beauty. A good ironical antidote would be provided by Eluard's entertaining pastiche of a delirium in the "Attempted Simulation of General Paralysis": "My great woman adored by all the power of the stars beautiful with the beauty of the billions of queens that adorn the earth the adoration I have for your beauty brings me to my knees. . . . My beauty and my beast think of me in paradise with my head in my hands."[15] To which a no less facetious reply could be given by Breton's own simulation of "Interpretive Delirium": "Do not count any more on me to help you forget that your ghosts are decked out like birds of paradise" (*IC*, 67). In order to avoid simulating in my turn this "interpretive delirium," I would like to suggest that if the ghosts of a future that may well have already taken place are indeed necessary to dispel illusions about the redeeming power of love, we need to investigate Breton's curious mixture of aesthetic philosophy and ethical zeal.

In much the same way as Lacan finds the pure and radiant beauty of Antigone in his reading of a play that has often been interpreted as the locus of ethics, Breton seems to posit a less pure but no less "convulsive" beauty as the "last word" of *Nadja*. Just before Breton closes with the superb and bewildering final page, summing up his conception of a "passionate" beauty that is both dynamic and static, he quotes Hegel in an enigmatic sentence that concludes the penultimate section. In fact, Breton exposes the rationale for his "all or nothing" attitude. He speaks directly to his new love, Suzanne Muzard, who has replaced Nadja and has "exploded" into his life with an intensity unknown before, and he explains that her irruption has not vitiated the ending he had intended to give to his narrative. This conclusion (the page on "Convulsive Beauty") seems to have been interpreted by the new feminine presence as purely subjective and libidinal, fundamentally dependent on love:

"It's still love," you used to say, and more unjustly, you would also say: "All or nothing."
     I shall never dispute this rule, with which passion has armed itself. At the most I might question it as to the nature of this "all"—whether, in this regard, it must be unable to hear me in order to be passion. As for its *various movements*, even insofar as I am their victim—and whether or not it can ever deprive me of speech, suppress my right to exist—how could they divorce me from the pride of knowing passion itself, from the absolute humility I should feel before it and before it alone? I shall not appeal its most mysterious, its harshest decrees. It would be as if I were to try to stop the course of the world, by virtue of some illusory power passion has over it. Or to deny that "each man hopes and believes he is better than the world which is his, but the man who *is* better merely expresses this same world better than the others. (N, 158–59, the latter refers to Hegel)

Breton quotes Hegel (as his footnote makes clear), a Hegel revisited by Croce.[16] Hegel rails at the *belle âme*'s belief that he can impose ideal values onto the world: the course of the world always proves the idealist wrong and defeats him by crushing his pretensions. Passion is considered as the very mechanism of historical dialectics and is not limited to a subjective emotion: passion thus defends the world against itself when it embodies the harsh and inhuman strength of "all or nothing" without which no change or revolution would have ever taken place. But in its very radicality, passion, as a force of the world, may also crush individuals; they cannot resist, "appeal" against, or avoid its decrees. Thus, Breton's personal attitude combines pride (for having known passion) and humility (because, having known it, he must admit to being powerless). The only hope he may therefore entertain will not lie in an effort to be superior to the world but rather in an attempt to reproduce it better than the others.

We are thus in a better position to understand the egotistic insistence on the question of the self exhibited in the first pages of the text. When Breton stresses his difference from other men, it is not a vainglorious or romantic cult of the self but an attempt to reach the only truth available to him: "I strive, in relation to other men, to discover the nature, if not the necessity, of my difference from them. Is it not precisely to the degree I become conscious of this difference that I shall recognize what I alone have been put on this earth to do, what unique message I alone may bear, so that I alone can answer for its fate?" (N, 13). The "message" he alone bears contains not just an already written text—which would rely too much on fate and predestination—but the combination of this unconscious encoding and all these other drafts and fragments such as *Nadja* itself. In their utopian convergence would lie the locus of the text as the Mallarméan "Book" capable of expressing the world in an absolute and final fashion.

The maximum transparency aimed at in the first pages is thus an ethical effort geared toward the best reproduction of a complex world. In *Nadja*, the figure Breton finds for this pellucid dream is, as we have seen, that of the glasshouse through which any account of his life will seem as if "etched by a diamond." In *Mad Love*, the glasshouse becomes the generalized trope of the "crystal forest" in which everything will be diaphanous: "The house where I live, my life, what I write: I dream that all that might appear from far off like these cubes of rock salt looked at close up."[17] Such a trope "crystallizes" a deep structural homology between the "world" and the "subject" and inscribes passion or desire as natural.

All this finds again its source in Hegel's *Philosophy of Nature* as translated into French by A. Véra. Hegel explains the process of differentiation and accounts for it by the means of the term "figure." A figure is the "material mechanism of individuality through which form manifests itself spontaneously."[18] The figure traverses three different moments: first, "magnetism," which corresponds to the "abstract principle" that is produced in its "free existence"; then "electricity," through bodies attracting and repulsing each other, thereby differentiating themselves; finally, "chemical processes" that realize a totality in which bodies represent different stages (PN, 1:561). For Hegel, the notion of figure culminates with the crystal: "The figure in its reality is the Crystal" (PN, 1:569). These references to Hegel underlie the passage from the *Magnetic Fields* in which the collaboration of Louis Aragon and Breton discloses the unconscious forces at work in spontaneous writing as much as they account for the definition of beauty as "fixed-explosive" in *Mad Love*. Beauty is indeed the becoming-crystal of all forms and all passions.

Such a becoming-crystal also encompasses the principle of individuation, the root of all differences. In Hegel's view, nature becomes the greatest artist:

> The form that deploys itself in crystallization is, as it were, a mute life that
> moves marvelously in purely mechanical productions that can apparently
> only be determined exteriorly, such as stones and materials, and that mani-

fests itself in particular formations as an organic and organizing effect. These formations develop freely and independently. And whoever has not been accustomed to observing what is regular and graceful in them will not take them for natural productions but will attribute them to the art and work of men. (PN, 1:566)

Breton tends to use Hegel's vocabulary whenever he attempts to articulate the unity of the mind and nature, and this appears more markedly after 1930. Indeed, the formulations of the *Second Manifesto of Surrealism* still evince a great ambivalence about Hegel, who is first quoted with due respect in connection with morality and "loyalty" in order to prove that any action is collective (OC, 1:792–93), then shown to have failed utterly: the following page admits the "colossal failure" (*avortement colossal*) of the Hegelian system that must now be replaced by historical materialism. Hegelian dialectics are declared wanting and deemed inapplicable to the new fields of investigation discovered by the surrealists.

Yet Breton keeps using the term *surclassée* when he writes that "philosophy is now overcome" (OC, 1:795), which translates very literally Hegel's *Aufhebung*. Much has been written about Breton's original version of Marxism and his brief stay in the French Communist Party. But once Breton has chosen his camp in the late thirties, opting for Trotsky over Stalin, he keeps referring to Hegel in his aesthetics. A good example is found in a text written in 1947 about Jacques Hérold's paintings and theories. Breton acclaims the recent publication of Malcolm de Chazal's aesthetic treatise and parallels some quotes with Hérold's pronouncements on "crystal figures" and "radiation" that are then linked with Hegel's terms:

> In the case of Hérold, it is clear that the accent is upon *magnetism*. In the words of Hegel, "magnetism achieves its gratification in the crystal despite the fact that it is no longer contained within it as magnetism." And he instructs us further that "the determinations of space should reproduce themselves in the determinations of the crystalline figure." (SP, 205)

Breton quotes from the long and fascinating discussion at the end of the first volume of Véra's translation of Hegel's *Philosophy of Nature*, in which the philosopher attempts to show how magnetism is the principle leading to the creation of crystal. Crystal is the realization of magnetism in natural bodies (PN, 1:621), but if magnetism finds a "satisfaction" in crystal, it does not remain as such in the body (PN, 1:610). Such a concrete figure allows Hegel to speak of an absolute interpenetration of form and matter (PN, 1:611). Magnetism remains deprived of finality, while the crystal is deprived of movement: these two missing elements will only be supplemented by the intervention of the spirit in nature when it understands how, for instance, crystallization is the externalization of the interior in the movement of nature according to the properties of space.

Breton's persistence in adopting these themes is striking: in 1956, when he praises the work of the painter Marcelle Loubchansky, he mimics even more literally the Hegelian reconstruction of the material forces operating in nature. His article concludes:

> In 1821, Hegel received as a present from Goethe a wineglass recalling symbolically the latter's *Theory of Colours* and dedicated as follows: "The originating phenomenon very humbly begs the absolute to give it a cordial welcome." Only a fragment of Hegel's letter of thanks has survived: "Wine," said Hegel, "has always been a powerful ally of the philosophy of nature, because it has demonstrated conclusively to the world that spirit also resides in nature." But, he added, a wineglass as instructive as the one which Goethe had given him was a veritable cosmic glass in which the sinister Ahriman joined Ormuzd, the child of light, to serve the folly of revelation [*zur Folie der Offenbarung diene*]. It is this glass which Marcelle Loubchansky carries to her lips.[19]

Breton alludes here to the abundant footnotes added by Véra to his translation of Hegel's *Philosophy of Nature* (PN, 2:113–14n. 1) concerning Goethe's *Urphänomen*—the first, original, or archetypical phenomenon being the opposition of light and darkness. In these pages of *Philosophy of Nature*, Hegel heaps abuse on Isaac Newton's theory of colors and speaks of the "ineptitude," "inanity," and "incorrectness" of his observations.[20] What is for Hegel, in his radicalization of Goethe's critique, Newton's "monstrous error"? (*HPN*, 143). He simply sullied the purity of light, admitting that light contains all colors in itself and that the experience of diffraction and refraction through a prism demonstrates how they all emanate from light. Goethe's theory of colors originated from the subjective and sensuous apprehension of color, not just seen as reflected through a prismatic glass, but constituted by an interplay of light and darkness.

The glass sent to Hegel by Goethe was a Bohemian tumbler covered diagonally half with black and half with white paper, so that the yellowish glass could appear blue when seen against the black surface: its simple presence was, according to Goethe, a direct refutation of Newton's theory. Newton (in a much more "scientific" fashion) appears closer to a physical theory of light when he explains that bodies derive their colors from the way they reflect light rays. Goethe, who derived considerable support from Leonardo's observations, had to postulate various physiological, physical, and organic factors that would account for differences in color. Fundamentally, Hegel agrees with Goethe, suggesting that color derives mainly from the metallic tainting of bodies, partly because his meditation seems "colored" by his study of crystals and precious stones. Hegel thus praises Goethe's "purity of his feeling for nature" (*HPN*, 148) and his belief that "white is visible light, *black* is visible darkness," only to engage then in a kind of associative and nonscientific symbolism. In this fashion, green, originally "the simple mixture" of blue and yellow, becomes "the neutral color" and is called "therefore the color of plants" (*HPN*, 152). Hegel's main point of emphasis is the fact that vision can be limited to the perception of color: "For sight there are only colors; shape belongs to touch, and is revealed to sight merely through the alternation of shade and brightness" (*HPN*, 160). Hegel's idealism is not devoid of Platonic overtones here, especially when he regards individuality as a "darkening" of a primal purity evinced by the transparency of crystal.

Moreover, Hegel's conceptual hesitation on the status of color should recall our discussion of Joyce's and Leonardo's greenish tints. Breton remains a Hegelian whenever he needs to address the issue of colored objects—even if he must, at times, invert the relative values and functions of light and darkness, as a passage of an essay on Picasso illustrates: "I have tried to define the external object, in its visual sense, as the product of a manifestation of the principle of darkness within the all-pervasiveness of light, a manifestation which succeeds in measuring itself on the surface through colour" (*SP*, 111). Hegel also anticipates Breton's haunted crystallography when he describes colors as specters:

> Colours are the particular modification of this relationship to light, so that they will have to be treated here. On the one hand they belong to the real individual body, but on the other hand they also merely waver outside the individuality of bodies. As yet, no objective material existence can be attributed to these shadowy entities; they are appearances which are simply dependent upon the relationship between light and a darkness which is still incorporeal. They are in fact a spectrum. (*HPN*, 122)

But during his vehement and misguided attack on Newton, Hegel refutes the theory of the specificity of the hues produced by the "prismatic spectrum" and adds: "(one might say spectre)" (*HPN*, 146), as if hoping to dispel these visual figments.

Breton appears less interested in the way Hegel praises Goethe for having replaced Newton with Plato than in the enigmatic passage in German about the "madness" or "folly" of manifestation: the irruption of light into the world becomes a sort of drunken epiphany, the sudden, Dionysiac revelation of all the powers and potentialities of nature. Indeed, this "pure" light reconciles the absolute and the archetypal. When extolling Marcelle Loubchansky's paintings for their visionary quality, Breton could just be commenting on Hegel's *Philosophy of Nature.* If the painter "restores to us the limpid gaze of childhood when the marvels of the aurora borealis conjugate themselves with those of the sky-blue robe" (*SP*, 346), it is also because the beauty she creates participates in the same tension between magnetism and the crystal-like fixity characteristic of Breton's own texts: "If it were ever a question of coaxing her secret from her, I think it would have to be sought in the direction of *magnetism.* . . . The secret would also have to be sought in the direction of the *diamond*" (*SP*, 346). The passing allusion to "aurora borealis" also evokes the passage of the *Immaculate Conception* in which Eluard and Breton invent a sort of Kama Sutra of surrealist lovemaking. Section 32 of this curious list reads: "When the virgin leans back with her body powerfully arched with her hands and her feet resting on the ground, or even better, her head and her feet, and the man kneels, it is *aurora borealis*" (*IC*, 105).

We may recall that this passage occurs in the subsection of the "Mediations" entitled "Love." These curious "Mediations" multiply devious points of entry used by Breton and Eluard to reach a condensed version of Hegelian dialectics. The subtitles ("Force of Habit," "Surprise," "There Is Nothing Incomprehensible," "A Feeling for Nature," "Love," "The Idea of Becoming") start with a pair of antithetical terms, surprise and habit, in order to establish the principle of historical comprehension through the interaction of contraries. When consciousness has started integrating the world as nature into its domain, it can reconcile itself to the idea of love and pure becoming. This abstract summary ought also to pay more attention to the ironic and playful mixture of collages, quotations, and parodies that dominates these texts (*IC*, 15–16).

The same argument reappears in the passage of *Surrealism and Painting* where Breton praises Max Ernst's strange assemblages of objects in certain collages: Ernst thus discovers new "relations" between the elements of our world. The gesture that creates these new relations is not deprived of violence, or indeed of arbitrariness, but always shows how human consciousness can surmount the randomness and cruelty of pure nature:

It is only natural, in fact, that we should be seized with horror by the things of this world ("Nature, nature!" we, too, cried out, sobbing, "the sparrow-hawk rends the sparrow, the fig devours the donkey and the tapeworm eats the man away!"); it is only natural that this horror should grip us when we consider certain episodes in Max Ernst's dream, which is a dream of *mediation*. The hateful separation of some of the parts is one more reason why we are determined to stake everything we possess. (*SP*, 26)

Indeed, Hegel reiterated that "mediation" was the crucial concept of his philosophy, a concept without which nothing could make sense—but with which he could make sense of everything, death and madness included. It will become clear that I believe André Breton to be a poet of mediation, a mediation he discovers through privileged encounters (with Chirico, Nadja, Ernst). This should counter the prevalent opinion that identifies surrealism with a literary and theoretical practice of lyrical immediacy.

It is important to note the shift from the first attempts at "automatic writing" as exemplified by the *Magnetic Fields* to the systematic exercises in the "simulation" of a psychotic delirium as exemplified in the *Immaculate Conception*. Ten years separate these two products of collaborative writing by Breton and Soupault in 1920, and Breton and Eluard in 1930. In the interim, Breton had met Nadja, written *Nadja*, and opted for a more systematic political commitment. This tremendous encounter with a female "muse" forced him to radicalize his notion of the concept as ghost. We have seen how *Nadja* opens with a scene of haunting—now that writing has replaced the frenzied and pathetic gesticulations of a woman who can be described either as a muse or as a case history in borderline behavior. For this reason, Hegel is all the more present in *Nadja* and the *Immaculate Conception*, despite Breton's apparent rejection of both idealism and speculative philosophy in the name of a clear political agenda.

The Hegel who is adduced by Breton is neither the Hegel of today nor the German philosopher of his immediate contemporaries. Breton is not so much concerned with the philosopher of history as with the philosopher of the spirit in nature, who deals with matter, form, color, magnetism, crystals, electricity, and so on. This corresponds to Breton's general aesthetic program outlined in *Surrealism and Painting* (thus roughly at the time of the encounter with Nadja):

Everything I love, everything I think and feel, predisposes me towards a particular philosophy of immanence according to which surreality would be embodied in reality itself and would be neither superior nor exterior to it.

And reciprocally, too, because the container would also be the contents. What I envisage is almost a communicating vessel between the container and the contained. Which means, of course, that I reject categorically all initiatives in the field of painting, as in that of literature, that would inevitably lead to the narrow isolation of thought from life, or alternatively the strict domination of life by thought. (*SP*, 46)

The utopia of a life identical with art and thought is a condensed version of Hegel's synthesis of the concept with the absolute and with its historical and empirical manifestations. To say that the surreal is the real would remain meaningless if this did not lead to a philosophy of relation or mediation. But since speed and economy are primordial for surrealism, the assertion of mediation must be made obliquely, less in a romantic fashion that would stress the power of the imagination than in a Freudian mode. The idea returns, and this return confirms the role of mediation, but it returns either as a ghost or as a slip of the tongue that nevertheless remains in consciousness.

Thus, Arp's fanciful distortion of *un nombril* (a navel) into *ombril* because one can say "*un (n)ombril, des ombrils*" leads Breton to a curious admission: "*Ombril*, a strange word, a slip of the tongue to which I would unhesitatingly apply the epithets tragic, snake in the grass, idea. . . . Idea motionless on the threshold of the mind, idea that the mind brushes against each day, as it passes, but does not confront!" (*SP*, 47). Such is the status of Arp's "ideas" produced by his wood reliefs: a shadow (*une ombre*), the shadow of a shadow, the snake lurking in our unconscious, always on the threshold of our waking minds and imaginations. Or, to take another example, when Breton quotes Ramon Lull in order to discuss Max Ernst's new painting, he begins by a reference to ghosts: "*A ghost is an abstract resemblance of things through the imagination*" (*SP*, 32). We can see how the equation between "ghost" and "idea" links the mind and the world through the intervention of the imagination. This is the way Breton has found to work with and against Hegel, to distort his well-know dictum ("Everything real is rational, and everything rational is real") in order to claim affiliation with a *surrationalism* that doubles and repeats *surrealism*. In such a context, the "crisis of the object" is interpreted in connection with the contemporary rationalist epistemology of Bachelard as early as 1936 (*SP*, 276).

All this stems from Croce's decisive influence on Breton in his lifelong dialogue with Hegel. I have already pointed to the fact that the quotation at the end of *Nadja* derives from Croce's essay on Hegel, whose French version Breton had read closely. *What Is Living and What Is Dead in Hegel's Philosophy*, Croce's critical account of Hegel's system, is no less important for Breton than it is for Joyce. It allows us to understand how the whirl of "surrational" insights that Nadja was able to arouse could lead Breton to a deeper awareness of the manifestation as mediation *and* as madness. In his chapter on dialectics, Croce examines the accusation of heady facility and abstruse glibness often made against Hegel. Antonio Rosmini, for example, had concluded an account of the dialectics of being and nonbeing with the allegation that "the system of Hegel finally only attempts to *render being mad, to introduce madness into everything*" (Croce, CQVM, 23). Far from denying such a charge, Croce quotes a famous sentence in the preface to the *Phenomenology of the Spirit* ("Truth is thus the bacchanalian revel, where not a member is sober; and because every member no sooner becomes detached than it *eo ipso* collapses straightaway, the revel is just as much a state of transparent unbroken calm"),[21] in order to praise madness as a "higher form of wisdom" (CQVM, 24), which destroys abstraction and launches dialectics as the only thought process capable of uniting life and thought. Croce also remarks that philosophy must be born from the womb of poetry (CQVM, 23), which provides a larger context in which to place Breton's wholehearted approval of the theme of a *"Folie der Offenbarung"*: it becomes identical with the Dionysiac drunkenness produced by natural and poetic "spirits."

Croce becomes more incisive when examining Hegel's theses on art and aesthetics. He sees Hegel as the victim of a sort of "panlogicism" intent on putting art in the shadow of philosophy. Croce attacks systematically Hegel's belief in the "death of art" (CQVM, 106), the domination of all art forms by philosophy that "thinks art" just at the moment of its demise. This is restated more cogently in Croce's *Aesthetic:* "The Aesthetic of Hegel is thus a funeral oration: he passes in review the successive forms of art, shows the progressive steps of internal consumption and lays the whole in its grave, leaving Philosophy to write its epitaph."[22] Croce demonstrates that the belief in an art reduced to an inferior philosophy invalidates the whole of Hegel's aesthetics. The same analysis applies in the case of Hegel's philosophy of history. Croce takes Vico as the model Hegel should have followed had he wished to avoid sweeping generalizations. Hegel pretends to be attentive to the idea of history but discards events as mere facts once they contradict his rational scheme. By a curious reversal, Hegel's philosophy of history ends up by negating real history (CQVM, 117).

On the other hand, Croce stresses the fact that for Hegel, nature does not know history (CQVM, 130). The combination of an ahistorical philosophy of magnetism and crystallography (closer to Bruno, according to Croce, than to Goethe), which provides a model of transparent organization for art, with a dynamic philosophy of history based on Vico's new science seems to offer a harmonious solution to Hegel's dilemmas. It is not necessary to wait with the owl of Minerva until night has fallen on nature and spirit alike. For the ghosts that appear at midnight herald a new world and prepare for a different type of "manifestation." This openness to the new entails that no one, not even Hegel, can stop the flow of time, as the conclusion of *Nadja* makes clear: "It would be as if I were to try to stop the course of the world, by virtue of some illusory power passion has over it" (159).

If we cannot arrest the course of history, art—especially painting—has the privilege of opening our eyes to the true magic of manifestation as such. It makes us believe in a surreal light coming from our eyes without which no vision would be possible: "I believe that men will long feel the need to retrace to its true source the magical river that flows from their eyes, bathing with the same light and the same hallucinatory shadow those things that are and those things that are not" (*SP*, 7). Perhaps art's power derives from this turning the river back to its source, thus starting anew a whole cycle of hallucinations whose cumulative effect will finally define a new type of passion.

This array of themes and quotations should suffice to show that the Hegel postulated by Breton has very little to do with the Hegel presented to the French intellectual public in the thirties and who was so influential on Bataille, Queneau, and Lacan—namely, the Hegel presented by Kojève. Kojève's central thesis begins with the notion of the "end of history": while Hegel saw Bismarck as the founder of the modern state that enacted a historical equivalent of absolute knowledge, Kojève saw in Stalin a new absolute master.[23]

Of course, Breton could never accept this thesis, any more than he could accept the idea that history is brought to a close once the spirit has passed through all the stages of its development. For Breton as for Croce, art can and indeed must lead the way whenever history reaches a dead end, since art already contains the categories that allow for an overcoming of the purely aesthetic domain. In this very subversion of art by itself, we can deduce not only an aesthetic system but also the lineaments of an ethical imperative that often appears as the extenuation or extinction of aesthetic axioms: beauty will be produced in a given and certain future because of its being coupled with the recurrent warning of "or it will not be at all!"

In a discussion of "mediation" and the "middle term," Hegel invokes a striking image: "In an army, the middle term is the general. Without the general, there may be a conglomerate of men, but there will be no army" (*PN*, 2:121). In fact, Breton seems to have assumed this role of "general of surrealism" without too many qualms because he believed in a collective movement unified by a sense of loyalty to a cause. This "general" might also have been called an "admiral" to follow another belligerent metaphor used in the *Second Manifesto of Surrealism* when Breton reminisces about the links between dadaism and surrealism and recent struggles among surrealists. Breton describes dadaism as the "torpedoing" of the "idea in the middle of the sentence which conveys it," in order to contrast this total dismissal of meaning with the way surrealism still retains a semblance of sense. But the meaning thus retained is no more than a "phantom ship": "Dadaism had wished above all to enhance this torpedoing. One knows that Surrealism had taken measures, by the way of a recourse to automatism, so that a vessel, any craft, would be spared from this torpedoing: something like a phantom ship (this image, which some thought they could use against me, even if it is worn-out, seems good and I take it up)."[24]

This allegory recalls a few lines from Breton's poem "Ghostly Stances" in *Earthlight*:

> The Jolly Roger from the time of any children's story
> Boards a vessel which is only the ghost of itself
> Maybe there's a hilt on that sword
> But in that hilt there's already a duel
> During which the two opponents disarm each other
> The dead one is the less offended party
> It's never the future.[25]

The "ghost of itself" suggests more nostalgia than terror; it signals a return to the age of childhood adventures, an imaginary world that negates the future.

A similar treatment of the imagination is provided by Yves Tanguy's dreamlike landscapes of regression bathed in a strangely amniotic light. This is how Breton describes these paintings, whose originality lies in their attempt at ascertaining the exact color of ghosts:

> We are behind the scenes of life, in that very place to which Gérard de Nerval had conducted us, where the figures of the past and those of the future "all co-exist, like the various characters in a drama with a still unformulated plot which is nevertheless fully fashioned in the mind of its author." But it was really Tanguy who made us see these wandering beings. His genius lies in having made himself master of their *spectral* essence—as Nerval has also said, to have "condensed in their immaterial, intangible mould a few pure elements of matter, meeting together and glowing suddenly like particles of dust dancing in a sunbeam." To succeed in this enterprise, Tanguy has wa-

gered with supreme confidence on the *poetic* accident of colour, to such an extent, indeed, that one could, I think, decompose his light into nasturtium, cock-of-the-rock, poplar leaf, well-chain, cut sodium, slate, jellyfish and cinnamon. (*SP*, 179)

In this highly personal variation on the prismatic decomposition of light, the ghostly colors retain their precise definitions (some derive from the pastel color-books; "cock-of-the rock," for instance, refers to a hue between ochre, melon, and faded pink), while peopling a metaphorical space with imaginary beings. While using the code of ekphrasis in a very idiosyncratic way, Breton's aim is not merely to describe certain paintings poetically. His real point is to prove that ghosts are not only seen but also painted.

Moreover, this accounts for the painterly quality of *Nadja*, with all the reproductions, photographs, and documents of the haunted life he once glimpsed. The iconicity of the novel enhances its proximity with the beautiful first edition of *Surrealism and Painting*. Like Chirico, Nadja created images and allegories capable of lending a definitive shape to "spectral essences." In order to approach these magnetic fields, ghostly stances are required. Their visual equivalent is the spectral rainbow of secondary colors pointing backward to the past and forward to an unknown future. Breton was fond of quoting Xavier Forneret's maxim: "*Tout dire se peut avec l'arc-en-ciel des phrases*" (Everything can be expressed thanks to the rainbow of language) (*SP*, 41).

The evocative term "cock-of-the-rock" reappears in the poem entitled "Not All of Paradise Is Lost" and provides an arresting metaphor connecting Hegel's crystallography and the unconscious scenography of ghosts who haunt the "other scene" of a purely poetic unconscious:

> Cocks-of-the rock move in crystal
> They protect the dew with pointed crests
> Then the charming emblem of the thunderbolt
> Descends on the banner of ruins
> The sand is reduced to a phosphorescent clock
> That says midnight
> With the arms of a forgotten woman[26]

Roland Barthes, Ghostwriter of Modernity

There can be no photograph without the withdrawal of what is photographed. The conjunction of death and the photographed is the very principle of photographic certitude: the photograph is a cemetery. A small funerary monument, the photograph is a grave for the living dead. It tells their history—a history of ghosts and shadows—and it does so because it *is* this history.
EDUARDO CADAVA, "Words of Light: Theses on the Photography of History"

It may seem rather arbitrary to link Barthes with Breton: Barthes, the world-renowned critic, theoretician of culture, and semiotician turned introspective and autobiographical, made no secret of the fact that he was tempted at the end of his life to write a "Proustian novel." He devoted his last seminar to the public "deliberation" of his "Preparation for the Novel." Would Barthes have written *Nadja*, a novel in which the "I" of the author is so central? It seems that the central encounter glorified by Breton is rewritten by Barthes's *Fragments of a Lover's Discourse*: instead of a modernist tale of passion, magic, and madness, we discover the countless clichés we use when our "postures" and functions are arranged by love, a postmodern puppetmaster. Despite his having trumpeted in 1968 the "death of the author," Barthes sensed a need to reintroduce the term "biography," even surreptitiously with his "biographemes," and found himself obliged to parade his subjectivity more and more—often as parody, in the case of the famous *Roland Barthes by Roland Barthes* in which he discusses his own work just as he had done previously in the same series with the work of Michelet.[1]

Much has been said about Barthes's "return" to realism, phenomenology, the imaginary, and Sartrian models: if death and perhaps his own inclinations had finally reconciled Barthes with Sartre (both died in 1980), Barthes could never be reconciled with surrealism, which he viewed as incorrigibly romantic and idealist. He preferred to mediate between a few great classical writers and the avant-garde of his time: Robbe-Grillet and Sollers are more likely to be praised than any surrealist poet. Yet the resurgence in his final years of the issue of novel writing, as well as his ambivalent stance on the issue of subjectivity, tempts me to link Barthes's demise with the central question posed by Breton at the beginning of *Nadja:*

> Who am I? If this once I were to rely on a proverb, then perhaps everything would amount to knowing whom I "haunt." I must admit that this last word is misleading, tending to establish between certain beings and myself relations that are stranger, more inescapable, more disturbing than I intended. Such a word means more than it says, makes me, still alive, play a ghostly part, evidently referring to what I must cease to be in order to be *who* I am. (N, 11)

It is clear that these questions can be heard in Barthes's later texts, which have a strange posthumous quality. The role of the ghost assigned to the subject is set off by the greater reality of the photographs that adorn *Camera Lucida,* just as Nadja and Breton's Paris partly derives its magic from photographs that replace descriptions. Breton thought that photography was proof that the descriptive novel had died.

Paul Valéry, who was initially a mentor for the young Breton, at the time of his early neo-symbolist poems, developed this thought in a speech he presented to commemorate the centenary year of the invention of photography.[2] Alluding to Plato's cave, Valéry suggests that modern science is fragmented into a variety of particular spectrographs: the universe is produced by humanity's diverse means of representing infinitely small or infinitely far events. According to Valéry, photography renders realism superfluous and description redundant. Language is given back to the writer as his own tool and medium. Breton could only agree with this thesis, since he attacked the "postcards" that were found in traditional novels and spoke of the "nonentity" of literary description in the *Second Manifesto of Surrealism* (OC, 1:314).

In the 1962 preface to *Nadja,* Breton adds that the abundant photographic illustrations aim at eliminating all description (OC, 1:645). The objects he wished to preserve in these illustrations had to be kept in a subjective perspective and were to be "taken from the exact angle of my vision when I had myself contemplated them" (OC, 1:746). Moreover, he notes that most objects seemed to resist this desire and proved unamenable to this reappropriation: he was not able to obtain permission to reproduce the Musée Grévin's wax woman attaching her garter, and the statue of Becque, walled in by planks, remained out of reach (OC, 1:746–48). Such a resistance pertains to what Lacan calls the real, which recurs as a hallucinatory chance encounter with an ever surprising otherness.[3]

This is precisely the field Barthes explores in his testamentary *Camera Lucida*. This last essay has been called Barthes's Proustian novel, which he dedicated to his mother who had recently died, yet whose photograph is conspicuously absent from the text, even when he discusses it at length. This text is also a sort of diary of a painful mourning process, a journal that poses the same question as Breton in *Nadja*, "Who am I?," but in a different and mournful key.

As Barthes writes in "Deliberation," a text to which I shall soon return, a journal is, at best, the limbo of the real text to come: "What the Journal posits is not the tragic question, the Madman's question: 'Who am I?' but the comic question, the Bewildered Man's question: 'Am I?' A comic—a comedian, that's what the Journal keeper is."[4] "Deliberation" begins with a surprising negation of its status as diary: Barthes thus publishes in *Tel Quel* a few pages from his diaries with the opening caveat: "I've never kept a journal" (*RL*, 359).

I want to quote a rather long passage from this nonjournal in order to analyze the link between the return to subjectivity and the identification of the subject with the role of the ghost.

At the (crumbling) Galerie de l'Impasse, I was disappointed: not with D. B.'s photographs (of windows and blue curtains, taken with a Polaroid camera), but by the chilly atmosphere of the opening: W. wasn't there (probably still in America), not R. (I was forgetting: they've quarreled). D. S., beautiful and daunting, said to me: "Lovely, aren't they?" "Yes, very lovely" (but it's thin, there's not enough here, I added under my breath). All of which was pathetic enough. And since, as I've grown older, I have more and more the courage to do what I like, after a second quick tour of the room (staring any longer wouldn't have done any more for me), I took French leave. . . . Finally I warmed up a little at the Flore, ordering some eggs and a glass of Bordeaux, though this was a very bad day: an insipid and arrogant audience: no face to be interested in or about which to fantasize or at least to speculate. The evening's pathetic failure has impelled me to begin, at last, the reformation of my life that's been in my mind for so long. Of which this first note is the trace.

(Rereading: this bit gave me a distinct pleasure, so vividly did it revive the sensations of that evening; but curiously, in reading it over, what I remembered best was what was not *written*, the interstices of notation: for instance, the gray of the rue de Rivoli while I was waiting for the bus; no use trying to describe it now, anyway, or I'll lose it again instead of some other silenced sensation, and so on, as if resurrection always occurred *alongside* the thing expressed: role of the Phantom, of the Shadow.) (*RL,* 368–69)

The "reformation" of his life seems to be the "decision" to write a novel instead of all those learned papers, seminars, and conferences. The excruciating details that speak of wasted time and missed opportunities would thus have the same function as the *Bal des têtes* at the end of *Time Regained.*

Like the Proustian narrator, Barthes experiences the turning away from the vanity of mundane pleasures—Proust's snobbism and devotion to some chosen figures of the Faubourg Saint Germain finds its counterpart in Barthes's adulation of a few novelists and artists from the Latin Quarter—and decides to commit himself to the serious task of writing. A certain pleasure in the writing act has been attained through this exact reviviscence of a lonely and disappointing evening. Barthes provides a glimpse of his *Passagenwerk* in the making, of his "Parisian nights" or *Soirées Parisiennes* of the following months, August and September 1979, by describing himself as a sort of ghost.[5] The concept of the "phantom," the thing resurrected but not exactly at the right place, corresponds to what Barthes expects of a photograph.

In keeping with Balzac's innate fear that each photograph taken by his friend Nadar might steal some layer in his private and precious spectral emanations, Barthes describes the triangle composed by the photographer, object, and observer as a sort of ghost dance:

> The *Operator* is the Photographer. The *Spectator* is ourselves, all of us who glance through collections of photographs—in magazines and newspapers, in books, albums, archives. . . . And the person or thing photographed is the target, the referent, a kind of little simulacrum, any *eidolon* emitted by the object, which I should like to call the *Spectrum* of the Photograph, because this word retains, through its root, a relation to "spectacle" and adds to it that rather terrible thing which is there in every photograph: the return of the dead.[6]

Barthes's subjective dereliction in his final years has been amply documented by his friends. Robbe-Grillet confirms this impression:

> In the final part of his existence, Roland Barthes seemed haunted by the idea that he was only an impostor: he had spoken about everything, Marxism as well as linguistics, without ever knowing anything completely. . . . To no avail, I replied that he was indeed an impostor precisely because he was a true writer. . . . He would smile, with that inimitable mixture of discreet

intelligence, friendship but also a certain distance, an aloofness from the world which would come upon him at any time then.[7]

This idea had already been launched by Robbe-Grillet during the Cerisy Conference of June 1977 devoted to Barthes, and it created a considerable stir. Although this could not be reduced to a private quarrel between the novelist of the *Nouveau Roman* and the critic, some historical elements should be recalled. In 1954 in the magazine *Critique*, Barthes published one of his first literary essays on Robbe-Grillet's *Erasers*. In the same venue, Barthes reviewed his *Voyeur* the following year.[8] In these texts, Barthes extols a pure writing that abolishes incidentals of plot and fable, destroys the "psychology of the characters," and merely records the surface of things and events, in a language void of any metaphor or blandishments of style. Robbe-Grillet embodies the utopia of a "writing degree zero," which had been developed in his essay with the same title published in 1953. Even if a few signs of disagreement appear in these three early texts (Barthes is quick to note that a "blank writing" is almost impossible, that writing always reverts to privileged recurrences or tropes), Robbe-Grillet remains a model, especially when compared to Butor. Ten years after *Writing Degree Zero*, Barthes wrote a preface to Bruce Morrissette's essay on Robbe-Grillet's novels, in which he denounces the return to the "traditional aims of the novel" and an abdication of the "revolutionary aspect of the work."[9] In various texts and interviews, Barthes comments more and more explicitly on the inadequacy of the writing of the *nouveaux romanciers* who were not able to realize their original project.

This explains how Robbe-Grillet could announce during the Cerisy Conference that Barthes had never written about his novels but had taken them as a pretext to speak of himself: "Thus Barthes the budding novelist had already started to develop in his texts." The novelist in Barthes might always have been subtly at work, combining a deceptive theory with obvious literary gifts in order to keep playing further with language. The novelist would consequently appear as a sort of literary imp who undermines the validity of theoretical pronouncements and displaces all the messages in an endless linguistic whirl. This is why, during this same discussion, Robbe-Grillet recalls an anecdote that also finds its place in the autobiographical *Le Miroir qui revient*. He explains how he was talking to a disappointed student just after Barthes had given his inaugural lecture (his *leçon*) at the Collège de France in January 1977. The student had exploded: "But he's said nothing at all!" Robbe-Grillet answered that therein lay precisely Barthes's genius: "Indeed, he has not said anything, he has slipped endlessly from one elusive meaning to another which also eludes us."[10] The student was angry because she was looking for a master, a guru, a sage, while Barthes was denouncing the "fascism" of all assertive language.

Barthes's atopicity was the only way of escaping from the recurrent risk of such normative and totalitarian language. Robbe-Grillet's praise is sound but also dangerous; it damns with faint praise. It is a little like praising a lecturer not for what he has said but for the richness of his voice.[11] The cruel truth hidden in these flippant remarks probably convinced Barthes that he was in fact not only hiding his homosexuality from his mother but also concealing his deep wish to be a novelist from himself. By a strange paradox, he had to become all the more spectral as he was split between the role of a central character whose tastes would color all his writings and the quasi-divine function of an author whose absence he himself had heralded.

This is why we can understand the convergence of two obsessions in the later Barthes: a return to the form of the journal and an exploration of family photographs. Moreover, this is why the passage I have quoted from "Deliberation" describes his reluctant visit to an opening of Daniel Boudinet's series of Polaroids: just such a bluish or greenish "Polaroid" from 1979 adorns the back page of the table of contents in *Camera Lucida*. While this can hardly be described as a family photograph, we cannot help allegorizing the small triangular shape that opens at the bottom of a double veil, against which a round cushion seems to force its way out as a fetus during its expulsion from the womb. But the birth we are witnessing is not just the birth of a novelist, or even the birth of a "happy" writer: Barthes's modernity lies in the fact that he embodies the Mallarméan opposition between the absolute work and the futility of everyday writing without any justification.

> The book, "architectural and premeditated" [Barthes is quoting Mallarmé], is supposed to reproduce an order of the world; it always implies, I believe, a monist philosophy. The Journal cannot achieve the status of the Book (of the Work); it is only an Album, to adopt Mallarmé's distinction. . . . The Album is a collection of leaflets not only interchangeable . . . but above all *infinitely suppressible.* (RL, 370)

This is why Barthes considers writing fifteen imaginary books in his *Roland Barthes* and concludes the list on the title of "Incidents": "*Incidents* (mini-texts, one-liners, haiku, notations, puns, everything that falls, like a leaf)."[12]

The writer who consents to a total identification with pure writing can only survive as the ghost of himself, the return of a private ethos that becomes the absolute test of truth and an absolute nothingness: this is what Stirner describes as the "unique" or "egoism" of the self in the *Unique and His Properties*—a treatise whose theses I shall address in the conclusion of this book.

The biographical theme of the ghostly self is not a discovery of Barthes's later years: a striking adumbration of it appears in an essay originally published in English in the *Times Literary Supplement* (in 1971). In this piece, entitled "Pax Culturalis," Barthes reexamines the opposition between nature and culture, which he himself had taken for granted in his early essays. He first examines the familiar truism that we live in a "bourgeois culture" and counters with the notion that any culture is bourgeois. Moreover, if "everything is culture," if even biological genes are constructed as a language, then this culture produces a paradoxical situation, being everywhere and nowhere, "without contours, without oppositional term, *without remainder*" (*RL*, 100). Such a culture will therefore be "without incident," "subject to a tireless repetition." Nothing will happen in this idealized version of the Hegelian "end of history" as envisaged by Kojève. Barthes adds to this entropic view that if this culture is indeed dead, then we are living off the "remains" of a decaying corpse: "Thus, culture is not only what returns, it is also and especially what remains in place, like an imperishable corpse: it is a bizarre toy that *History never breaks*" (*RL*, 100).

The illusion of a peaceful but lethal entropy dissolves when we pay attention to the various languages vying for supremacy: "In our culture, in the *Pax culturalis* to which we are subject, there is an inveterate war of languages: our languages exclude each other" (*RL*, 101). Barthes adduces the example of the lack of communication he experiences when conversing with a salesman in the Nouvelles Galeries: although both speak French, they can hardly go beyond banal truisms. Such an exchange lacks the particular excitation a Charlus would feel when chatting up elevator boys in Proust's *Recherche*. Barthes views this lack of communication as another mourning (*deuil* in the French original) and grieves for an impossible transparency.

The cultural world is thus made up of monadic and idiolectal entities that only jostle each other: "My neighbor is bored by this Brahms concerto, and I regard this variety sketch as vulgar and that soap opera as idiotic: boredom, vulgarity, stupidity are various names for the secession of languages" (*RL*, 101–2). Grief and mourning are subjective expressions by which we lament the lack of an ideal community, whose realization Barthes sees elsewhere, in a mythical China seized by a "cultural revolution" (this is written in 1971), whereas Europe has only the choice between a "high" and dead elite culture and a trivialized phantom: "One can say that in petit-bourgeois culture, in mass-culture, it is bourgeois culture which returns to the stage of History, *but as a farce* (Marx's image will be recalled)" (*RL*, 104). The unique alternative is thus between a "return of the ghost" of the dead culture or the "return as farce," the travesty of inadequate ideologies. No doubt Barthes saw himself as caught between the roles of the madman who asks: "Who am I?" and that of the comedian, fool, or jester who asks: "Am I?" (*RL*, 372).

The only alternative for Barthes, who despite all his surprising theoretical about-faces nevertheless remained steadfast in his effort to abide by an ethics of signs (announced as early as *Mythologies*),[13] is thus to speak of himself, of his own idiolectal choices, likes and dislikes, in the hope that the tone will at least be just and able to touch us. Or, more precisely, he opens his album in the hope that he will touch us whenever describing how he himself has been touched by certain photographs. When he opposes the operator, spectator, and spectrum in his pseudoscientific terminology—whose aim is to let the "ghost" emerge from the spectrography of the camera—he deliberately withholds from his analysis the function of the operator.

This is the aspect of *Camera Lucida* that has disappointed most photographers and professional critics—even a close friend and publisher such as Denis Roche, himself an avant-garde poet and novelist, and above all an excellent photographer, has expressed his dismay. Roche's frustration appears when, for instance, Barthes reduces Wiliam Klein's views of Moscow to their documentary importance, whereas "their revolutionary esthetic is obvious."[14] Roche grants that the importance of *Camera Lucida* is as a sort of novel or journal that reinstates the subjectivity of the observer. If we follow Roche's hint, this text would be the equivalent of Nietzsche's last letters, which are indeed alluded to at the end of *Camera Lucida*.

Barthes attempts a sentimental analysis of photography that leads him to the admission of basic feelings of pity and love—but in imitation of a Nietzsche who threw himself in tears on the neck of a beaten horse, when he had "gone mad for Pity's sake" (*CL*, 117). *Camera Lucida* finally exposes the subtle connection between madness and the "prick" of the *punctum*—but this needs a narrative in the first person and past tense: "I then realized that there was a sort of link (or knot) between Photography, madness, and something whose name I did not know. I began by calling it: the pangs of love" (*CL*, 116).

> Pity. I collected in a last thought the images that had "pricked" me (since this is the action of the *punctum*), like that of the black woman with the gold necklace and the strapped pumps. In each of them, inescapably, I passed beyond the unreality of the thing represented, I entered crazily into the spec-

tacle, into the image, taking into my arms what is dead, what is going to die, as Nietzsche did. (*CL*, 118–17)

It is only on the antepenultimate page of *Camera Lucida* that we realize that the treatise on photography is closer to the journal of a madman who is crazed by grief and mourning.

A first hint had been given early on, during a discussion of the doubling effect of photography: "Even odder: it was *before* Photography that men had the most to say about the vision of the double. Heautoscopy was compared with an hallucinosis; for centuries this was a great mythic theme. But today it is as if we repressed the profound madness of Photography" (*CL*, 12–13). Such a madness can only be perceived by a subject who becomes aware of his fascination, of the deeper madness underlying this fascination: this would be the principle by which seeing is more than seeing. The particular "madness" of photography consists in making us *see* death as the main referent: "The Photograph (the one I *intend*) represents that very subtle moment when, to tell the truth, I am neither subject nor object but a subject who feels he is becoming an object: I then experience a micro-version of death (of parenthesis): I am truly becoming a specter" (*CL*, 14). Thus, the central question is not just "Am I?" or "Who am I?" but "Am I alive or dead—when I see a photograph, or when I am (become) a photograph?" In order to reach this truly disquieting problematic, Barthes needs to prick or pierce the equanimity of a purely cultural (entropic) contemplation. For this, he has to produce his first rhetorical machinery, the opposition between the *studium* and the *punctum*.

Such a binary opposition is not reached immediately in *Camera Lucida*; it is only after Barthes has stated his dissatisfaction with all previous discourses on photography as an art or a genre. What he stresses from the start is a desire to stick to the particular, the "this" of photography, to reach an "ontological desire" that links the image back to the source, back to the absent person or object. ("What is a ghost? Stephen said with tingling energy. One who has faded into impalpability through death, through absence, through change of manners" [*U*, 154].) It is only after asserting his main thesis, using phenomenological terms quite new to his pen—"Death is the *eidos* of that Photograph" (meaning a photograph of himself [*CL*, 15])—that he can elaborate a "structural rule" (*CL*, 23).

Noticing that he is struck, interested, "hailed" only by certain photographs, he wonders what in the photograph attracts his eye. Starting from a picture by Koen Wessing that depicts soldiers in Nicaragua patrolling in a poor village while two nuns pass by, the "co-presence of two discontinuous elements" (*CL*,

23), yields the main rule: only a detail can focus attention. Hence the opposition between a studium reducing photography to a generality (connotations, politics, history of art, referential or documentary value) and the punctum that "rises from the scene, shoots out like an arrow and pierces" the subject, thus seizing upon the subjective cathexis of the eye:

> A Latin word exists to designate this wound, this prick, this mark made by a pointed instrument: the word suits me all the better in that it also refers to the notion of punctuation, and because the photographs I am speaking of are in effect punctuated, sometimes even speckled with these sensitive points; precisely, these marks, these wounds are so many *points*." (*CL*, 26–27)

Barthes's decision to wait for the "accident which pricks me" in any photograph leads to a remarkable discussion of several photographs.

This movement toward a subjective glance is less surprising than it seems. Many commentators have discussed the curious recantation in *Camera Lucida*, deploring the fact that Barthes seems to have forgotten all his previous analyses of the "photographic message" as an historical and political construction that frames the referent and constitutes its meaning by surreptitiously endowing it with all sorts of values.[15] After all, Barthes was one of the first to define the rules of semiological, mythological, and culturalist interpretation of such messages as advertisements or political images (Kennedy's vibrant and triumphant profile, and a black soldier under the French flag are two of many examples with which the "semiological" Barthes worked in a critical and caustic manner).

A relatively early text devoted to an exhibition of political photographs (with the aim of exposing the horrors of repression, torture, and execution perpetrated against Guatemalan Communists) in the French text of *Mythologies* questions the saturation of meaning evinced by some political photographs: because they presuppose a whole interpretation and are bound to their interpretive context, they finally leave us cold, only allowing us to measure the infinite distance between the mangled bodies and ourselves. "We can no longer *invent* our own reception in front of a synthetic nourishment which has already been perfectly assimilated by its creator."[16]

Against this reduction (no doubt, performed with the best intentions), Barthes opposes the *numen* of the photograph, thanks to which interest can be awakened. Only thus can the photograph trigger pity, compassion, and political sympathy, for it then presents the "amplified sign of instability," an "immobile aggrandizement of the unfathomable," "a troubling challenge, dragging along the reader of the image towards an astonishment less intellectual than visual, because precisely it holds him through the surfaces of the spectacle, through its optical resistance, and not immediately through its meaning" (M, 120–21). The good photograph is like a good painting: it does not allow for an easy reduction of its surface to a cultural or political meaning; its material resistance to codification excites the decoding activity. All the seeds of the later conceptual elaboration are to be found in the photographic text, and the punctum just provides a rationale for the subjective decentering that is identical with this flash of meaning that will have to become a "floating flash" (CL, 53).

The punctum elaborates on another, earlier, floating notion, which he had called the "third meaning."[17] This "nonconcept" already refuses the characteristics of semantic stability and iterability that define a philosophical notion: it is the moment when an image produces a sort of nonmeaning that touches me for its formal properties. With the punctum, the point that touches me by revealing that I need not fear, since the enormous catastrophe I fear has already taken place, is indeed identical with what William Talbot had called the "the Pencil of Nature." The critical discourse only adds what was already there: "Last thing about the *punctum*: whether or not it is triggered, it is an addition: it is what I add to the photograph and *what is nonetheless already there*" (CL, 55). We can list these strange supplements. We find in succession:

the two nuns already mentioned, when contrasted to the soldiers in
    Nicaragua (CL, 23, 47);
the strapped pumps of a young black woman in a James Van der Zee
    photograph (CL, 43);
the bad teeth of some Little Italy children in a photograph by William
    Klein (CL, 44–45);
Tristan Tzara's large hand with unclean nails in a portrait taken by André
    Kertész in 1926 (CL, 45);
the dirt road on which a blind violinist is led by a boy in a photograph by
    Kertész (CL, 45, 47);
the "slightly repellent" spatulate nails of Andy Warhol, where he hides his
    face in his hands, in Duane Michals's portrait (CL, 45);
the boy's huge Danton collar and the girl's finger bandage in Lewis
    Wickes Hine's portrait of two idiot children in an institution (CL, 51);
the black boy's crossed arms (but not the other boy's hand resting on
    Brazza's thigh) in a group picture of Savorgant de Brazza and two boys
    by Nadar (CL, 51);

something indescribable floating between the eyes, skin, hands, and shoes
of Robert Wilson, which makes him someone Barthes would like to
meet (*CL*, 51–53, 57);
the kilted groom holding the bridle of Queen Victoria's horse (*CL*, 57);
Robert Mapplethorpe's outstretched arm and radiant smile that defines a
kairos of desire;
and then, the absolute punctum, the unseen photograph of the mother in
the Winter Garden (*CL*, 67–70).

Any attempt to systematize these "details" would be idle; if Barthes shares
with Freud the idea that details can allow us to reconstruct the effect and af-
fect of a work of art,[18] then these details can never add up to a few personal
obsessions. Despite the private or subjective elements thus exposed, Barthes's
points cannot be easily reduced to visual fetishes.

In one case, the punctum seems to deflect the too obvious allusion to homosexuality when the boy's hand caresses de Brazza's thigh: precisely because
this curious gesture is a little too obvious, the punctum must be elsewhere. In
the case of the black woman's strapped shoes, Barthes revises his judgment
and devises another explanation—which implies that the punctum is not immediate but needs a certain temporality to unfold itself:

> This photograph has *worked* within me, and later on I realized that the real
> *punctum* was the necklace she was wearing; for (no doubt) it was the same
> necklace (a slender ribbon of braided gold) which I had seen worn by some-
> one in my own family, and which, once she died, remained shut up in a
> family box of old jewelry (this sister of my father had never married, lived
> with her mother as an old maid, and I had always been saddened whenever
> I thought of her dreary life). (*CL*, 53)

Barthes could not have admitted more openly the private nature of these
associations, which imply an entire family romance to be understood. A complex Freudian game of displacement—from shoes to neck, a similar buckle or
band—and condensation is at work. For instance, if the straps on the shoes do
not mean much to most viewers and thus appear as a "private" punctum,
Barthes's second elaboration shows the necklace to be a token to sterility that
allegorizes the way too strong or close family "attachments" can ruin a life: a
new insight into the central role of the straps is then provided. In the same
way, although Barthes comments at length on the picture of his mother when
she was five and opposes it to two other pictures—one of her from 1913, an-

other where she is holding her son, Roland (reproduced in *Roland Barthes by Roland Barthes* with the somewhat ironic caption, "The demand for love")[19] — we cannot see the central picture of the mother. As Barthes says, it would remain pure studium for the outside observer and could never concentrate the love he feels for her.

The first part of this redoubled essay (whose shape is carefully constructed so as to give twice twenty-four elegiac "songs") concludes on the idea that the referent of all photographs is death; the second part concludes that the referent of all photographs is the mother. In fact, we can understand how these two mothers mingle and mesh. In the pages where Barthes comments on his mother's absent photograph, he only gives us a portrait by Nadar, without any discussion. This beautiful woman with white hair is simply presented as "Nadar: The Artist's Mother (or Wife)" (*CL*, 68). Only a few pages later do we find the moving admission: "Ultimately I experienced her, strong as she had been, my inner law, as my feminine child. Which was my way of resolving Death" (*CL*, 72). (In the next chapter, we shall see how Mallarmé resorts to a similar dialectics of entombment and generation for his dead son, Anatole.)

The paradox is that Barthes becomes both his own father and mother in a strange logical twist: "If, as so many philosophers have said, Death is the harsh victory of the race, if the particular dies for the satisfaction of the universal, if after having been reproduced as other than himself, the individual dies, having thereby denied and transcended himself, I who had not procreated, I had, in her very illness, engendered my mother" (*CL*, 72). Indeed, the mother becomes the punctum par excellence since she embodies the culmination of particularity and cannot be subsumed by any generality about generation and race. Barthes knows that to "engender" his mother he has to write about her in this strange narrative, which is a meditation on a single photograph. This passage ends with Barthes's comment on the loss of any dialectical recuperation of the dead object: "From now on I could do no more than await my total, undialectical death. That is what I read in the Winter Garden Photograph" (*CL*, 72). It is tempting to read Barthes's book as less a Proustian novel than as a Mallarméan *tombeau*, since it is not only a tomb for his mother but, as with a *Tomb for Anatole*, a tomb for his mother and himself united in a single entity.

Another photograph seems to confirm this idea. It is reproduced in the first part of the essay, when Barthes describes an old Mozarabic house from the Grenada Alhambra by Charles Clifford. This photograph "touches" Barthes, who does not say whether that is because of a punctum or not: "This old photograph (1854) touches me: it is quite simply *there* that I should like to live"

(CL, 38). In an effort at elucidating such a wish to "inhabit" certain pictures, thus perhaps to "haunt" them (instead of being haunted by them), Barthes quickly links these places to a maternal function and to a regressive desire to return to the mother's womb:

> Looking at these landscapes of predilection, it is as if I *were certain* of having been there or of going there. Now Freud says of the maternal body that "there is no other place of which one can say with so much certainty that one has already been there." Such then would be the essence of the landscape (chosen desire): *heimlich*, awakening in me the Mother (and never the disturbing Mother)." (*CL*, 40)

We could highlight the Freudian elements of this photograph, which depicts a house resembling a tattooed body with its elaborate yet faded Arab fresco, two windows serving as eyes, and the huge arch as human legs. It takes some time to discover a young boy sitting on a slab, his back pressed against the right-hand side of the house. Dwarfed by the enormity of the building, he stares into the void, while behind, in the distance, are a cypress tree and then, quite distinctly, three white crosses. This house is simply the entrance to a cemetery: the *heimlich* had already contained the *unheimlich* as the return of inevitable death. Yet this death, if it is not dialectic, is tamed, incorporated within a sweet regressive fantasy that carries the subject back to somewhere within himself (*CL*, 40).

In stark contrast to this almost lyrical tone in the midst of an elegiac mode, the abrupt announcement of the mother's death marks a rupture in the book at the beginning of the second part: "Now, one November evening shortly after my mother's death, I was going through some photographs" (*CL*, 63). The second beginning of the investigation into the essence of photography is explicitly linked with mourning: "I had acknowledged that fatality, one of the most agonizing features of mourning, which decreed that however often I might consult such images, I could never recall her features (summon them up as a totality)" (*CL*, 63).

The mother's very image, even more than her death, remains "undialectic" because it cannot be transformed into Hegelian negativity, a Proustian search for a lost time, or a Sartrian recapturing of an eidos in a flash of the imagination: "The Photograph does not call up the past (nothing Proustian in a photograph)" (*CL*, 82). On the contrary, its two dimensions and glossy paper only testify to a certain "nevermore" of the reality that "That has been."

What Barthes discovers in this personal odyssey is a certain truth, the truth that something had taken place which seems to confirm a realism: "The realists, of whom I am one and of whom I was already when I asserted that the Photograph was an image without a code[20]—even if, obviously, certain codes do inflect our reading of it—the realists do not take the photograph for a 'copy' of reality, but for an emanation of *past reality*: a *magic*, not an art" (*CL*, 88). I shall now try to prove that this position—a "magic realism" (which in a confusing way could evoke a school of novelists in which one generally puts Marquéz and Rushdie)—has deep affinities with Breton's sur- or superrealism. Barthes, like Breton, sees reality as haunted and as projecting emanations that can even be recorded, not only by paintings as in the case of Chirico, but directly by cameras.

For the invention of photography supposed the joining of two techniques: the purely optical apparatus of the *camera obscura* used by painters to verify the laws of perspective, and the chemical discovery that certain metallic emulsions can be modified by light rays and thus retain a trace of them. Barthes downplays the optical side (which would entail an analysis of the framing mechanism, therefore of the entire ideological apparatus that determines and overdetermines the countless choices any shot presupposes) in order to perceive the real magic of photography, which solely derives from the chemical operation:

> For the *noeme* "That-has-been" was possible only on the day when a scientific circumstance (the discovery that silver halogens were sensitive to light) made it possible to recover and print directly the luminous rays emitted by a variously lighted object. The photograph is literally an emanation of the referent. . . . A sort of umbilical cord links the body of the photographed thing to my gaze: light, though impalpable, is here a carnal medium, a skin I share with anyone who has been photographed." (*CL*, 80–81)

And curiously, for Barthes, this light is above all white and black—which is why he almost never mentions color photographs in his essay: he says that he feels that "color is a coating applied *later on* to the original truth of the black-and-white photograph" (*CL*, 81). This is also perhaps why the only color photograph in the book is the blue-green tint of Boudinet's Polaroid, a color that should match that of the mother's eyes (in the early black-and-white pictures of his mother, he recognizes "quite a physical luminosity, the photographic trace of a color, the blue-green of her pupils" [*CL*, 66]).

By the same token, Barthes relishes the thought that the silver in the emulsion remains somewhat alive. Photography participates in some magical transubstantiation (light becomes metal) and thus avers the consubstantiality of the gaze to its object. The striking image of the umbilical cord (one could think of Stephen Dedalus gazing back at God through Eve's absent navel) suggests a bond that belongs to the religious or mystical.

If photography is thus both a resurrection and a haunting by means of a two-dimensional image, could we not say—as Beckett once said, jokingly— that the inventor of photography was not Niepce or Talbot, but Veronica? Noting that the wonder and astonishment he experiences in front of photographs is nothing short of the religious, Barthes adds: "Photography has something to do with resurrection: might we not say of it what the Byzantines said of the image of Christ which impregnated St. Veronica's napkin: that it was not made by the hand of man, *acheiropoeitos?*" (*CL*, 82). Barthes goes even further when, ignoring modern techniques of trick photography, superimposition, collage, and distortion, he states that each and every photograph operates as an ontological proof, "a proof no longer merely induced: the proof-according-to-St.-Thomas-seeking-to-touch-the-resurrected-Christ" (*CL*, 80). This "proof" would reconcile St. Thomas, the skeptic who needed to touch, and Veronica, the pitiful woman who happened by chance to preserve an image printed by Jesus's own blood. If it is true that each time I look at a photograph I am led to meditate on the mystery of light that binds me to its chemical origins, then the punctum indeed belongs to the mystical: it is always an arrow shot from God at an ecstatic St. Theresa.

The Holy Shroud of Jesus would thus be the conceptual model upon which photography is founded. Georges Didi-Huberman has studied the paradoxical nature of this object, whose fabrication cannot really be explained, but which embodies a fantasy of total reference.[21] Pierre Madaule, a novelist who happens to be a friend and disciple of Maurice Blanchot, has incorporated the wealth of syndonologic studies into a fiction work, *Véronique et les chastes.*[22] Madaule notes that one of the extraordinary facts about the Holy Shroud is that it could supply a *negative* image of a man, be it Christ or not, at a time when photography had not been invented. When Secundo Pia was asked to photograph the *sudarium* in 1898, he saw a man's face appear, which then was shown to represent the positive image that would have been produced by a volume directly applied on a veil. This veil is supposed to be dated from the fourteenth century. Although most specialists believe that the shroud was fabricated about that time in Burgundy, no one can explain by which technique the "print" could have been made.

The shroud would thus embody the concept of an "authentic fake"[23] through which the two mysteries of transubstantiality and consubstantiality would merge into one. In Barthes's terms, such a mystical model would correspond to a writing that would take place by itself. The direct inscription of traces on paper would immediately testify to the reality of an event—like a haiku, it would thus describe what is without any commentary. One would not have to be embarrassed by all the machinations of great fiction or the trappings of conventional novels; a true trace would be inscribed just as the subject who beholds it disappears in front of its light. A ghost, or the ghost of a ghost? Photography: the absolute magical and realistic writing, a writing that could abolish all writing, bequeathing to us the sense of ethical reverence and the supreme politeness of silence.

Mallarmé's Crypts

In a short article written in 1910–11, Freud tells the story of a man who, just after his father's death, often relived that sad event in his dreams: "He had repeatedly dreamt that *his father was alive once more and that he was talking to him in his usual way. But he felt extremely painful that his father had really died, only without knowing it.*"[1] The key to this apparently "nonsensical" dream is found by Freud once he adds "as the dreamer wished" or "as the dreamer wished it" to the last sentence of the dream-narrative. The dream's meaning lies in the son's repressed wish that the father should die quickly, as a release, and in the subsequent guilt this dream had been triggered. But in this case, as Freud writes, there is no evidence that "any actual crime has been committed." The dream must be solved along the lines already traced by a neurotic fantasy: "One is bound to employ the currency that is in use in the country one is exploring—in our case a neurotic currency" (*SE*, 12:225). Starting with a discussion of Pierre Janet's "loss of the function of reality," the article culminates with the example of the dream whose enigma is happily "solved" by Freud, which moreover confirms the autonomy of the pleasure and reality principles.

This dream was later added to and summarized more succinctly in the *Interpretation of Dreams:* "His father was alive once more and was talking to him in his usual way, but [the remarkable thing was that] he had really died, only he did not know it" (*SE*, 5:430). The more copious commentary takes some time to stress that the wish for the father's death had arisen from "merciful thoughts." In order to account for the apparent absurdity of the dream, Freud needs to connect it with a "stirring up of the dreamer's earliest infantile impulses against his father" (ibid.). Freud ought not to belabor the impression of "absurdity" produced by such dreams, for indeed, as Mallarmé will show us, they can also be taken at face value: it is an essential element of mourning that dreamers and mourners alike rue the fact that the loved ones should appear to be unaware of their sad condition. Death is unconscious—but this lack in knowledge creates a sort of logical scandal.

The context into which the dream had been inserted in 1911 as a footnote was only devoted to "absurd dreams." Two years later, Freud again adds two seemingly unrelated and arbitrary comments about the emotional ambivalence usually felt for dead people and the possible identification between the dreamer and a dead person. Freud first notes that certain dreams show someone first as dead and then as alive: these fluctuations could stem from some indifference on the part of the dreamer who would seem to think: "It's all the same to me whether he's alive or dead" (SE, 5:431), in order to erase, repudiate, or alleviate intense contradictory impulses toward the deceased. Then in a second moment, Freud offers a curious rule for the interpretation of dreams where the dreamer associates with deceased figures:

> If there is no mention in the dream of the fact that the dead man is dead, the dreamer is equating himself with him: he is dreaming his own death. If, in the course of the dream, the dreamer suddenly says to himself in astonishment, "Why, he died ever so long ago," he is repudiating this equation and is denying that the dream signifies his own death. (SE, 5:431)

This looks like a strange logical loop: if the dreamer dreams of dead people without noticing that they are dead, then he dreams of himself as dead; if he appears to be aware of their death, he rejects the identification.

The only case of a dream concerned with a dead person other than the dreamer, thus not a mere projection, would seem to be the first type of dream, in which the dreamer both recognizes the demise of the dead person and that same figure's ignorance of his expired condition. The dreamer cannot escape through indifference, for he has the added burden of doubly mourning the deceased: aware of the loss for himself and of the absence of any feeling of loss for the other, who apparently happily survives as long as the dream lasts. Yet this type of dream creates pain, anxiety, and emotional discomfort. As Freud says at the end of his new paragraph: "But I willingly confess to a feeling that dream-interpretation of this kind is far from having revealed all the secrets of dreams of this character" (SE, 5:431).

The dreamer who dreams of his own death and the dreamer who dreams of his father's death have something in common (besides being projections of Freud's psyche—much of the Interpretation of Dreams found its inspiration in Freud's father's death): both are haunted by a nonknowledge that blurs the usual distinctions between life and death. This forces them to see the deceased as a potential ghost who attests to the tenacious survival of the unconscious. These Freudian insights should enable us to approach a complex knot linking

Mallarmé's work to the horrible experience of his son's death. The touchstone of such an experience remains knowledge, a knowledge of death that is reserved for the survivor and orients the dream of an absolute book toward new challenges.

In Freud's article (quoted at the beginning of this chapter), the artist is mentioned just before the dream of the dead father. The artist is called upon to confirm the important function of a purely imaginary creation, although he normally manages to return to reality: if he originally turns away from reality and takes shelter in a life of fantasy, he soon returns to the world of his fellow men through his own creations since he can "mold his phantasies into truths of a new kind, which are valued by men as precious reflections of reality" (SE, 12:224). The artist becomes a hero, king, or creator without having brought any real change to reality because he has given life to a universal feeling of dissatisfaction with pure and simple reality: "But he can only achieve this [becoming king and hero] because other men feel the same dissatisfaction as he does with the renunciation demanded by reality, and because that dissatisfaction, which results from the replacement of the pleasure principle by the reality principle, is itself a part of reality" (ibid.). It is thus not narcissistic self-aggrandizement that is accepted as a universal symbol by other men, but, because art gives expression to a pain everybody has suffered, it can then reach universality. "Reality" includes both the "reality principle" and the consequence of this principle, which is the uneasiness provoked by its demands. Artistic duplication of reality conforms to this dual aspect: even as it denounces the reality principle, it mirrors universal pain whenever loss is felt.

Accordingly, the artist who attempts to transform the intensely private loss of a loved one into a work of art has to progress through some kind of "absurd" dream in order to return to a reality shared by all. When he seals a recently erected tomb, the artist or poet not only sings of a common fate but offers rhetorical strategies by which symbolical survival is made possible. The notes Mallarmé jotted down shortly after his son's death provide a moving example of a poetic "concession" made to death in the hope of completing the work of mourning.

Mallarmé's son, Anatole, whose health had always been poor, became very ill and died when he was eight years old. The poet's grief was immense and found its expression in a series of jottings published only in 1961 with a long introduction by Jean-Pierre Richard. The two hundred fragments seem to promise a *tombeau* for Anatole, a *Tomb for Anatole*, less a "consolation" for the grief-stricken parents than the incorporation of the dead child into a work of art that would somehow defeat death.[2] Anatole, who resembled his father, will have to

become a "child of the work." He must be both the magnum opus, a tomb for
the deceased heir, and an endless work of mourning, during which the father
takes up his son's struggle against death, a malevolent being who attacks the
weaker of the two:

> what! enormous
> >   death — terrible
> >   death
>
> — —
>
> to strike down
> >   so small a creature
>
> — —
>
> I say to death   coward
>
> alas! it is within us
> not without //
> he has dug our
> >   grave
> >   in dying
>
> concession[3]

The whole text, which we cannot place with certainty as either a series of
preparatory notes for a special poem or as stray elements for the great "Book"
we have already encountered in the introduction, seems to be founded on a
particular type of rhetorical trope, the concession. In the context of the notes,
"concession" first means a plot of land in a cemetery that is granted for a certain number of years or indefinitely (if indefinitely, the French phrase is "perpetual concession"); but the entire movement of the notes shows that Mallarmé
also alludes to the rhetorical strategy of granting a point in order to attack more
comprehensively, surrendering a position in order to find a more powerful
argument. Both meanings are linked in the sense that the rhetorical adversary
is also the cause of there being a cemetery plot in the first place. The adversary
is death:

> >   death!
> Oh! you believe that
> you will take me
> thus — to this
> mother

—to me
                    father

— —

I admit that you can

                        do much (148)

The boy's body cannot be disputed as death's possession, but there is a point
where death can be "thwarted":

                        want

to thwart death

— —

(Oh) listen the woman
                    her tears
Oh! I see
that you are strong, clever—
            etc. (29)

This "enormous death" will indeed haunt the survivors as they express their
grief in various ways, for its triumph is also the triumph of interiority: death
now inhabits the parents' souls. The concession that will be granted or built
will therefore find its real locus in the poet's mind.

In fact, this concession is never far from a confession. Mallarmé keeps deploring his "bad blood," he fears he has bequeathed a constitutional weakness
to the child, an "evil race" (122–23). However, the concession is not a negation
in the Freudian sense, although it follows the same logic in inverted order:
instead of negating to affirm, using the cover of a negation to bypass censorship, this concession affirms in order to negate. It is thus identical to the movement by which the parents negotiate a way through their son's death, in terms
that seem very Hegelian since they combine interiorization, negation, and idealization: "child, planting / idealization," "+ true return / into the ideal" (16,
35). Or again:

so as not to see him
    but idealized—
afterwards, no longer him
alive there—but
seed of his being
taken back into itself—
seed allowing
to think for him (33, translation modified)

This strategy replaces the more immediate rhetorical consolation that simply states: "No, you are not dead." This appears too obviously as a sweet illusion, as the parents' understandable but misguided wishful thinking:

> when the too powerful
> illusion of having him
> always with us
>
> no, you are not one of the dead
> —you will not be among
> the dead, always in us (126)

The haunting quality of these shorthand notes derives from their exploring all the possible positions taken by grieving parents, and it feeds on the necessary contradictions this entails. In one fragment, for instance, Mallarmé criticizes the bitter delight the parents may take in routine visits to the cemetery, the need they feel to "renew / laceration / pain" (126), and remarks that this is already unfair for the absent:

> unjust for the one
> who remains below, and is
> *in reality* deprived
> of all that
> we connect him with. (127)

There even seems to be some *jouissance* in the grief:

> No, you are not one of the dead
> —you will not be among
> the dead, always in us
>
> becomes a
> (not bitter enough) delight [*jouissance*] for us (126–27, modified)

This accounts for the fact that the son may retort with sinister "laughter" from within his father (134). The only way to avoid this unethical movement is to follow the path of disavowal in the hope of reaching a deeper truth.

The incorporation of the child into the surviving parents relies on the mechanism of interiorization and sublation (*Aufhebung*), but also demands the dialectical machine of negation. Death is not simply an ineluctable fact or an unconditional given, for it has to be linked phenomenologically to a consciousness. In this case, the awareness or consciousness of death finds its limit in the ignorance of the child:

to feel it burst
(the void) in the night
the immense void
        produced by what
            would be his *life*
—because he does not
know it—
that he is dead (31)

It seems that we have not moved out of Freud's dream, although the narrated event comes straight out of reality. The child cannot know because he was too young when he died. Besides, who could be expected literally to "know" his or her being dead? The paradox of death is in his asymptotic limit of knowledge.

treacherous blow
of death—of
evil without his
            knowing anything
—my turn
to play with it, for the very
reason the child knows
nothing⁴

This becomes the hinge, the turning point of a future reversal; the worst blow also offers the best weapon with which the poet may hope to foil death's power in a strange game. In the division of roles, it seems that the mother will be the one who simply deplores the dead son's blindness, whereas the father seizes the idea it suggests:

he knows nothing of it!
—and mother weeps—
                idea there
yes, let us take everything
on ourselves, then his
    life—etc.—
for sinister
    not to know
        and to be no more. (38)

In another passage, this ignorance is not identified as "sinister" but rather as "happy":

no death—you will not
deceive him—
—I take advantage of the fact
that you deceive him
—for his happy
ignorance
—but on the other hand
I take him back from you
for the ideal tomb (129, modified)

The tomb will be both literal and metaphorical, a crypt ("ancient egypt—/
embalmings—/ days, operations / crypts" [27]) and a poem. But if death has
deceived the child by taking him by surprise, this very ignorance can be doubly taken up by the father's anguished knowledge. In fact, the notes reflect a
complete ambivalence about the ethical problem of exploiting the child's death
for a poem. The poem will eternalize the father's suffering and reassure the
child still unaware of his own death ("I want to suffer everything / (thus—) for
you / who do not know—/ nothing will be / taken away (but / you) from the
hideous mourning" [130, modified]).

Part of the peculiar pathos of these notes originates from the return of the
child as a ghost, who then wishes to know the horribly hidden "secret" of his
own demise:

what do you want, sweet
adored vision—
who often come
towards me and lean
over—as if
to listen to secret (of
my tears)—
to know that you are
dead
—what you do not know?
—no I will not //
tell it
to you—for then you
would disappear—(149–50)

The return of a beloved ghost embodies the same paradox as the famous rider
over the Lake of Constance: if he knew the truth about his own death, he

would not return. Mallarmé has devised a dramatic articulation in three parts, in which the last part is dominated by the return of the dead child:

—to see then
how II—"the
(which will be the)
(of) sickness and
the little phantom"—
would be framed—
—III returning [*revenant*, "ghost" for Auster] //
above, towards
the end of II—
dead— (158–59, modified)

But the parents' desire to hide the hard fact during the child's illness has already created an unevenness, an inequality in knowledge (the child's development will be arrested, he is "in me / the future / man you will not / be" [150]), which can be considered as the worst of betrayals:

oh—let him
not know
anything of it—never
suspect it
— —
(during sickness
—but from which treason
   death
        ignored[5]

The complexity of these notes derives from the serial temporality they stage: the child dies several times; the mother cries "he is dead" when he is only very ill, which suggests a frenzied dialectization in the construction of the ideal tomb. Such conceptual haste risks detouring mourning toward some kind of infernal travesty:

if he heard us
how angry he would be
— —
  to suppress him
  thus
        sacrilege without

his knowing it!   tomb
          shadow

— —

no, divinely
                for not dead
          and in us (100, modified)

This fragment concludes on a possible "transfusion" of the child into the parents, a metamorphosis into those who guard his memory. The mother will accept him into her earthly bosom, while the father will attempt to erect a monument. But there is the risk that all this could lack solid foundations, for in the game there remains some duplicity, shared by the child and the parents:

seen, come back dead, through
illness—eyes, want
to pour out light.
          —pretend, agree
to play, with indifference

— —

          he knows without knowing
          and we weep for him without
letting him know

          enough tears—this would
introduce death— (141, modified)

The simple admission of truth—without the detour of concession or negation—would result in a jarring parody triggering a sinister laughter:

Indeed Sir
     indeed you are
                         dead
At least this is
what your announcement
letter

— —

and laughter from within
myself—hideous! (134, modified)

But the "laughter from within" manages to unite father and son, since this same sequence ends on:

you will see
clearly, o my—dearly
beloved—that
if I could not
embrace you
squeeze you in
my arms
—it is because you were
inside me (134–35)

As always in this series of dialectical reversals, the blessed ignorance of the child can be converted into the most radical denial of death's sway:

much better
that he does not know it
— —

    we take on all
       tears
       —weep, mother
       etc.
—transition from one
state to another
    thus not dead
    death—ridiculous enemy
    —who cannot inflict on the child
    the notion that you exist! (77)

Mallarmé goes even further when he suggests that not only can death not convey an idea of its power to the dead child, but also, it ignores itself:

death—whispers softly
—I am no one—
I do not even know who I am
(for the dead do not
know they are
dead—, nor even that they
                die
—for children
at least (61)

"At least"—the phrase betrays again the extenuation of a concession: in this pathetic rhetoric, "least" has priority over "last." Death provides the parents with a "last" that confronts the ignorance of children and appears to be defeated. The following pages attempt to generalize the statement to every human being, in a probing and hesitant syntax that reflects the poet's uneasiness:

> for as soon as
> > (as one is
> I am—(I
> dead) I cease
> to be—(63)

Indeed, the poet is groping toward an age-old topos, the classical argument used in consolations (at least in non-Christian consolations, such as Seneca's— for Mallarmé systematically shuns any reference to a divine agency). "At least," he admits to being engaged in a work of "consolation":

> —this consolation in its turn,
> has its foundation—its base—
> absolute—in what
> (if we <ma> want
> for example that a
> dead being lives in
> us, thought (82)

The first argument proposes that, as long as the dead are not forgotten, they survive ideally; this is followed by the traditional idea that death, not being perceived by the subject experiencing it, cannot really frighten anyone. This insight, which retains some dynamic urgency when applied only to blissfully unaware children, risks being reduced to banal common sense. But the preceding words show that this reasoning would be too reductive:

> heroes—sudden
> deaths
> for otherwise
> my beauty is
> made *of last*
> *moments*—
> lucidity, beauty
> face—of

what would be

me, without myself (62–63)

Mallarmé clearly incorporates the dead child into his own crypt, which does not prevent him from identifying with the boy's point of view. "Me, without myself" does not simply describe the father, looking like the child, without the child, but rather the boy being turned into a ghost. The "shadow" takes upon itself that part of ignorance which being dead implies: the father becomes a ghost in his turn. His knowledge of the dead son's ignorance is displaced to the writing self, in a movement of enunciative "disappearance" so characteristic of Mallarméan poetics:

—I

am not—

but in an ideal

state

— —

and for the

others, tears

mourning, etc—

and it is my //

shadow not knowing

of myself, who

dresses in mourning (64–65, modified)

Death is thus unconscious and, even more crucially, it can be said to structure the unconscious as *writing*—a lesson developed a few years later by Mallarmé's spiritual heir, Jules Laforgue.[6] This death destroys any belief in personal identity and traverses generations to convey the idea that the father is no less dead than the son, both having always already died as bearers of language.

The grown man carries within him a series of little corpses, including those of his son and of himself. This produces a complex pedagogy, since the moment of truth, the point at which Anatole can begin to understand without merely turning to dust or disappearing, is postponed to the future still open to the adult:

you look at me

I still cannot tell you

the truth

I do not dare, too little one

What has happened to you

— —

one day I will
tell you
    —for *man*
I do not want //
you not to know
your fate

— —

and man
dead child (44–45)

The first occurrence of "man" seems to imply that Anatole will keep growing older in spite of his death: "idealization" keeps him alive in his parent's minds. The second occurrence generalizes this to a statement that absolutely negates the romantic notion according to which "the child is father to the man." As Serge Leclaire has shown in his study of primary narcissism, the murder of the "wonderful child" embodying all the fantasies of omnipotence is a necessary, though painful, process.[7] This murder is identical with the labor of mourning each person must perform when considering the successive selves he or she has been.

One reason why Mallarmé cannot believe that "the child is father to the man" is that he seems to guess that all revolves around the child's name, which has been chosen by his parents as a kind of pun. *Anatos* etymologically means "harmless" or "not well armed," thus providing a translation of Mallarmé as "*mal armé*" (badly armed), which corresponds to the father's self-reproach of not having "given / adequate blood" (191). Deprived of defenses against death, the child has simply obeyed his predestined fate, falling into the grave only to turn into *anatolé*, meaning a celestial body, star, or moon rising above the horizon. Between the grave in the cemetery plot and the apotheosis into the sky, Anatole, the harmless and innocent second child (he had been preceded by Geneviève), is "refined out of existence" in the most cruel way but enables his father to write down his name which translates his own family name eternally among the constellations. This upward rising literally embodies the father's spiritual cravings:

    little body
put to the side
by death

a hand
that a moment
 before was him

 —and shout, almost without
paying attention to this
body put aside—
 O my son
as toward a heaven
spiritualist instinct (178, modified)

The double risk of the poetic attempt to uplift the child is that this might on
the contrary drag him down under the earth. Mallarmé is aware of the connection between the writing (composition) and the work of decomposition; the
idealization is paid for at the price of a gnawing image suggesting physical
decay.

I write—him
 (underground)
   decomposition
mother sees—
 what she should
  not know. (180)

The mother thus remains on the side of not knowing, while the father is capable of carrying the weight of both consciousness and the unconscious.

not to know his
happiness
 when he *is*
there—. . . found that
 so natural

— —

 link
  to unconsciousness
   of death— (182)

The drama of the child's death thus defines a sort of negative cogito, whose
formula would be: "I do not know <that I am dead>, therefore I am," provided
one might add: "—everywhere," or "—in us." This is why the true locus of the
act of mourning is neither in the graveyard nor the idealized constellations
that carry the boy's name, but in the survivors' home:

true mourning in
the apartment
— not cemetery —

furniture (183)

"Furniture" thus metonymically condenses mourning and immortality: "In this way furniture / immortality" (159). The relocalization of the crypt into an apartment becomes the theme of a whole poem that attempts to rephrase the work of mourning and avoids the stalemate of these notes (which were not taken up as such for any subsequent work). The poem describes an interior haunted by the absence of a youthful heir and focuses on one piece of furniture, the console illuminated by a last ray of the sun:

Does all Pride smoke out evening,
A torch put out by a shake
Without the immortal jet
Surviving abandonment!

The ancient chamber of the heir
Of many a rich fallen trophy
Would not even be warmed
If he came in by the passage.

Inevitable agonies of the past
Clutching as though with claws
Disavowal's sepulcher,

Under the heavy marble
It enisles no fire lit
But the flashing console.[8]

The final line can be construed in two ways, since console can be either a noun or a verb: a curious consolation can be expected from that piece of furniture whose peculiarity consists in being supported by the wall, its two feet otherwise unable to sustain the heavy marble top. That typically cluttered bourgeois apartment is visited by the momentary glory of a solar fire whose last flash of lightning (*que la fulgurante console*) suddenly replenishes it with light and presence. The heir's empty and unlit chamber finds a temporary solace, and the marble — not just the console's top but a tomb's slab — rightly functions as "disavowal's sepulcher."

While we might rightly object that a purely biographical reading of the poem limits its infinite suggestiveness, the hidden allusions to Anatole help to make sense of the letter itself (thus it is not necessary to imagine a chimneypiece in the room).[9] Indeed, the fact that Mallarmé could resume writing and situate these poems in the long series of "tombs" for friends and writers (Poe, Baudelaire, and Verlaine being the most renowned) defines a Mallarméan genre in itself. This genre is imbued with the same discretion and subtle dialectics of negation, whose paradigm would be provided by the last lines of Paul Verlaine's tomb:

> Verlaine? He's hidden in the grass, Verlaine
>
> Only to find there in naive accord
> With lip not drinking and with unchecked breath
> A so shallow rivulet, much maligned death.[10]

The French text yields a submerged pun on *"nier la mort"* that can still resound in *"Un peu profond ruisseau calomnié la mort."*

If, as Leo Bersani writes, Mallarmé can be understood as *the* poet of the sublime and of sublimation,[11] I hope to have shown that sublimation relies less on sublimity than on a rhetoric of concession and disavowal. Mallarmé was the first writer aware of the negative power of language—for him, to write was to subtract from the world, as we shall see in the next chapter—but also confident in its restorative powers. The drama of the poet is not that the "man dies" as he described it repeatedly in his letters and essays[12]—after all, this only fits the poetic program Mallarmé had devised for himself—but that he should survive his heir; this bequeaths to him the impossible task of having to survive his own ghostly disappearance. The result of such a constitutive impossibility is often a poetry of fragments, all the more powerful as it explores the tensions of the impossible dialectization of mourning:

> death is not   prayer
>   of mother
> nothing   —playing
>   death
>   <remedies>   she
>   "so that the child
>   does not
>   know
>
>   — —
>
>   and father benefits. //

      no more life for

       —

  me
       and I feel
  I am lying in the grave
  beside you. (78–79)

What remains is the poignant dirge addressed to Anatole, destined to remain a
son and whose stubborn (Barthes would say "undialectical") death partly resists mourning and idealization: he cannot be totally sublimated, nor just re-
deemed by the idea. His ghostly eyes keep staring, unblinking, into a frozen
futurity.

         that future eyes
  filled with earth
              never
  cloud over
  with time (146)

Verlaine and Mallarmé between the Angels and the Ghosts of Languages

The L of HAULTIN only disappears to leave room for the GH of HAUGHTY, and this GH would have very gratuitously appended itself to the I of the French verb *déliter*, which gives DELIGHT, had it not been for the reinforcement brought to the penultimate of the verb from which the last syllable falls.

Let us not forget GAS, our *gaz*, from the Flemish GEIST, which corresponds to our *esprit*, as does GHOST in English.

MALLARMÉ, *Les Mots Anglais*

If the importance of English in Mallarmé's choice of a teaching career is generally known (indeed, the bulk of published pages he devoted to the study of English quite outweighs his poetic production), it more often goes unnoticed that his mentor and friend, Verlaine, also nurtured his poetry at the inexhaustible source of language instruction. Mallarmé's early choice of English seems to have been determined by his youthful devotion to Edgar Allan Poe. In the letter to Verlaine called "Autobiography," he explains that he "learned English simply to read Poe better."[1] He adds that he left for England with the hope of acquiring a profession, the wage of a language teacher having become necessary following his marriage. The material necessities prompting such a career choice are always emphasized. I would like to show that Mallarmé managed to transform these into a fate—his particular poetic fate—teaching himself slowly, through many academic or pseudo-academic essays, how to master language as such. The discovery of language as more than a tool probably goes back to Vico's forceful insights in the middle of the eighteenth century but corresponds more decisively to the "linguistic turn'" of modernity exemplified by Mallarmé and Nietzsche, a "turn" away from the ideology of rational discourse that can appear to be groping toward the birth of a new "modernism."

Verlaine, who gladly played the irresponsible dunce cursed and blessed in turn by destiny, and then Valéry after him marvel at the complete selflessness of Mallarmé who, despite the horror that his profession caused him, remained a teacher of English almost his entire life. Valéry, always ready to attest to his hero's exquisite self-denial, recounts Mallarmé's recriminations against the hell of teaching. Valéry could not fathom how someone who always refused to present arguments directly or to instruct except by suggestion or allusion could live the life of an educator. "Moreover, he never spoke of his ideas except through figural language. Explicit instruction strangely repulsed him. His profession, which he loathed, had something do with this aversion."[2] It seems more logical to see in this paradoxical disjunction a structuring mechanism rather than a life or a career—but, above all, a fundamental relation to language. This relation to language is most clearly brought out in opposition to the lighter and more playful practice of Verlaine.

Verlaine had, then, also played English teacher in Rethel, a small town of the Ardennes, where he spent two years teaching—and drinking—from 1877 to 1879, and he gladly kidded Mallarmé about their common vocation. As Mallarmé recalls: "So, he was fond of many an English quotation, pompously, as if in possession of some language which is exceptional or within the reach of few people, including, that's true, a small number of poets" (OC, 874). It has often been pointed out that the strange mannerisms that distinguish Mallarmé's prose style often come from an imitation of English idioms. Thus, when he responds in 1897 to an inquiry of Monsieur Clerget about Verlaine's career and life (this was just one year after his death), numerous Anglicisms ("mainte" echoing "many," "un qui" recalling "one who," etc.) seem to parasite his text. But Verlaine had, above all, invented a pedagogical trick, a "device of his invention" that he wished to communicate "with pride" to his colleague during their exchange of "pedagogical confidences":

> [Verlaine] had (so I understand) accurately viewed the persistence of the guttural intonation or stridence—the teeth against—that was inveterate among the English attempting our language, as an undeniable mark, as the aptitude to pronounce correctly and effortlessly their own tongue: this supreme feat which a conscientious French teacher demanded of his pupils, why not get there right away, by inculcating in them, even when reading Boileau, the flawed pronunciation common to the compatriots of Dr. Johnson . . . in accordance with such a fortuitous linguistic mystery, since voices, distorted in an authentic grimace, must lend themselves better, perhaps, to the miracle of foreign elocution which will surely take hold by itself, internally, by a force. (OC, 874)

Moreover, Mallarmé relates how Verlaine required his students at Rethel (among whom he must already have distinguished Lucien Létinois, his future spiritual "son") to greet him every morning not in English but in French with a strong English accent: "Verlaine, then, had arranged it that he would never enter class without his children standing up and greeting him with this refrain (it can only be transcribed by borrowing from the spelling used in the scenes and songs of comic opera): '*Baonn-jaur, Maossiun Voeu-laine!*' the moment when the instructor was to take the rostrum" (*OC*, 875). Perhaps this ingenious pedagogical tool was nothing but a clever device to throw a sumptuous and grotesque veil over the poverty of the teacher's faulty pronunciation?

Indeed, the principal of Rethel had forewarned the students that, while their teacher knew more English than all of them put together, he pronounced it quite badly and they had to make allowances. Of this fact, Verlaine almost prides himself when, toward the end of his life, famous and celebrated, he is invited in 1893 to lecture in Belgium and England. The idea that one can learn the pronunciation better by distorting one's own idiom can provide a key into the complex detours used both by Verlaine and Mallarmé.

The several passages of correspondence in which Verlaine plays around by writing in English demonstrate that his knowledge of grammar is quite spotty— he uses "to wait" with a direct object and is unaware of some elementary distinctions between adjectives and adverbs. What remains crucial for him, as for Mallarmé, is this game of false translations and literalisms. We should not be misled by the superior knowledge of a learned and serious Mallarmé, an instructor capable of publishing translations or school textbooks.[3]

As is well known, the history of symbolism in France can be written as the declension of successive translations of the English "spleen," from Baudelaire to Mallarmé and passing by the small jewel that is the "spleen" of the *Romances sans paroles:* "The roses they were all so red / and the ivy was all black. / Dear, if you merely turn your head, / all my old despair comes back."[4] This collection displays Verlaine's anglophilia with the titles of the section "Watercolors," all in English. Even if Poe serves as a link between Baudelaire and Mallarmé, a breach develops between the former's work as a translator and the metalinguistic function of English for Mallarmé and Verlaine. Whether they translate or not, the other language serves, in effect, to make their own tongue look alien. They have to alienate themselves from their "natural" mother-tongues in order to make them fully their own. Add to this either the effects of disjunction toyed with by the great city, London, everyone's place of vice, the metropolis where Verlaine lived in degenerate circumstances with Arthur Rimbaud (and the city that will witness the birth of Anglo-American modernism—I will return to this point in a later chapter), or Mallarmé caught in a distressful passion with his future wife whom he must marry if he wishes to prevent her return to Germany.

If England enables him to go and live his dream—even if it means letting it fall back into the quotidian once the ferry is taken and the Parisian cobble-stone regained—English serves to review or revise language. Verlaine was well aware of this, as is illustrated by the poem "There," from the collection *Love:*

> "Angels!" only corner shining in London this evening,
> Where a little gas blazes and a crowd prattles away,
> It's strange that, like a very stubborn hope,
> Your memory haunts me and forcefully winds
> Around my spirit a red and black regret;
>
> Shop windows, songs, omnibus, and dances
> In the half-fog where the taste of rum flows,
> Yet, propriety, respect for the rhythm,
> And even in the stupor a certain decorum,
> Until the hour when mist and night thicken.
>
> "Angels!" days long gone, dead suns, torrents run dry;
> My old sins lurked for years along your paths,
> All of a sudden blushing, woe! and astonished
> At truly delighting in your decent pleasures,
> Them, just the opposite, coming from Paris!
> . . . .
> It is Grace which amiably passes by and makes a sign,
> O primitive simplicity, it returns!
> Dear, humble, new beginning! Noble flight
> of the hour toward the blue sky, ripener of golden fruits!
> "Angels!" A name *seen again*, calm and fresh as a swan! (*OP*, 289)

A poem of conversion, that text which Verlaine himself said seemed "conventional" (*OP*, 962), initiates an ideological rewriting of life—the sins arriving from Paris discovered Victorian morality in England. So long as one exhibits the drunkenness of décor, but with the decorum of salvation!—which relies, however, on a Mallarméan lesson that is probably well buried. For, as a letter makes clear, the poem evokes a section of London. Verlaine writes to a friend: "'Angels' is a section of London, lower-class but relatively *bonhomme:* something like our Faubourg Saint-Antoine or our Batignolles, near the Fourche" (*OP*, 963). The comparison with the Fourche clearly indicates that the poem concerns that large intersection in the north of London that leads to Islington, which is still called "Angel."

The English angel is pluralized in Verlaine's memory, as if to gesture toward its double etymology: Latin (the poem was even erroneously printed with the title, "Angelus"!) and Anglo-Saxon. As Mallarmé recalls: "Who were the Saxons? Angels: Angles, just as they called themselves" (*OC*, 905). Verlaine's faulty memory makes his language hiss in an English fashion, sticking in the S's that do not exist on the level of the great city but, rather, exclusively in the ear, the site of a lyrical transfiguration—all this so that divine (that is, Latin) grace may resonate there. It is hardly pagan "Greece," then, that could still dangerously subtend "grace" with overly tempting "golden apples."

Confirming what Mallarmé wished to demonstrate—while committing several errors and absurdities, the necessary accompaniments to any mythical attempt to articulate the truth about language—in *English Words* (of which Valéry could say that it contained his entire poetic and, above all, his entire science of language), every language takes shape through an interweaving of branches originating from at least three sources. It is this multiplicity that enables the poet to polyphonically exploit his own language.

In a famous passage when Mallarmé laments that day and night exchanged their "natural" features (since *jour* possesses an obscure timbre and *nuit* a clear timbre), he is not yielding to a Cratylism of the poet but, on the contrary, founding a complex poetics upon a linguistics of absence: the poet's task is born from the poverty and inadequacy of natural language and his duty is to enrich it: "We know that *verse could never exist alone:* it philosophically remunerates the deficiency of language, a superior complement" (*OC*, 364). If a single language, doing away with the diversity of languages, imposed itself upon us like the unique stroke of truth, there would be no need for poetry. Babel is surely the *felix culpa* of humanity.

In "Crisis of Verse," Mallarmé takes stock of the period's literary evolution, which he shows to be moving toward an "exquisite crisis, fundamental," a crisis that seized hold of French poetry following the demise of Victor Hugo. Hugo had reduced everything to verse and, moreover, had "confiscated" poetry by identifying himself with it, by becoming the founder of the Republic and the bard of the French alexandrine. However, a general weariness of the alexandrine, explicitly identified by Mallarmé with the national flag ("due to the lassitude brought about through abuse of the national cadence: whose employment, like that of the flag, must be reserved for exceptional occasions" [*OC*, 362]), encourages once again more experimental poets to attempt "side games," more or less radical breaches. The greatest freedom prevails:

> What is remarkable is that, for the first time, in the course of any people's
> literary history—concurrently with the great general and secular organs

which, in the style of a latent piano, exalt orthodoxy—someone could devise an instrument with his individual playing and hearing as soon as he blows, strokes or strikes it scientifically; use it only on exceptional occasions and thus dedicate it to Language. (OC, 363)

These multiple heresies—the "choices" of particular devices in an anarchy of experimental efforts—evoked by means of free or mixed verse arranged in musical fashion by a Verlaine, do not seem dangerous to Mallarmé so long as they are viewed as a recourse, an often desperate recourse to the pure language that is impossible by definition to set down in words.

Pure language, that pre-Babel dream, represents the horizon of poetic hope: to materially inscribe the truth on a page. What underlies the belief in a pure language, beyond the opposition between *langue* and *langage*, beyond the notion of a "lack" that reinscribes negativity in—and legitimates—the process of creation, is the possibility of envisioning a science of language. "Science" for Mallarmé is almost always reduced to a central science, that of language which, if it is not "deified" as Valéry remarks of the written thing (O, 1:621), remains the object of a knowledge to be acquired. Such a knowledge is never "pure" in the sense that it cannot abstract itself from a particular spoken language: it is linked to a fundamental "piety" of the writer who received his mother tongue as a legacy ("if he, recreated by himself, took pains to meticulously rescue from his junk pile a piety of 24 letters as they are, by the miracle of infinity, fixed in his own language" [OC, 646]). The randomness of this dispersion of letters gathered in one language, his and ours, postulates the existence of a place: at once an historical locus determined by nation and language, an ontological site to be cleared away for the "disaster" of future creation.

In fact, one of the poet's earliest writings suggested the plan of a "method" that articulated the preeminence of a science, "the Science of Language" (OC, 849–56), in relation to which all other sciences could be organized. In the years 1865 to 1869, Mallarmé attempted to acquire a method of the human intellect, comparable to that of René Descartes, just when he struck down in his mind the old "plumage," God.[5] Mallarmé declares:

Every method is a fiction, and useful for demonstration.

Language appears to him as the instrument of fiction: he will follow the method of language (determine it). Language reflecting upon itself. In the end, fiction seems to him the very process of the human intellect—it is fiction which puts in play every method, and man is reduced to will.

Pages of discourse on the Method (underlining it).

We did not understand Descartes, the foreigner grabbed hold of him: but
he provoked the French mathematicians.

It is necessary to recapture his movement, to study our mathematicians—
and to make use of foreign lands, Germany or England, only as a sort
of counter-test: in this fashion, helping us through that which they took
from us.

In any case, the hyper-scientific movement is coming only from Germany, England cannot, because of God whom Bacon, her legislator, respects,
adopt pure science. (OC, 851)

I have quoted this long passage because it seems to describe in advance the
European geography of languages and the intellect that Mallarmé endeavored
to tour exhaustively, in a curious there-and-back between abroad and domes-
tic, the foreign land being useful only for the purposes of recovering what it
stole from France. But without that theft, France would never have realized
what was her most precious possession.

This text was written before the Franco-Prussian war, which will subsequently
add a new epistemological obstacle to progression in this maze—as is illustrated by a passage drawn from *La Dernière mode* concerning the Wagnerian
cult on the rise in France. In 1874, Mallarmé mentions in his "Chronicle of
Paris" the arrival at Châtelet of a new conductor who is looking for beautiful
and powerful scores. For Mallarmé he cannot be anyone but Wagner: "Or,
indeed, only one thing could be done, to seize absolutely the 'Tannhaüser'
and, by a display of extraordinary glory, avenge it for the outrage once caused
in the name of France by a hundred ill-mannered boors: a solution which is
all the more impossible, since the arms, since Alsace, since the blood!" (OC,
818). Mallarmé is referring to a cabal raised against *Tannhäuser* at the Opera
of Paris in March 1861 and proposes a belated but exemplary act of reparation.
He refuses the jingoist nationalism that both withdraws into imaginary frontiers and ignores the oblique trajectory required by writing, a journey necessarily diffracted by the Other—a big Other made up of works, texts, and monuments.

If the music of Wagner comes back to haunt the margins and sometimes
also the center of the Mallarméan text—whose author is a paradoxical Wagnerian, close to the circle of Parisian enthusiasts like Dujardin, but also excessively circumspect about the effects of forced mythologization—that is because
Mallarmé seeks, above all, to recover from Wagner and from music as a whole
that which poetry seeks to attain with words. The same text highlights these

movements of there-and-back, starting this time from France: "For want of a French piece, exceptional and captivating all of Europe, and as the program must, above all, be completely national, why not present an extract of some of our remarkable masters, to which I would add, however, an Italian and a German act: since it was our genius to make Italy, Germany, and the world understand German, Italian, and French music" (OC, 818).

The same back-and-forth effect can be observed in the arts and philosophy and, of course, in the relations between languages. When Mallarmé concludes a long discussion on the processes of the formation and ramification of English word families, he writes: "The formation of words, indeed, it is necessary to leave that task to the English themselves: we, French, can analyze them. Very well: for a word is almost never viewed with such precision as from the outside, where we are: that is, from abroad" (OC, 975).

Indeed, where are we? According to Mallarmé, we are always "from abroad." Whether we are in our national setting or not, we draw from foreign lands that test and countertest, which permits us to experience independently—and exclusively—the national heritage. The effect of a more perspicacious vision to draw from elsewhere, from an exteriority, is not reduced to the trite notion of the "analytic" intellect of the French whose own words, as we will see, can easily be formed in synthetic fashion. The privileged position accorded the French in this last example refers back to historical imports and exports of word stocks, reactivating the force of the past, of wars and conquests, of struggles for domination, in the pure science of philology: "Science having found in Language a confirmation of itself, must now become a CONFIRMATION of Language" (OC, 852). These terms, extracted from the previously cited notes for a method, confirm what Mallarmé understands by science: the science of language, which he also calls in his letters, "linguistics," extends beyond traditional philology—even as it still makes use of its discoveries, as is demonstrated by *English Words*, and transcribes, by a game of concept translation, absolute knowledge into knowledge of language.

The name of Hegel is imperative here, given the role that he played in the great crises of 1866 during which Mallarmé founded his aesthetics on a vision of the beautiful and nothingness, which corresponds to Hegel's notion of absolute knowledge. Hegelian friends of Mallarmé, such as Lefébure and Villiers, provided him with a new logic in which the absence of God signifies the absolute, while English empiricism, which does not consider the question of the absolute, falls back into theology. Villiers later drew the most precise approximation of the "hero" of the drama, which would be taken in by the great "Book," and it is in him that Mallarmé hails an almost total knowledge, since he is familiar with "Saint Bernard, Kant, Aquinas, and principally one designated by him as the Titan of the Human Intellect, Hegel" (OC, 491).

During the elaboration of his "Poetic Method," after the crises of Tournon and Besançon, which led him to the verge of suicide, Mallarmé moved between three languages—English, French, and German—that were, first, "languages in which one thinks" before languages in which one speaks. But already, during the distressful period preceding his decision to marry Maria Gherard, even before settling down in London, he had written to his great friend and confidant, Henri Cazalis: "All that, my dear Henri, I will not tell it to Emmanuel, because he is French, and I tell it to you because you are a little German."[6] "That" concerns the hope entertained by the young student to be able to mold Maria little by little into his "reflection." A young Maria, who, in addition to having replaced his sister Maria, initially appeared to him to be an Englishwoman! It was only afterwards that he realized his mistake and tore up a first love letter drafted in English.

A meditation on reading, "that desperate practice," and on the pure conditions of poetry, the Mallarméan gesture implies a trilingual translation—a notion indispensable to any attempt to grasp the unity of his works divided between an abundant series of commentaries, critiques, essays, and scholarly works in prose, and some rare, joyous poetic pieces haunted by the absence burrowed at their center by the great book never written. That complex strategy is definitively grounded in an absence more radical, perhaps, than the absence of language: the absence of the world.

As Valéry suggests in regard to a Mallarmé he called the "Master": "A man who renounces the world places himself in a position to understand the world" (O, 1:621). It is this renunciation, rather than Hegelian negativity or Poe's principle of perversity, that makes possible the link between the poet's subjective, lyrical progression and the knowledge of language: it demands that poetry think and, above all, accomplish with words a complete bracketing of the world—onto which the self-fulfilling gesture of the writer raises itself.

Elsewhere the transformation of the "little teacher" of Tournon—transferred to Besançon due to his lack of authority and parents' complaints—into the "Maître" who declares to the press that "the world is made to lead to a beautiful book,"[7] or preemptively asserts, during the anarchist bombings in Paris, that "the bomb is the book" (after the affair of Fort Chabrol), enables an entire French landscape of the start of the Third Republic to be drawn, with emphasis placed on the power of the education system. It is thanks to the discreet but effective support of Henry Roujon, private secretary of Jules Ferry at the Ministry of Public Education, and then director of the Ecole des Beaux-Arts, that Mallarmé was not, on several occasions, dismissed: Roujon got rid of the most threatening files, the reports of inspectors and principals.

From the Commune to the Dreyfus Affair, Mallarmé traverses all the crises, including the Panama crisis, without ever really taking a stand, masked by the ironic politeness that permanently protected him, persuaded, at bottom, of the inanity of such upheaval from the perspective of the only truly important problem, the creation of the great "Book." If his sympathies for the anarchists were recalled by Julia Kristeva as well as his private positions in favor of a review of the Dreyfus trial,[8] it cannot be forgotten that his first responsibility as an author and literary editor was *La Dernière mode*, whose public consisted of Orleanist countesses and legitimist baronesses.

It is, however, in that upscale, excessively curious magazine—a genuine literary *hapax* since Mallarmé, as is well known, covered all posts there—in that "gazette of the high-life" (Mallarmé deplored the fact that "high-life" was not included in any French dictionary), that he attempts for the first time to demonstrate that "language instruction" is at least as useful as sewing or the arts of charm:

> What! Grammar itself can be interesting! If you would please to convince yourselves of it, Ladies, leaf through . . . the New French Grammar . . . [which] shows you, to you, that a language, far from leaving its formation to chance, is composed just like a marvelous piece of embroidery or lace: not a single thread of the idea which vanishes, this hides but only to reappear a little farther behind that. (OC, 828)

Mallarmé, who signs this article, "Madame de P.," will have the opportunity to develop that logic embroidered between languages by closely studying the English language. Valéry could thus see in *English Words* a work that holds the secret of his mentor's quasi-scientific method.

As in *La Dernière mode*—so attentive to cross-dressing and the question of the feminine point of view—Mallarmé displays in *English Words* a decided preoccupation with ascertaining the place from which he observes language: "Simply to study English from the viewpoint of French, for one must hold to a position from which the eyes can be thrown forward; but nevertheless, it must first be verified that this observation site is good" (OC, 902). This site, however, is the French language whose evolution comes to an end around the eleventh century—which is excellent, in Mallarmé's view, since it can then be included within the more prolonged evolution of English. English achieves a superior fusion of Gothic derivations and transformations of *langue d'oïl* or

Norman, which suggests several stages of the importation of Latin metamorphosed into vernacular and learned idioms. From this point, Mallarmé goes back even further to Sanskrit roots that are then broken apart into "themes." These minimal assemblages proving the kinship of Indo-European languages will soon lead to a subtle play of auto-translation: these languages will revive their common but disjointed idioms in a sort of incest or generalized inbreeding.

Before examining the interweaving of themes and hybrid versions generated between languages, before accurately taking stock of Mallarmé's apparently paradoxical project, *to think German in order to be able to speak English in French*, it is best to dwell longer on the notion of ownership from the point of view adopted by one language toward another. Such a sense of ownership can receive the name of "patriotism"—a patriotism which is, in truth, quite special. As Mallarmé writes in his own textbook, *Les Mots Anglais*, a French person learning English will not merely broaden his or her linguistic horizon but also travel back in time, toward the past of the French language:

> A thousand reasons to know English, fluently for its literature and its gift for ubiquity, or methodically, for our sake, in order to put forward claims of a very early role in its formation (as is done here on every page): but there is nothing more valuable in it than to come upon French words of old, if one has the special patriotism of the well-read to whom falls the past and contemporary treasure of his language. (OC, 998)

It seems, then, that the meticulous philological examination of "English words" permits an exploration of French that is far more extensive than if it had been conducted directly. Moreover, it could not have been conducted directly, for lack of an "observation site."

Philological analysis of English prompts the secret interaction between life and death, which regulates the evolution of every language. English cannot be said to have entirely sprung from French, but the interplay between the two germane languages produces a diffracted and altered memory of the language: "To find like old and effaced titles to be given back to the living, here; and there, an entire evocation of types dead in their original idiom but which have not disappeared at all somewhere else" (OC, 998). He then includes a list of words extinct in French but which have survived barely changed in English.

Letters, too, can come back to life, like the letter "s," which remains silent in French plural endings but is sounded in English. Its "whispering" could relate to an enigmatic passage of fragments on the method concerning the word "s": "S, I say, is the analytic letter; dissolving and disseminating, par ex-cellence. . . . I find in it the occasion to affirm the existence, outside of all verbal value other than that which is purely hieroglyphic, of speech and of scribble, of a secret direction vaguely indicated by spelling and which mysteri-ously converges toward the pure general sign which must indicate verse" (OC, 855). Verse silently inscribes a plural in the singular, and this plural sets loose Cratylic reveries on the "natural" evocation of sounds. The vast English whis-pering is a poetic rumbling that already murmurs—potentially—beneath the French language.

A good number of French words were devoured, transmuted, and digested by English, which can occasionally stem from Greek (such is the case with "the," according to our amateur philologist) by circumventing the French and Latin networks; beyond the real scientific rigor of the treatise and in spite of some extravagances, one ultimately arrives at a notion of translation that im-plies both filial respect for the strictest sort of literality and a play of blurredness, of tremulousness, precluding any identity of language with itself. Concluding his book, Mallarmé points English in a double direction—toward both future and past—by hailing it as the "contemporary Language par excellence, which reflects the double nature of our period, retrospective and advanced" (OC, 1053).

This language is closely akin to the principal character of the text: "Here pushing forward, there recollecting, to the future, to the past, *under a false appearance of the present*" (OC, 310). The only "present" acknowledged by the English language, always double, Gothic and classical, Anglo-Saxon and Franco-Latin, refers back to "the political Europe" still to be created (OC, 1049) or to the Indo-European legends. Whichever may be the case, there exists no absolute origin that science can establish: "A Reverie forbidden to Science . . . to investigate whether such an element, because it is the primi-tive, is supreme" (OC, 1048). In relation to the heterogeneous crucible of En-glish, the purity of German only betrays a "poverty" (in rhymes, for instance). The irony of root exchanges gives rise to the fact that one of the "household" English words, "family," derives not from Saxon but from Latin—thus from a relatively "foreign" root.

Within this linguistically expanding horizon, myths and legends of Aryan or Sanskrit stock are condensed by the poet in his French version of an En-glish book that he translates under the title of *The Ancient Gods*. This dictio-nary of comparative mythology is closer to being rewritten than translated and, in parts, the translator's personal comments displace the subject at hand. One such addition deals with the recurrent theme of all myths, which is none other than the "tragedy of nature," the renewal of the seasons, and the daily drama of the sun which is born every day and dies every night (OC, 1169).

It is useful to read the translator's note that concludes the volume, which also deals with problems of translation. Starting with the differences between languages in transcriptions of the names of ancient gods and heroes, Mallarmé stresses the fact that French is almost the only language to assume the privilege of translating those names (OC, 1277). This entails both loss and gain, since we thereby gained a repertoire of terms that are now naturalized and indispensable to poetic reverie, but these translations can also derive from the caprices of pedants and lead to confusion, such as in the case regarding Artémis and Diane: "I respect the instinctive eagerness of French to translate, but I admonish it for not knowing where to translate," remarks Mallarmé (OC, 1278). For this reason, he rejects "Ulysse," which would be better replaced with "Odyssée" (but still does not dare to rechristen Zeus as Zée!).

Any translation entails a certain degree of destruction—reminiscent, in fact, of the damage inflicted by the scholarly interpretation of myths (whereby Oedipus is restored to the sun cults following the tendency at the time of German-inspired anthropology): "What pleasure mingles with our surprise at seeing familiar myths slowly evaporate, through the very magic implied by the analysis of ancient speech, into elemental water, light, or wind" (OC, 1276). In this text, which associates the solar with the scholastic, the analytic with the synthetic, we can observe the systematic ambition of someone who, even while modestly laboring away at the diffusion of knowledge by advancing toward a greater familiarity with that Indo-European wealth of legends that constitutes a sort of unconscious memory of the "European family" evoked by the *English Words*, also attempts to modify profoundly his own language, but remains well aware that a language is not regenerated by arbitrary decisions, whether in the realm of translation or of poetic creation. "A portion, even the restricted and technical portion of a language, does not change in an hour, unless a group of individuals discovers an immediate interest there" (OC, 1278). It was this "interest" that the project of the great "Book" aimed at sparking, so that the work would appear anonymous and Mallarmé himself would be limited to the role of "translator" of a text from which he would be effaced as author: "the same copy with ten different translations!"9

These observations allow us to appreciate what is surprising in Mallarmé's activity as a translator. Indeed, *Thèmes Anglais* does not present so many French sentences to translate into English but rather French transpositions of English proverbs and idiomatic expressions, with the idea that, "retranslated by the student from their French source into their original English form, they are retained in his memory" (OC, 1058). Certain sentences, such as "The same and the same, like Nan and Nicholas" seem to have been whispered to Mallarmé by a grinning Verlaine.

When Mallarmé translates Poe, he exhibits a similar literalism, with an important nuance: Mallarmé never translates Poe's poems into verse; he does not reproduce the breaks, blanks, and page arrangements but rather furnishes paraphrases printed without interruption. These "translations into prose" reveal a knowledge of English more extensive than that of Baudelaire, the first translator of Poe, as well as curious errors that sometimes emerge in places where Baudelaire translates correctly. Indeed, the bias of paraphrase can seem absurd in the case of purely musical poems, such as "The Bells," which displays an alliterative music based on echoes, internal rhymes, and tintinnabulation effects of pure sound. Mallarmé realizes that this poem is untranslatable but nonetheless strives to render it in French—that is, in the language that can absorb it (and not on the page) as a signifying dissemination.

A brief examination of some absurdities in this poem's translation suggests that many of Mallarmé's felicities are aggravations of initial errors. Error becomes productive and positive since it assaults the language and fashions a new sort of French, halfway between a misunderstood original and an excessively faithful paraphrase. In this fashion, "to the mercy of the fire" becomes for Mallarmé à merci du feu; "keeping time" is read allant, avec elles, d'accord; and "seem to twinkle with a crystalline delight" produces that typically Mallarméan expression: cligner, avec cristalline délice, de l'oeil.[10]

Another error is the translation of "people" as le peuple instead of ceux qui. Thus, "And the people—ah, the people—/ They that dwell up in the steeple . . . They are Ghouls" becomes "Et le peuple—le peuple—ceux qui demeurent haut dans le clocher . . . sont des Goules." This signals a curious return of the repressed: the repressed of the foule (the crowd, mob) crops up through the Gothic style of certain evocations. In fact, foule originates from the idea of a place where one is foulé—that is, pressed, squeezed by the multitude. The link to Freudian repression is hardly without grounds.

This throng, in another text, will ultimately yell out [hurler] its emptiness at the poet who was initially shouted down ("the crowd, when it will have, to the fullest extent of its furor, exasperated its mediocrity, without ever returning to anything else but primary nothingness, will yell out [hurlera] to the poet, an appeal" [OC, 499]). The crowd literally hurls toward the poet, something like a fate that resonates in him, since he has been elected because he burrowed without fear into that "primary nothingness" and could, for instance, look right into the "great blue pits which the birds spitefully bore" into the sky. To bur-row into that nothingness, from Wagner to Poe, from Hegel to Descartes, while crossing through the no less methodical doubt of Hamlet, "bitter prince of the reef," does not mean only compensating language for the price of its deficiency, paying tribute to its constitutive shortcoming. The erotic vision of the faun turns into a doubt ("My doubt, the hoard of ancient nights, divides / In many subtle branches"), which also circulates among languages, carries out hazard-ous or coerced rapprochements, migrations from trunks to secondary branches, risings of the sap from tellurian roots to translucent limbs, leaves. The effects of geminating and dissemination, which branch from bough to bough (for instance, in Mallarmé's peculiar French syntax, "*en maint rameau subtil*" is derived directly from the English "many a"), bring to bear (*opèrent*) on objects and enforce the relation to cosmology that is implied by the most current sen-sibility just as by the most ancient mythology. In this case, to operate (*opérer*) means both to effect and to cut off, to prune and to graft in the site elected by language.

For if it is always a question of "remunerating the defect of languages," it is futile, even sacrilegious, to try to supplement natural creation: "Nature takes place, one will not add to it; only some cities, railroad tracks, and various in-ventions making up our material. . . . Equal to creating: the notion of an elud-ing object, which is lacking" (*OC*, 647). Or even, in the response to an already cited inquiry: "Things exist, we are not to create them; we are only to grasp the connections; and it is the threads of these connections which make up the poems and orchestras" (*OC*, 871). Connections and gaps, arrangement in a network, and the burrowing of a lack are then almost synonyms. The revived language of the poet opens this gap which the absence of the object renders "pure": not "pure idea" but absence of idea and object, a *poeisis* to be written on the double signifying face, musical and literary.

It remains, however, to situate that which returns to languages and also to ascertain the site of poetry: is verse written in a maternal tongue that fastens it to a ground, or does it only take aim at the blue of the sky? A youthful poem still glorified "France of the blue sky" and "its beautiful pure sun," while stu-pidity figured as an obstacle and an abutment: "And the impure vomiting of Stupidity / Forces me to hold my nose in front of the blue sky" (*OC*, 8). Can (or must) one translate expressions such as "*rien n'aura eu lieu que le lieu*" (nothing will have taken place except the place)? In view of Mallarmé's lec-ture in England on "Music and Literature" and of the notes for the great "Book," it seems that Mallarmé partially sought a national acknowledgment of the poet's role, envisaging, for example, the creation of a sort of Office of Letters.

We could even infer that the general scheme putting in play the initiates, the creator's friends, and the masses rallying together the whole of France, mattered to him at least as much as the act of writing itself: "Every nation, where writing shone (in the absence of the foundations of pious cement which I admired [referring to Oxford and Cambridge]), possesses a sum which can only be designated as its literary 'Capital': [for] us, [it is] French" (OC, 637). Aside from that English patience that labors for the future in the tranquillity of the "cloisters" of culture (Oxford and Cambridge)—a patience that "remains in advance"—there is also the German model of a new musical fervor in which nationalism and aesthetic ecstasy coexist in disturbing fashion.

Between these two foreign models, Mallarmé always dutifully embraces a saintliness, a piety of the "Book," that alone permits a suspension, an escape, a "flight in itself": "This flight is needed—in itself; one could [ask] again: but, itself, does it not already become far, to take refuge?" (OC, 637). Where to take refuge, toward which foreign land, from which interior exile? Which subtracting and abstracting power must one exert in order not to deprive the act of writing of its significance? In the great Wagnerian celebration inaugurated by music, the nation believes it has rediscovered its roots: "Everything, like the functioning of a celebration: a nation testifies to its transfiguration into truth" (OC, 371). According to the already mentioned principle of the "absence of present" inseparable from literary fiction, one must throw back the empty illusions of "the impatient" that demand from the poet a response to "the need to act": "Suicide or abstention, to do nothing, why?—A unique time in the world, because owing to an event which I will always explain, there is no Present, no—a present does not exist. . . . For lack of the Crowd's adopting a position, for lack of—everything" (OC, 372). And if the crowd takes a stand, sweeps along everything and everyone with a cohesive force blind to national values, poets, and machinations, it will do nothing but concretize the lack: unable to suffer the absence of languages and the absence of the world always evoked by the poet, it will founder in the worst of moral faults. Mallarmé continues, "He who would admonish his own time is misinformed, when what is past has ceased and a future is delayed or both confusedly mingle together again in the hope of camouflaging the gap" (OC, 372).

If it is not, then, of the present, the crowd can only occupy the site of an unawareness, a blindness tied precisely to the being of the site enveloped by the throng with its motley body. Faced with such a lack of understanding, the poet will sensibly content himself with diversions to pass the time: all that remains is from "time to time to send to the living his calling card, *stances* or sonnets, so as not to be stoned by them, if they suspected him of knowing that they are not taking place" (*OC*, 664). For the poet's duty is in reality to demonstrate in person—in spite of the calumnies heaped upon him, obscurity, preciosity—that "literature exists and, if you wish, alone, apart from everything" (*OC*, 646).

That is why, in this conflict of "settings apart," of excisions and bracketings, it is so essential to know what is meant by "to take place." The "Book" takes place, and it even takes place entirely on its own: "Depersonalized, the volume, as much as one disengages from it as author, demands that the reader approach. So, know that, in the midst of human secondariness, it takes place entirely on its own: done, being. The buried meaning moves and arranges, in unison, pages" (*OC*, 372). These expressions recall a recurrent motif of the notes for the "Book" that set down the oldest intuition supplying meaning and grounding the whole work: "I found that it had been, written as early as 1867." "*J'ai trouvé que cela était*" is reached after the poet has "ventured" into the "sensation of Darkness Absolute." Here is the exact context of the account: "Destruction was my Beatrice. I can speak of this now because yesterday I completed the first sketch of my work. It is perfectly outlined; it will be imperishable if I don't perish. I looked upon it, without ecstasy or fear; I closed my eyes and *saw that it existed.*"[11]

This ontological radicalism hardly fails to anticipate the capture of that being-there, "out there" as it were, of things evoked by the later Roland Barthes. There are abundant examples among the fragments intended for Mallarmé's "Book": "One will know if something or nothing" (f. 100 A), "proof that it is" (f. 128 A), "proving that this *is* that" (f. 112), and "the time to prove that this is that" (f. 113 A). Would it be a question, finally, of a direct "proof" that could do without the countertest of the foreigner? Curiously, however, by a descent recalling that of Igitur at the midnight of creation, the scene of the anonymous drama of reading-translation put on stage by the dreamed about feat of the "Book" will suggest, in a novel sense, a recourse to national categories. The preparatory notes assert: "city and life = homeland" (f. 4 A). Igitur already bestowed a cult upon his ancestors and upon the unconscious of his family while he tried to vanish into the "purity of his race," which he would identify with the absolute. The same goes for the stakes of "A Throw of the Dice Will Never Abolish Chance": if the poem, which mimics the throw of the dice executed by all creating thought, does not wish merely to recover its fortune from pure music or language, it must institute a cult consecrating both the writing of absence and the effects of those "absences" on the public.

The "Book" also aims, then, to win back from religion a fundamental structure—even if it must be emptied of its original meaning—and from nationalism its secret (the secret of race), yet without falling prey to the illusions that each convey:

> When the old religious vice, so glorious, which diverted natural sentiments towards the incomprehensible in order to confer upon them a dismal grandeur, will be diluted by the waves of obvious fact and daylight, it will not remain diminished since devotion to the Homeland, for example, if it must find sanction other than in the field of battle, in some general rejoicing, requires a cult: being of reverence. (OC, 397)

The mysteries of religion preserved, at least in a coded, encrypted form, the buried and now forgotten secret ("Indeed, it was impossible that in a religion, even though neglected since then, the race would not have placed its intimate, unknown secret" [OC, 397]). If Mallarmé agrees to "carry out excavations in order to exhume ancient and magnificent intentions" from religion or from the corpse of God, must he not also, then, dig a hole and proceed by burrowing through the somewhat rotten soil of the nation?

The art that will dare to unearth these compacted "intentions" will play out anonymously once again the rite of the Eucharist or "real presence" incarnated by the officiating priest at the mass. Fiction mimics the rite, which is itself only another mime: "That the god may be there, diffuse, total, mimicked from afar by the effaced author . . . then renders, struck by the authenticity of words and light, triumphant of Nation or of Honor, of Peace" (OC, 394). This "solemnity" works itself out like an arabesque divagation around the altar that must, however, be neither desecrated nor described too closely: "The cloud around expressly: since to clarify . . . would be to surprise the ritual and betray, with a gleaming, the sunrise of an officiant's cope, in place of the head priest festooned with incense to conceal it, a nakedness of place" (OC, 394).

I could point to numerous "gleamings" in the prose of the later Mallarmé who inherits the surplus of orphic ambitions handed down to poetry—I would like for the moment to limit myself to this observation: that the young Mallarmé, quite Wagnerian, Hegelian, and more pro-German than a good number of his friends, claims to be "antinational" (he therefore protests that critics of Wagner had wasted the opportunity to "show a hostile nation the courtesy which undercuts belligerent headlines" [OC, 324]), while it is when the work emerges in its most "refined" form that he encounters the necessity to conceive of the national.

At first, the national is reduced to the chauvinist defense of French soil and makes up a part of that current, common discussion that he compares to the exchange of small coin. The poet who strives, of course, to "give a purer sense" to the words of the tribe must combat this reductive and conservative tendency: "A vocabulary is owned in common, by the poet alone and by all, whose work, I concede, is to perpetually restore the standard meaning, just as the national soil is defended" (OC, 854). In fact, the poet's place appears in a certain interior exile, and, given the manifestations of chauvinism in art, whoever investigates modernity is duty-bound to "leave the soil of his country," "to take hold materially of the foreigner's route" (OC, 324).

The poet, who inhabits the interregnum of time, in a time not of the present, uses this tactic to part from himself by various reveries—in short, "to be somewhere where one wants and feels oneself to be a foreigner" (OC, 326). But once this "somewhere" returns to the "nakedness of place," set aside for the fatal throw of the dice, the setting in motion of the memory of language and race brings the anthem back to the secret of an original politics, buried in the heart of the father who has become the son of his (dead) son, in the hope of being thereby the grandfather of the entire race. Paradoxically, it is when beauty is created against the background of absence that it suggests a recourse to a utopian community that shares it in common. Paradoxes, to be sure, for one might still have to conceive both of a territory that would be national without the site of a cult and of a cult that demands from the masses collective acclaim for a slain hero.

This death, for which the notes of the "Book" elaborate several scenarios, is surely the demise that Mallarmé reserved for himself in his laughable inability to finally create the absolute work to which he devoted his entire life. Is it hardly accidental, then, that he died of a laryngeal spasm while struggling with the fantastic creation of the "Book"? It is not so much that physical demise serves as an indication of the "elocutionary disappearance" of the poet (OC, 366) who disappears—with a vengeance—into a pure but inaudible language, but rather that the crisis which seized him is called in French by a name derived from English, *faux croup* (spasmodic croup): a *faux coup* or false throw of the dice that grabs you in the throat, parodying the final throw of the dishonest croupier.

We might say that Mallarmé was paradoxically "choked by modesty" (a phrase which in French is often used in the negative [*Il n'est pas étouffé par la modestie*] as an understatement expressing haughtiness or conceit). Mallarmé would have literally died from the discrepancy between his sublime aspirations and the awareness that he would never fulfill them. Death, in its role of absolute master, remains always untimely: more so perhaps in Mallarmé's case, with the surprise we must imagine seizing him and barring his utterance and from his utterance. Like Rainer Maria Rilke's Orpheus, the poet identifies with a pure trace, his exile becomes writing, in a last metamorphosis not devoid of pathos: "Finally, the shadows of ink all invaded where one hears nothing but crime fluttering about, remorse, and Death. So, then, I avert my gaze, and the sobs, snatched from my soul not so much by this nightmare but rather, by a sensation of exile, traverse the silent darkness. What, then, is the homeland?" (OC, 263).

This chapter began with the idea that Mallarmé's main effort had been to mediate between the sibilant "angels" of the English language and the "ghost" of Hegel's *Geist*—or, in other words, to combine Hegel's ghostly phenomenology of negativity and Poe's more picturesque and Gothic specters and apparitions. Indeed, Mallarmé needed to think the *Geist* of history and science (both converging around language) in German or as a German idealist philosopher would, in order to translate the specters of plurally disseminating English echoes: such a combination was indispensable if he was to create the new poetic idiom of the French language.

The consequence of this momentous project was that Mallarmé remained caught between the ghost of all ghosts, the absolute but impossible "Book" that might embody his French "solution" (or dissolution or, indeed, his "operation") for a radically new poetical language and the *angelus novus* of a pure language, a "new angel" similar to the figure that Walter Benjamin evokes so well after Paul Klee's painting, an angel who can see the chain of historical events as "one single catastrophe which keeps piling wreckage upon wreckage," even though a storm blowing from Paradise "propels him into the future with his back turned, while the pile of debris before him grows skywards."[12] Mallarmé would have gladly concurred with Benjamin that this storm can be identified with a doubtful progress, but he may have had to wait to the last gasp of this fateful "*croup*" to meet his own ghost, or the ghost of his son Anatole, to see a specter who was suddenly talking with an angel's tongue and speaking all the languages at once, but without him.

Broch's Modernity as Crime, or the Sleepwalking of Theory

Mallarmé's meditation on the totalizing "Book" implies the contingent inscription of the vanishing author in a futile everyday life, from which at least a few postcards are occasionally sent to contemporaries. A rigorous reflection on the interaction between the theory of modernity and its social locus of production can lead to the radical thesis of Dragonetti. In his study of Mallarmé and the ghost of the "quotidian," Dragonetti claims that the perfect realization of Mallarmé's book was his own correspondence.[1]

It is true that Mallarmé systematically worked with a view to the social inscription of his writings, especially toward the end of his life, when he wrote poems for anniversaries, banquets, commemorations, burials, all the rituals that surround the busy life of a literary maître; on the other hand, he multiplied his *loisirs de la poste*, a genre of his own invention, in which the address of his correspondent became the pretext for a brief poem, often a quatrain that the mail carrier had to decipher in order to deliver the message. At the same time, he identified his poems with gifts for friends: they were written on fans, fruits, packages containing candies or coffee. For lack of the absolute "Book," poetry seemed condemned to fulfilling the function of miniature decorations: ornamentation appeared as the bourgeois rewriting of an ontological futility, a systematic post-Pascalian *divertissement*.

Dragonetti follows the theme of the "ghost" through all these circumstantial writings, showing how the real ghost—less Anatole than the locus of Anatole's writing, had he survived—is the impossible, tyrannic, and totalitarian *bouquin*. Even if I must acknowledge some skepticism at such painstaking exegetical feats, which transform each and every letter sent by Mallarmé into fragments of an aborted *ars poetica*, I admire the forceful and easy solution to Mallarmé's apparent contradiction: just as he was describing to his disciples the absolute task of a "supreme fiction," his real activity consisted in rhyming addresses and a few rare sonnets. A somewhat similar, yet not identical contradiction is at work in the position of a writer who, not unlike Mallarmé, wished to rehabilitate ornamentation from a theoretical point of view: Hermann Broch.

What a limited victory it would be for Mallarmé to have overcome the moldy feathers of a vanquished and ghostly God, if the host is to be distributed in so many gifts, all gilt-wrapped! Surely, the resistance of the "crowd" to an elitist practice was in Mallarmé's mind, as he understood how imaginary bogeys were resurrected in the very place of this dead God.[2] These new ghosts, such as the recently revived spirit of nationalism and sectarian intolerance, or its necessary complement, the ideology of race and soil, were indeed fast returning.

In Mallarmé's time, these ominous returns of the half-repressed "political unconscious" manifested themselves first in the cultural campaign against Wagner, then in populist agitation triggered by Boulanger, followed by the scandal of Dreyfus's condemnation. This divisive and decisive case was to have momentous implications for the following century. For historians such as Zeev Sternhell, it marks the birth of all subsequent right-wing totalitarian and racist ideologies.[3] It is not a coincidence that the Dreyfus case plays such a role in Proust's *Recherche:* its very mention suffices to have all the characters in the novel express themselves on issues of class, race, and politics, and prepares for the general dissolution of values in *Time Regained* during the World War I episode.

The very phrase "dissolution of values" recalls a recurrent theme in Hermann Broch's works. At the end of his trilogy, the *Sleepwalkers,* written in response to Proust's and Joyce's modernist masterpieces, the series of historical narratives gives way to an entire theoretical system elaborated in ten philosophical or historical "digressions" and interlaced with the stories of the third volume, all entitled "Disintegration of Values" (*Zerfall der Werte*).[4] Broch's novels and essays appear as the indispensable counterpart to Mallarmé's view of writing as the key to the ultimate mystery: both are radical thinkers of a totality that is no sooner postulated than it exhibits its lacks and cracks; both write in a moment of crisis, from the French fin de siècle to the sweeping irruption of totalitarian practices in Germany and Austria in the 1930s. The final episodes of the *Sleepwalkers* take place in a small Alsatian town not far from Trier and depict a failed revolutionary coup, which also alludes to the turmoil of Austria in the late twenties, whose outcome was the Anschluss with Nazi Germany. Broch could only anticipate the Anschluss in his novel, but it had dramatic consequences for him: arrested as a Jew, he then revised his short story focused on the last days of Virgil. After a moment of precarious freedom he opted for exile to England and then the United States, where he was able to finish the monumental novel, *Death of Virgil.*

Broch's multiple facets are truly astonishing: he was an industrialist who nevertheless took part in discussions over trade-union formation, who astutely got rid of the family textile plant before the crisis of 1929 and found himself poor but free to devote all his time to artistic pursuits, not limited to writing and music but also encompassing mathematical, philosophical, and logical studies, playwriting, and posturing as the Jewish dandy in avant-garde circles. Broch, a friend and admirer of Karl Kraus, a literary rival to Musil, a devoted admirer of Joyce, who despite his early assimilation by his bourgeois marriage to a Catholic wife (they soon separated), paraded his mistress Ea von Alesch in the avant-garde cafés, entirely belongs to the Viennese intellectual milieu in which radical experimentation contributed to a redefinition of modernity while always being balanced by cultural critique.[5]

Although Broch defines himself as a *Großstadtjude*,[6] his novels' scope is never strictly limited to the Viennese atmosphere: *The Sleepwalkers* addresses the whole of German culture, and the unfinished *Bergroman* variously called the *Spell* or the *Temptation* takes place in a village in the Tyrol mountains. *The Sleepwalkers* is not only Broch's response to *Ulysses*,[7] but also an indictment of a whole period that can be described as "modern" or more specifically "modernist."

The trilogy is made up of three interconnected narratives underpinned by dates and general categories that provide them with a conceptual framework. Although the English translation presents them as Part One: *The Romantic* (1888); Part Two: *The Anarchist* (1903); and Part Three: *The Realist* (1918), the original text puts the dates first, then names and concepts side by side, and lists: "1888—Pasenow, or Romanticism," "1903—Esch, or Anarchism," "1918—Hugenau, or Realism (or Matter-of-Factness)." The three dates may look arbitrary if we think of the literary periods: 1888 is generally associated with the ascension of Wilhelm II to the throne and the flowering of the neo-symbolism called *Jugenstil*, a style that Broch later identified with the beginning of Vienna's "gay apocalypse" in his late essay on Hugo von Hofmannsthal. The relevance of 1903 is even harder to ascertain, except that anarchism as a movement saluted by Mallarmé (when he claimed that "the Book was the Bomb") had died out in central Europe, while still remaining powerful in Russia and Spain. Nineteen-eighteen saw the disastrous end of World War I for Germany and Austria and the consequent abdication of the Emperor, as well as the disappearance and "balkanization" of the old Austria. To link it with the new ironic style known in Germany as "*neue Sachlichkeit*" (a term usually reserved for the painting of Grosz and Dix) is less arbitrary. It soon becomes clear, however, that Broch's notions of romanticism, anarchism, and realism go beyond the categories of literary history and imply a historical and ethical system whose major concept is that of "value."

The novel, published in 1931–32, seems strangely prophetic, announcing the arrival of a *Führer* on a scene of absolute despair and loss of all values. The last pages describe the anguish of the isolated individual who feels the need for a guide:

> There awakens within him a doubly strong yearning for a Leader [*Führer*] to take him tenderly and lightly by the hand, to set things in order and show him the way; a Leader who is nobody's follower and who will precede him on the untrodden path of the closed circle and lead him on to ever-higher reaches, to an ever-brighter revelation . . . the Healer who by his own actions will give a meaning to the incomprehensible events of the age, so that Time can begin anew. That is his yearning. (S, 647)

The lone individual to whom these words are addressed is nevertheless a curious character; the passage takes Hugenau as a paradigm of the "new man." Hugenau or the "realist," under cover of the confusion created by a revolutionary insurrection in a small town in the Mosel region, has just murdered Esch, the naive idealist, and then seduced Esch's wife in order to embezzle her money.

This same Hugenau is presented as walking on the "road to Zion," having forgotten his crime, overhearing the voice of mystical comfort that claims (this is the last sentence of the book): "Do thyself no harm! For we are all here!" (S, 648). Never has a novel ended on such an ambivalence of values, an ambivalence or a tension between antagonistic perspectives—is Hugenau finally redeemed? Is he the embodiment of a new "realism" that must destroy older and doomed values? Or is he, on the contrary, the new political subject, ready to call Hitler to his help? The ambivalence is rendered all the more poignant as the issue of the inversion of values is problematized in the very narrative. I shall start from a few remarks on style and ornamentation in order to present Broch's lifelong quarrel with modernism.

The Sleepwalkers is a novel whose form imitates its content: the first part depicts the marriage of a Prussian cadet and uses a self-contained form that so closely resembles Fontane's novels that it verges on parody. The finale of the first section ironically sends the reader back to the conventions that govern such a genre: "Nevertheless after some eighteen months they had their first child. It actually happened. How this came about cannot be told here. Besides, after the material for character construction already provided, the reader can imagine it for himself" (S, 158). The second part moves more freely from naturalistic technique to inroads into the characters' psyches, especially when Esch travels in a sort of religious trance to meet and accuse Bertrand, whom he holds responsible for all that is wrong in the world. The third part abandons a unified narrative, juxtaposes different voices and styles ranging from poetry to theoretical discourse, from self-contained stories to Platonic dialogues, in a narrative fragmentation corresponding to the theme of moral disintegration.

One of the philosophical asides, the third subsection of "Disintegration of Values," begins with a remark on the primacy of architecture for the understanding of any historical period: architecture owes this privilege to the way it can make "style" visible to all. What is rendered visible is thus not only style, but man's obdurate effort to negate time by creating a lasting artistic structure that concretely embodies historical values.

> For certainly style is not a thing confined to architectural and plastic art merely; style is something which uniformly permeates all the living expressions of an epoch. . . . For whatever a man may do, he does in order to annihilate Time, in order to revoke it, and that revocation is called Space. . . . And in this also can be seen the peculiar symptomatic significance of ornament. For ornament, detached from all purposive activity, although produced by it, becomes the abstract expression, the "formula" of the whole complex of spatial thought, becomes the formula of style itself, and with that the formula of the entire epoch and its life.
>
> And in this, it seems to me, lies the significance, a significance that I might almost call magical, of the fact that an epoch which is completely under the dominion of death and hell must live in a style that can no longer give birth to ornament. (S, 397–98)

The narrative "I" who signs these pessimistic reflections can be identified as Bertrand Müller, a depressed philosopher who lives in Berlin and rarely leaves his room, but who meets a Salvation Army girl who can bring him a message of peace and hope. He is a double of the infamous Bertrand who is repeatedly accused of sodomy by Esch. This doctor in philosophy is in a position to interpret actions that might otherwise pass as irrational.

His theory of style and ornamentation also applies to Hugenau's shady dealings with Esch's wife and the newspaper they manage. The following section of the "Disintegration of Values" stresses Hugenau's emblematic quality: he literally embodies his epoch, whose values he constantly acts out:

> But with this extremely intimate connection between the substance of logical thought and the positive and negative values which action embodies, the scheme of thought which governs a man like Hugenau and compels him to act in one particular way, which determines his business methods for him

and makes him draft contracts from a certain standpoint—that is to say, all the inner logic of a man like Hugenau—is given its own place in the whole logical framework of the epoch, and brought into essential relation with whatever logic permeates the productive spirit of the epoch and its visible style. (S, 415)

One single life can thus play the same role as an ornament, both condensing and summarizing differentially the prevailing logic of an era:

And even although that rational thought, that rational logic, may be nothing but a thin and as it were one-dimensional thread which has to be wound round and round the multiplicity of dimensions presented by life, nevertheless that thought, projected in the abstraction of logical space, is an abbreviated expression of life's multiplicity and prevailing style, much in the same way as ornament is an abbreviated spatial expression of the visible style-product,—a projected abbreviation of all the works that embody style. (S, 415)

Thus, there is a deep affinity between a story narrating the rise of a deserter, seducer, embezzler, and finally, murderer, with the fate of a purely functional contemporary architecture:

Hugenau is a man who acts with singleness of purpose. . . . Behind all his purposefulness there lies a logic that is completely stripped of ornament, and the fact that this logic should demand the elimination of all ornament does not seem a too daring conclusion to draw; indeed it actually appears as good and just as every other necessary conclusion. And yet this elimination of all ornament involves nothingness, involves death, and a monstrous dissolution is concealed behind it in which our age is crumbling away. (S, 416)

Broch's hidden historical *Witz* seems to have completely reversed the famous phrase by which Loos could attack ornament as "crime": it is the very lack of ornament, or the activity producing this lack, that is called criminal.

To understand fully the context of this discussion, we have to go back a few years to one of the earliest pieces by Broch. In 1908–9, Broch jotted down some notes on art, culture, and society, which the editor entitled "Culture 1908/1909" and among which we find a piece called "Ornaments (The Case of Loos)."[8] Broch writes in response to the agitation that had surrounded the disclosure of the first public building designed by Loos, the Goldmann and Salatch store on Michaelerplatz. The violent reactions of an angry public generated a sort of quarrel of the ancients and moderns; Broch refuses to identify with either camp. He defends Loos against insults and declares his work to be clear and fine. Loos indeed seems revolutionary insofar as he buries the preceding aesthetic of the turn-of-the-century *Jugendstil*. Loos was extremely sarcastic whenever he had to discuss buildings by van de Velde (he wrote that if one were to lock up a prisoner in a cell designed by van de Velde, it would be a marked aggravation of the sentence), and Broch seems to concur when he denounces in the *Sleepwalkers* the "comic absurdities of a Van der Velde" (S, 391).

Neither eclecticism nor neo-Gothic are viable, and the story of Hanna Wendling is exemplary: her rather empty married life is only brightened by the prospect of decorating her interior, for which task she duly reads her favorite magazines, the *Studio, Interior Decoration*, and *Vogue* (S, 398–99). As the philosopher muses, all this testifies to the fact that the present architecture is unable to launch a new style; instead it is reduced to producing mere symptoms, which are so many "writings on the wall" (S, 391).

Broch cannot accept the basic premises of Loos's theory. He calls his aesthetics an "industrial aesthetic" (*Ingenieurästhetik*), since it rejects everything that is not functional or useful. Indeed, Loos's fundamental tenet was "The meaning is the use," a maxim soon taken up by the Viennese circle intent upon developing logical positivism. For Broch, this tendency boils down to a banalization or a systematization of Enlightenment rationality. Loos appears as heir to the *Aufklärung* in that he trusts a universal "common sense" capable of destroying all prejudices. Even if these ideas are true, they are dangerous: such is the paradox of Broch's position when he writes in his 1908–9 notes on culture: "Even if Loos's ideas are precious from a pedagogical point of view, they are impossible elsewhere, because they are so true." Loos embodies a pure reason that wishes to control everything, a sort of Heideggerian *Gestell* linked with a technocratic calculation of possibilities.

In his early notes, Broch imagines ancient culture under the shape of an old man who is castrated during his sleep by a young and ambitious rival: this contains the seeds for the plot of the *Sleepwalkers*, if Esch can be equated with a more ancient form of culture (Esch, a travesty of the biblical prophet, has simply come at the wrong period). The comparison entails another link: the annihilated ornament used to call up sexual potency. "Ornament was a musical expression of sex, of the spirit of all art, a quintessence of culture, a symbol of life that was clearer and more condensed than any rationality" ("Culture 1908/1909"). Ornament then appears as more than the part that would stand for the whole: being deprived of any utility, it can express the whole in a poetic way, pointing to what Broch later called "lyricism," or an idiom capable of joining the extremes of rationality and irrationality in a memorable phrase, a recurrent musical movement, or a striking visual symbol.

The notes written in 1908–9 thus respond to Loos's famous essay "Ornament and Crime," published in 1908 in the *Frankfurter Zeitung*.[9] Loos postulates a theory of eroticized art: for him, any form of art is erotic, and the first model is that of the cross, which expresses copulation (the horizontal line stands for the supine woman, the vertical line for the man who penetrates her). Whereas Loos implies a development away from these early impulses toward a greater clarification and more enlightened self-awareness, Broch insists that the irrational impulses cannot be eliminated and should be taken seriously: no aesthetic system can be free from anthropological elaboration. While Loos sees art as a sublimation and repression of infantile drives and an advance of civilization that conquers its own barbarity, Broch refuses what he calls a Freudianized puritanism. If both agree on the equation linking ornament and sexuality, Loos sees the function of art as overcoming all these dangerously irrational and regressive impulses leading precisely to "crime" and excesses in all sorts of debased primitive rituals, while Broch stresses the positive value of ornaments: "For Loos's theory is merely an acceptation—a very self-conscious one—of modernity's incapacity to create ornaments, and should not be understood as an appreciation of ornaments in general."[10] This sentence occurs in an essay written in 1912, which develops the insights of 1908 and attempts to sketch a whole aesthetic system.

These "Notes Toward a Systematic Aesthetic" start from a theory of "ecstasy" as the "manifestation of the will"—in a terminology that evokes Schopenhauer—to focus then on a discussion of Loos and ornaments. Indeed, Loos himself expresses an appreciation of ornaments if they are produced naturally and naively: he concludes his "Ornament and Crime" with the famous tale of the shoemaker who is happier if he can add decorative frills to the leather of his shoes. As a "real aristocrat," Loos refuses to spoil this innocent pleasure in the display of traditional skill. But our epoch had reached a stage when ornaments can only be thought of in a nostalgic way; if they are produced as "contemporary art," they are either superfluous or reactionary. Like the tattoos on the bodies on criminals, ornament is "criminal" in that it forces us to regress to infantile fixations.

In the 1912 essay, Broch counters with the idea that decorative art is still possible. Ornaments are not regressive: they enhance or highlight our perception of aesthetic proportions. Broch's theory of ornament is inseparable from his theory of style, a term he prefers since it can also apply to mathematical demonstrations (to illustrate what "style" is, Broch gives two examples of geo-metric figures, with calculations and formulae). Even when he notes that Loos's insights seem influenced by the Freudian school, Broch refuses to have re-course to a psychoanalytic theory of sublimation. His own concept of style owes its systematic character to Otto Weininger's vitalistic emphasis on "rhythm."

A text published in 1908 provides Broch with a specific terminology: in Wilhelm Worringer's *Abstraction and Empathy*[11] he finds a synthesis of insights deriving from Schopenhauer, Weininger, and Riegl. Worringer, quoted by Broch, states at the beginning of his third chapter: "Ornamentation provides a sort of paradigm in which one can distinctly decipher the specific features of absolute artistic will *(Kunstwollen).*" If Broch never exactly uses the Scho-penhauerian term of "artistic will," his notion of the "whole" is not far from an absolute will that underpins all historical periods. Broch believes in the possi-bility of assessing the "differential expression of the unified and unifying fun-damental concept of the whole"[12] provided by an ornament. An ornament is a detail that provides a synecdoche and points to the whole, thus affording a bridge between time and space: music and architecture exchange their prop-erties when an appogiatura builds a development, transition, and folding back onto the beginning with sounds and in time: the same could be said of a cor-nice, molding, finial, and all the traditional elements of style. If architecture is, as Goethe said, "frozen music," then music is spatialized time, since it affords a sense of unity that abolishes the very element in which it is perceived. The ornament is the minimal unit allowing the transformation of successivity into instantaneous spatiality. The ability to perceive such a process negates death, affirms vital sexuality, and is described as "ecstasy" by Broch. In the conclu-sion of Broch's "Notes," Kandinsky's idealist aesthetic, as summed up in *About the Spiritual in Arts* (1912), squarely replaces Loos's abstract and modernist func-tionalism.

Broch's insights seem to anticipate the theories of a writer who was a close friend and whose name resembles his, Ernst Bloch, who, in *Spirit of Utopia*, written in 1915–16 and published in 1918, also calls "ecstasy" the spatialization of time. The chapter entitled "Production of the Ornament" expresses hu-manity's sense of wonder when contemplating a work of art: "What a deep mystery, time is transformed into space."[13] Bloch posits his "principle of hope" as the foundation of ethics and of revolutionary impulses. The proximity of Bloch's *Spirit of Utopia* to Broch's essays has often been noted and may ac-count for the strange messianic and eschatologic proclamations of the second and third parts of Broch's trilogy. Bloch also mentions the Schopenhauerian idea of a "waking dream" (*Wachtraum*) during which one hesistates between the "not yet known" and the "deepest wonder": no doubt, the figure of Christ as the archrevolutionary looms large at the end of Bloch's philosophical essay.[14] Like Broch, Bloch suggests the return of archaism disguised as modernity—and this will define the site of Nazi mythography. But they do not find a model in a clean utopian image of American metropoles, where highrise skyscrapers testify to humanity's sublime elevation out of anarchic primitivism. By their recurrent appeal to the positivity of an "irrational" hope in messianic revelation and salvation, Bloch and Broch necessarily counter Loos's puritan radicalism.

In the face of Loos's purified modernism, Broch seems to hesitate between two positions: the first is the "reactionary" position of one who keeps looking backward, glancing nostalgically toward the time of an indissociable unity of forms and values, celebrating a unified sensibility before the famous "dissociation," which Eliot identifies with the English revolution and Broch with the rise of Protestantism. Such a nostalgia for the lost values of a totality of beliefs has already been depicted as "romantic" in the novel. Pasenow embodies the regressive desire to be reassured by encompassing systems of values, such as the army: the army provides a uniform in which he can hide his wounded *schöne Seele*. If Broch identified squarely with this position, he would appear less as an Austrian Joyce (a title he claimed for himself after the publication of the *Sleepwalkers*, with the help of Brody, his publisher) than an Austrian Eliot: his sympathies for Catholicism would find a good match in Eliot's blend of royalism and Anglo-Catholicism. But the consequence of romanticism is always the production of inferior art, namely *Kitsch*. And kitsch is defined by Broch in all his essays as an inversion of values, as radical evil in the field of art.

The second position would be closer to that of Bloch, Musil, or Kraus, with an added dimension—the narrative dimension, which cannot completely "contain" the theories it exposes, and which at times seems even at odds with some of their logical consequences. The richness of the *Sleepwalkers* derives precisely from this inadequacy of the novelistic strands for the philosophy that the novel claims to illustrate.

A third position, which Broch never fully explores, would have consisted in drawing Loos closer to a contemporary postmodernism and in stressing the fact that Loos was not averse to the use of ornaments—he merely prohibited the creation of new ornaments in a period that could not give birth to them in any justifiable way. His famous project for the Chicago Tribune Building in 1922 consisted of a Doric column transformed into a proud skyscraper: the date often associated with "high modernism" also saw the birth of postmodernism in architecture. This seems to pave the way for the discourse of contemporary architecture, in its flaunting of decoration pillaged from all past periods and in its deconstructive playfulness and polyphony of styles. Broch, all too prone to denounce this tendency as "irresponsible" and ethically unsound, in short, identical with the production of kitsch, would have to wait until after World War II to reach a more balanced appraisal of such a parodic playfulness—in a movement that I shall describe later.

Returning to the prewar scene of Viennese modernism, Walter Benjamin notes how Kraus and Loos could be perceived as two accomplices in a general debunking of Viennese philistinism: Benjamin quotes Loos's famous remark, "If human work consists only of destruction, it is truly human, natural, noble work," and describes Kraus's and Loos's negative critique as ethically purifying and politically justified. "One must have followed Loos in his struggle with the dragon 'ornament,' heard the stellar Esperanto of Scheerbart's creations, or seen Klee's *New Angel*, who preferred to free men by taking from them, rather than make them happy by giving to them, to understand a humanity that proves itself by destruction."[15]

Broch draws a similar lesson from Kraus's and Loos's ferocious and relentless cultural critique, seeing a link between Loos's preference for a Jerusalem of white, spotless, almost abstract walls over a capital that looks like a museum of clichés, and Kraus's apocalyptic vision of the end of humanity. If Loos praises funerary architecture as the only true monumentality of this century, this can herald for Broch a new utopia. It signals another beginning requiring the zero time, the absolute annihilation before starting anew. The apocalyptic tone that resounds so forcefully at the end of the *Sleepwalkers* cannot be so easily absolved of the suspicion that it, too, is merely another, subtler variety of kitsch.[16] In order to examine this point more closely, let us examine Broch's passage introducing the remarks on architecture in the third volume of the trilogy:

> The horror of this age is perhaps most palpable in the effect that its architecture has on one; I always come home exhausted and depressed after a walk through the streets. I do not even need to look at the house-fronts; they distress me without my raising my eyes to them. Sometimes I fly for consolation to the so highly commended "modern" buildings, but—and here I'm certainly at fault—the warehouse designed by Messel, who is none the less a

great architect, strikes me only as a comic kind of Gothic, and it is a comic effect that irritates and depresses me. It depresses me so much that looking at buildings in the classical style scarcely suffices to restore me. And yet I admire the noble clarity of Schinkel's architecture. (S, 389)

Before noting the curious ambivalence of tone, we can simply stress that the opening paragraph in section two of "Disintegration of Values" clearly links the theses outlined with a subjective point of view. It cannot be Broch who is speaking, but a character: the "theory" is never dissociated from a personal sensitivity, verging at times on squeamishness (in view of all the real horrors of the war as evoked in other parts of the novel), not far from suicide or madness, almost understandable in the context. The narrator's dissociative and quasi-schizophrenic *Weltschmertz* projects itself on buildings, without finding an "objective correlative" to the present epoch's anxiety: caught between Karl Schinkel's masterful neoclassicism (Schinkel built all the famous monuments in Berlin at the end of the nineteenth century, doing for Berlin what Haussmann had done for Paris) and Messel's curious blend of modernism, functionalism, and post-Victorian neo-Gothic, he appears to be a reluctant aesthete, although he denies it: "I am not an aesthete, and unquestionably never was one, although I may unwittingly have given that impression, and I am just as little addicted to the sentimentality that yearns for the past, transfiguring dead-and-gone epochs" (S, 389–90). Indeed, Loos consistently praised Schinkel's neo-classicism for its purity.

In the *Sleepwalkers*, Müller's position appears clearer when he mentions the controversial AEG industrial hall designed by Peter Behrens. Is it the same character who wanders in the Berlin streets who also wonders whether his taste could be shared by someone like Hugenau? This remark occurs in a later section of "Disintegration of Values" that seems to come more directly from the author's pen, since there is no narrative link between the philosopher Müller in Berlin and Hugenau, active in the Mosel city where Esch and Pasenow are also.

Has the man who deals in pipes or textiles anything in common with the feeling for style that is evident in the shops built by Messel, or Peter Behrens's turbine power-houses? His private taste will certainly run to pinnacled villas and rooms cluttered with knick-knacks. . . . It is also a matter of indifference what direction is taken by the architectural or other taste of a business agent of Hugenau's type, and the fact that Hugenau had a certain aesthetic pleasure in machinery is likewise without importance; the sole question of any

moment is whether his ordinary actions, his ordinary thoughts, were influenced by the same laws that in another sphere produced a style devoid of
ornaments, or evolved the theory of relativity, — in other words, whether even
the thought of an epoch is not a vehicle for its style, governed by that
same style which attains visible and palpable expression in works of art. (S,
414–15)

Broch gives away the rationale of so many disturbing ambiguities. Through
its many-layered narative, his novel attempts to recreate the "style of the age"
and helps the reader understand how the "spirit of the age" (*Zeitgeist*) penetrates everything, thus rendering meaningful the most irrational or absurd
impulses. One of the most striking and dramatic actions of the novel, the moment when Hugeneau murders Esch by plunging a bayonet into his back, is
accordingly presented as a sort of dream sequence, a kind of trance that will
soon be forgotten by the survivor. Esch is walking like an automaton in the
night, followed by Hugenau: "And then it overwhelmed him like an illumination — he lowered his rifle, reached Esch with a few feline tango-like leaps,
and ran the bayonet into his angular back. To the murderer's great astonishment Esch went on calmly for a few steps more, then he fell forward on his
face without a sound" (S, 614). Nothing prepares the reader for such a foul
action, yet it seems the only logical solution when viewed as the conclusion of
Hugenau's conquering attitude.

In the same way, the philosopher Bertrand Müller is also a "sleepwalker"
caught up between rational and irrational positions. This is confirmed when
his friendship with Marie, the Salvation Army Girl, and Nuchem Sussim, one
of the Jewish refugees from the east, grows and entangles him in the repressed
attraction between Marie and Nuchem (who is married and has children).
The philosopher is portrayed as poor, undernourished, prone to hallucinations, and even preoccupied with his own suicide. His disintegrating comments
on style, his weary admission of a threatening and increasing state of alienation are as symptomatic as Hugenau's cold logic and dispassionate murder:

> I try to philosophize — but where is the dignity of knowledge to be found to-
> day? Is it not long defunct? Has Philosophy itself not disintegrated into mere
> phrases in face of the disintegration of its object? . . . It often seems to me as
> if the state I am now in, the state that keeps me here in this Jewish house, is
> beyond resignation and is rather a kind of wisdom that has learned to come
> to terms with a completely alien environment. (S, 557)

All the characters face the philosophical problem of the dissolution of any stable concept of "reality"—and the leitmotiv of the theoretical passages is "Can this age, this disintegrating life, be said to have reality?" (S, 557, but also 373, 559, 627).

The original trauma of the war has brought about a radical questioning of all foundations, which is condensed in the formula: "Are we, then, insane because we have not gone mad?" (S, 374). If we had been sane—let us say, in 1914—we would have gone mad by the end of the war: thus, we must have been insane in 1914 (which also accounts for the war itself). If the militarist ideology, which caused so many people to embrace willingly the possibility of their own death, or all the "ideologies of hatred" seem absurd, yet they penetrate deeply the unconscious logicality of a whole period. "Our common destiny is the sum of our single lives, and each of these single lives is developing quite normally, in accordance, as it were, with its private logicality" (S, 373)— Broch coins the ironic expression *Unterhosenlogizität* to evoke an "undergarment" logic of the private sphere. The spectacle of contemporary history corresponds to what Stephen Dedalus called the "nightmare of history," and it is recurrently described in strongly apocalyptic terms: "Amid a blurring of all forms, in a twilight of apathetic uncertainty brooding over a ghostly world, man like a lost child gropes his way by the help of a small frail thread of logic through a dream landscape that he calls reality and that is nothing but nightmare to him" (S, 373). This is why the first section concludes like the last section (in the passage already quoted at the beginning) and thus the whole book concludes on an ambivalent appeal to the saving *Führer*:

> But if there were a man in whom all the events of our time took significant shape, a man whose native logic accounted for the events of our age, then and only then would this age cease to be insane. Presumably this is why we long for a "leader," so that he may provide us with the motivation for events that in his absence we can characterize only as insane. (S, 375)

The novel was finished in 1930 and published in 1931, and Broch was later to enhance the prophetic quality of these pages. Yet, even if they denounce the mechanism by which a society devoid of values will crave for a providential leader such as Hitler, they nevertheless pose a problem for the reader of its theses on history: if the author of these axiological meditations seems alienated and mystified, how can one give them more than symptomatological value? How can one reach beyond the limitations of individual logics and private worlds to find some central point of view?

Broch alludes systematically to a Platonic point of view, yet insofar as he presents himself as an historian, he never fails to stress his post-Einsteinian position. In the *Sleepwalkers* this generates the sweeping reconstruction of the disintegration process whereby values gradually lose their moorings in a total-izing system of beliefs, such as existed in the Middle Ages. Broch does not lament such a vanishing of faith, as Henry Adams or Matthew Arnold would, but interprets the evolution in terms of his mathematical logic of values. What has been lost by the disappearance of the fixed point of reference identified as God is simply the position of an infinite point outside the system of values. But it was precisely this transcendent exteriority that ensured the whole system's consistency. Broch then provides a logical diagram with which we can inter-pret the atomization of values:

> In certain geometrical figures an infinitely distant point is arbitrarily assumed
> to lie within a given finite plane, and then the figure is constructed as if this
> assumed point were really at an infinite distance. The relation of the various
> parts to each other in such a figure remains the same as if the assumed point
> were really at an infinite distance, but all the masses are distorted and fore-
> shortened. In somewhat similar fashion we may conceive that the construc-
> tions of logic are affected when the logical point of plausibility is moved
> from the infinite to the finite: the purely formal logic as such, its methods of
> inference, even its substantive associative relations, remain unaltered, —what
> is altered is the shape of its masses, its "style." (S, 419–20)

If contemporary cosmogony has stopped believing in a first cause, does this new skepticism imply a pure relativism? The loss of an overall "style" may be linked with the awareness that the world cannot be independent from a con-sciousness that posits it. The world can be perceived as a "reality" only if value systems relate its different elements to the whole; but these value systems can-not be posited in the void of a presupposed absolute. Broch follows Hegel in his critique of absolute idealism, without necessarily accepting his speculative dialectics:

> Hegel levelled against Schelling the (justified) reproach that he had pro-
> jected the Absolute into the world "as if it were a bullet from a pistol." But
> that applies with equal force to the concept of value projected by Hegelian
> and post-Hegelian philosophy. Simply to project a concept of value into his-
> tory and summarily to describe as "values" all that history has preserved may
> be permissible at a pinch for the purely aesthetic values of the creative arts,
> but it is otherwise so sweepingly false that it drives one in contradiction to

maintain that history is a conglomeration of non-values, and to deny out-
right that there is any value-reality in history. (*S*, 561)

Broch is criticizing the contradiction involved in Hegel's view of a "world-
spirit" that judges everything from the elevated perspective of a "High Court
of History": this posits an absolute at the end of a history that thus necessarily
becomes retrospective. History can only be said to be rational in an absolute
sense when it is ended. This critique leads Broch to the first "thesis" of his
"epistemological excursus":

> History is composed of values, since life can be comprehended only in the
> category of value—yet these values cannot be introduced into reality as ab-
> solutes, but can only be thought of in reference to an ethically-motivated
> value-positing subject. Hegel's absolute and objectified "world-spirit" was
> such a subject introduced into reality, but the all-embracing absoluteness of
> its operation could not but result in a *reductio ad absurdum*. (This is another
> example of the impassable limits imposed on deductive thinking.) These
> values are not absolutes, but only finite postulates. (*S*, 561)

As the discussion of architectural ornament and fictional characters has shown,
Broch contradicts Hegel in what appears to be his systematic ratification of the
dominant values enshrined in a monumental history: the discarded and fleeting impulses, the irrational and contradictory longings have a place only insofar as they obey the dialectics leading toward *Aufhebung*. Broch counters with
a character such as Hugenau, who "may be a person of no value, even a de-
stroyer of values," yet "as the centre of his own system of values . . . is a ripe
subject for biography and history" (*S*, 561). In that respect, Hugenau is not
different from a symptomatic ornament, or from the no less symptomatic absence of ornaments: "Even the histories of inanimate objects, as for instance
the architectural history of a house, are made up from a selection of those facts
which would have been important to the respective subjects if they had a will
to create values" (ibid.). Without a "value-positing centre" any event loses its
reality and "dissolves into nebulosity."

Similarly, culture is borne by values; it is "value-formation," a point of view
that could lead Broch to some vague culturalism or relativism. He has therefore to assert all the more forcibly his second thesis, which posits the "absolute-
ness of the Logos," embodying the force of law (in a Kantian sense) without
which nothing would be recorded in history. The Platonic logos posits a formal unity that can be perceived in concepts or art works as soon as they reach
some transcendence.

Broch's third thesis attempts to mediate between a sort of Husserlian radical logicism and a neo-Hegelian cultual relativism:

> The world is a *Setzung* [position] of the intelligible Self, for the Platonic idea has never been abandoned nor ever can be. But this position is not projected "like a bullet from a pistol," for nothing can be posited but value-making subjects, which in their turn reflect the structure of the intelligible Self and in their turn fashion their own value-positions, their own world-formations: the world is not an immediate but a mediate position of the Self, it is a "position of position," "a position of position of positions," and so on in infinite iteration. (*S*, 563, modified)

It is important to note here that the English translation of *Setzung* as "product" misses the point: Broch is talking of the way subjects posit and construct the world as reality while obeying the structure of an absolute rationality. The mediate notion of such a construction supposes the introduction of an "ideal observer" into the field of observation: an observer without whom, according to Einsteinian principles, no fact could be measured, but ideal in the sense that the observer still adheres to an absolute logic of the system as such, similar to Eco's notion of an ideal reader (equivalent to the ideal author) of a text.[17]

In the novel this function is embodied by the double figure of the author of these very notes: while they are clearly ascribable to Bertrand Müller on the one hand (a philosopher who shares more than a name with the enigmatic Bertrand of the first two parts of the trilogy), they are very close to the essays Broch was writing in the twenties and thirties and derive much of their meaning when situated in the philosophical controversy surrounding logical positivism. Broch tries to refute Carnap's view of purely rational language games: this is why he stresses both the primitive attitude of the value-bearing subject and the Platonic background of a logos governing all positions. His logical phenomenology takes into account the unconscious and anthropology, while remaining devoted to a narrative dramatization of the clashes between different value systems.

Broch's diagnosis of the present age is undoubtedly pessimistic: whereas the culmination of perfect style lies in the mutual interpenetration of rational and irrational elements, the modern zeitgeist has unleashed the powers of reason, losing touch with the Platonic concept so that it clashes with its own infinity:

> The pure Ratio, arising through dialectic and deduction, becomes set and incapable of further formation when it grows autonomous, and this rigidity annuls its own logicality and brings it up against its logical limit of

infinity,—when reason becomes autonomous it is thus radically evil, for in annuling the logicality of the value-system it destroys the sytem itself. (S, 627)

When reason and life are pitted against each other as free and autonomous realms, each system initiates its own "private theology." This then produces splinter subsystems all striving for full acknowledgment. Their slogans gesture toward such an absolute status: "art for art" or "business is business" would be two symptoms of modernity, as well as all racist, nationalist, and militarist ideologies. These partial systems merely caricature the absolute Platonic center they have lost, thus becoming all the more despotic.

Hugenau's very person radicalizes the loss of values, since he embodies the paradox of a "man liberated from values" who nevertheless symbolizes a whole epoch in which "commercial values" recover their domination after the revolutionary gale has subsided. If Hugenau allegorizes the triumph of modernism, his radicality is also haunted by the ghost of a rationality of the irrational.

As an individual, Hugenau manifests the triumph of individualism (he exploits or dispatches all those who are in his way) and heralds a new era of mass murder and irrationality. If he has been clever enough to take advantage of the revolutionary uprising for his own ends, when he falls back into normalcy, he remains a sleepwalker, because his actions become automatic while he remains in some uncertainty:

> In this predicament of the European spirit Hugenau was scarcely involved at all, but he was involved in the prevailing uncertainty. For the irrational in man has an affinity with the irrational in the world; and although the uncertainty in the world is, so to speak, a rational uncertainty, often, indeed, merely an economic uncertainty, yet it springs from the irrationality of the superrational, from an independent reason that strives towards infinity in every province of human activity, and so, reaching the super-rational limits of its infinity, overthrows itself and becomes irrational, passing beyond comprehension. (S, 640)

Thus, Hugenau cannot fit squarely into the role of the bourgeois conformist seemingly reserved for him: he still embodies a subject of values and in that role keeps proving, willy nilly as it were, that he is connected with the "ideal subject" of values. In the midst of his business dealings, for instance, he will suddenly refuse to serve a customer just because he senses something strange in his expression (S, 641). Similarly, he feels isolated from his fellow citizens by a strange zone of silence (642).

Hugenau's portrayal is thus unforgettable and may be called Broch's most subtle and tantalizing character, because this despicable man still testifies to a sense of haunting that goes beyond his consciousness: his uneasiness in normal everyday gatherings betrays his subliminal awareness that things and values are threatened by a nameless dissolution—the same dissolution that started affecting Joachim von Pasenow when he could not help seeing his bride-to-be's face slowly merging into the landscape. Hugenau is a reluctant and parodic Hegelian, who is only redeemed because his irrational actions have been motivated by a desire to reach absolute freedom. He is vaguely aware of the need for symbols without which the "visible world would fall asunder into unnamable, bodiless, dry layers of cold and transparent ash" (S, 642): his suppressed anxiety calls up the curse of pure contingency, of the arbitrary and fortuitous yokings of things, events, and names.

> Would not the racing bicyclists have to scatter to the four winds if they were no longer combined by a common uniform and a common club badge? Hugenau did not ask such a question, for it exceeded the grasp of what might be called, not without reason, his private theology; yet the unasked question irritated him no less than the elusiveness of the experiences that worried him, and his irritation might, for instance, discharge itself in boxing his child on the ear for no reason at all on the way home. Having relieved his feelings in this manner, however, he found it easy to come back to sober reality, thus confirming Hegel's maxim: "Real freedom of will is a harmony between the theoretical and the practical spirit." (S, 643)

The last pages of the *Sleepwalkers* can seem paradoxical: the ethical and absolutist points of view consistently set forward by Broch lead him not to indict Hugenau but to condone his actions in the name of a striving toward absolute freedom. The rhetorical flourish of a series of invocations gestures toward some revolutionary desire beyond any sense of good and evil:

> Oh, agonizing compulsion towards freedom! terrible and ever-renewed revolution of knowledge! which justifies the insurrection of the Absolute, the insurrection of life against reason—justifying reason when, apparently at variance with itself, it unleashes the absolute of the irrational against the absolute of the rational, justifying it by providing the final assurance that the unleashed irrational forces will once more combine into a value-system. There is no value-system that does not subordinate itself to freedom; even the most reduced system is groping towards freedom, even the outcast victim of all earthly loneliness and detachment, the man who achieves no more

than the freedom to commit a murder, the freedom to enter prison, or at most the freedom of a deserter, even he, the man stripped of all values. . . . Each man must fulfill his dream, unhallowed or holy, and he does so to have his share of freedom in the darkness and dullness of his life. (S, 644)

This "truth" is something that Hugenau would want to convey to others, yet cannot find words for. In a final dialectical twist, Hugenau is transformed into a figure of eternal damnation: he becomes Ahasuerus, the Wandering Jew, doomed to wander over the earth because of his sin, waiting for the time when the "absolute zero" of values can start producing or positing new values.

Ironically, Broch plays with the cliché that identifies modernism with a "lost generation," a phrase coined by Gertrude Stein, popularized by Hemingway, and applied to the entire period of modernism:

Inexperienced, helpless, and insensate, the men of this generation are delivered to the icy hurricane, they must forget in order to live and they do not know why they die. Their path is the path of Ahasuerus, their duty is his duty, their freedom is the freedom of the hunted creature and their aim is forgetfulness. Lost generation! as non-existent as Evil itself, featureless and traditionless in the morass of the indiscriminate, doomed to lose itself temporally, to have no tradition in an age that is making absolute history! (S, 646)

In this exalted rhetorical upsurge, Broch launches all the major themes of his subsequent essays and novels—such as the interversion of aesthetic and ethical values that defines kitsch for him—and yet seems to reach a point of utter undecidability in his theory of values:

Whatever the individual man's attitude to the course of the revolution, whether he turns reactionary and clings to outworn forms, mistaking the aesthetic for the ethical as all conservatives do, or whether he holds himself aloof in the passivity of egoistic knowledge, or whether he gives himself up to his irrational impulses and applies himself to the destructive work of the revolution:
he remains unethical in his destiny, an outcast from his epoch, an outcast from Time,
yet nowhere and never is the spirit of the epoch so strong, so truly ethical and historical as in that last and first flare-up which is revolution . . . the last and greatest ethical achievement of the old disintegration system and the first achievement of the new, the moment when time is annulled and history radically formed in the pathos of absolute zero! (S, 646–47)

Even more strangely, Hugenau newly refigured as the wandering Jew is presented as yearning toward the leader who would point to Zion ("his road is the road to Zion and yet the road we must all take" [S, 647]). The leader transfigured into a Messiah ("our hope that a Messiah will lead us to [Zion] remains imperishable" [S, 648]) provides a bridge between the individual and the "brotherhood of all creatures." He speaks in the silence of the logos and announces a new fraternity of all men.

Having reached this bombastic culmination, the reader is likely to have forgotten how the passages from the "Disintegration of Values" stem from the sick and divided mind of Bertrand Müller; it is no coincidence that he also appears obsessed with Zion and eternal exile, yearning for community in the strange triangle of love uniting him with Marie and Nuchem. About his own state Müller says: "Nothing has survived—flung to the winds is my ego, flung into nothingness; irrealizable my yearning, unattainable the Promised Land, invisible the ever-brightening but constantly receding radiance, and the community that we grope for is devoid of strength yet full of evil will" (S, 558).

In the face of Bertrand's anguish and alienation, Nuchem's Talmudic wisdom provides a sort of positive yardstick. Nuchem merely says: "The law is imperishable. God is not until every jot and tittle of the Law has been deciphered" (S, 559). Nuchem is also described as being quite amused by the philosopher's favorite quotes of Kant or Hegel, after he has resumed his work, his "thesis on the disintegration of values" (S, 439): "[Nuchem] had an immeasurable respect for books, but he could laugh uproariously over a few lines of Kant, and was astonished when I did not join in. So it seemed to him an extraordinarily good joke when he found this maxim while looking over Hegel: *The principle of magic consists in this, that the connection between the means and the effect shall not be recognized*" (S, 439). Bertrand Müller fails to see the humorous side of these passages and thus assumes that Nuchem Sussim has a deeper understanding of philosophy. One could almost conclude that Hegel's very serious and rationalistic definition of the principle of magic is so hilarious for Nuchem because it is identical with the principle of Witz or with jokework.

The Freudian Witz, of which Broch was inordinately fond, is the only acceptable alternative to what the *Sleepwalkers* posits as the Jews' "abstract modernity."

The Jew, by virtue of the most abstract rigour of his conception of infinity, is the really modern, the most "advanced" man *kat'exochen*: he it is who surrenders himself with absolute radicality to whatever system of values, what-

ever career he has chosen . . . — it looks as though the current of the absolute
Abstract which for two thousand years has flowed through the ghettoes like
an almost imperceptible trickle beside the great river of life should now become the main stream. (*S*, 526)

In that sense, the Jew radicalizes what the Prostestant dissolution of values had
started. It is not surprising that Hugenau should almost become a Jew at the
end of the story. Interpreted in this light, it may seem that Hugenau's final
elevation to the position of Ahasuerus is nothing but a cruel joke, inverting
Hegel's famous "cunning of reason."

In the same way, when Dr. Litwak, a sort of rabbi, tries to intervene to stop
Nuchem from going out with Marie, Müller retorts rather cruelly: "Stop him
from what? From wanting to go to Zion? Leave him that harmless pleasure"
(*S*, 462). This refers of course to the canticles sung by Marie and to her sublimated virginity, but also to Nuchem's yearning for a freedom that entails a no
less radical negation than Hugenau's sinister deeds.

The paradox of this novel is that because it problematizes the point of view,
linking it with the issue of values and value systems, it must leave readers in a
state of hesitation over their own values — like sleepwalkers, pondering the relative weight of ethics and aesthetics, or the possibility of redeeming Hugenau
or damning him. In fact, if readers condemn Hugenau, they will condemn the
whole present period without having any possibility of overcoming its lethal
contradictions. Broch's resolute mediation between Kant and Hegel, between
a sense of the absolute demands that can be made in the name of pure legality
and a sense of the historical cynicism derived from a need to identify the real
with the rational provides a system that attempts to encompass everything, rational and irrational, Platonic logos and positivistic dissolution, fiction and
theory — yet leaves theory dangling from an impossible point of utterance.

When readers realize this apparent contradiction, they can only laugh —
and reread. But this laughter is as discontinuous as the individual actions that
posit values — all "positions of positions of positions" — whereas Hegel's "trans-
finite and indefinite unity" postulates a totality that is both a recapitulation of
all moments and a constant reassertion of the absolute.

For Broch, the absolute inheres in the structure of the subject's will, and
the irrational nature of this position posits its agency as irreversible, ultimately
responsible for all actions. The three narrative moments have juxtaposed three
characters with three sets of values: romanticism is reactionary, anarchism is
progressive yet parodic, caught up in a contradictory desire that asserts what it
negates, while realism (*Sachlichkeit*) introduces the simple constatation that

"it is the way it is": ethical dishonesty, but the only hope for a radical transmutation of all values into something new.

The question remained alive for Broch at the time of the writing of the *Sleepwalkers*, a novel that poses without solving the problem of new values. In a letter, he wonders about the problem of modernity, or what he calls the "new problem": "What direction does the longing for enlightenment and salvation take in times of disintegration and dissolution of old value systems? When the longing can no longer fuse into these systems? Can a new ethos emerge out of the sleep and the dream of the vilest everyday?"[18] This leads to a forceful questioning of the desire for totality, a desire that should not be reduced to an assertion of the totality.

All of Broch's characters appear as sleepwalkers, in a *Schwebezustand*, a state of hesitation between the "nevermore" of ancient values and the "not yet" of new values. Esch exemplifies this urge when he confronts Bertrand and announces that he will denounce publicly his homosexuality (the sexual mark of infamy awaiting the eternal "aesthete"): he only betrays the childish "desire that someone should come to pay the debt of sacrificial death and redeem the world to a new innocence" (*S*, 296). But after he has acted out his dream in a sort of trance, he cannot recover sleep and return to his old "anarchic" values, as an italicized paragraph states: *"Great is the fear of him who awakens. He returns with less certainty to his waking life, and he fears the puissance of his dream, which though it may not have borne fruit in action has yet grown into a new knowledge. An exile from dream, he wanders in dream"* (*S*, 303).

Sleepwalking can be defined as an intermediary state embodied by all the main characters of the novel at one point or another. They share a sort of dreamlike precision and a hallucinatory acuity of vision that characterize all of Hugenau's actions: he acts with a sense of security because he remains suspended in a dream that began when he decided to desert. Everything that follows is given gratuitously, as it were; he rediscovers the world like a child and begins a period of "vacation."

This intermediary state is thus close to what Broch would later call "twilight state" (*Dämmerzustand*) in his theory of "mass psychosis" elaborated during his American exile. This theory, which attempted to interpret the conditions of the overwhelming triumph of Nazism in Germany and Austria, also aimed at providing a new basis for "absolute democracy," a democracy that could be made immune to such aberrations. In Broch's paradoxical phrase, democracy must become "totalitarian" (it must convince people of the truth and strength of its total idea) if it wishes to withstand the perverse appeal to irrationality that Nazi leaders so adeptly exploited. In a way, democracy must be "awake" and cannot allow any "sleepwalking."

For reasons both personal and theoretical, Broch was never able to complete his political theory of democracy, which he envisaged as "totalitarian," precisely in order to prevent the return of dictatorship. The fragments that have been published are tantalizing, showing how Broch hoped to solve some of the contradictions still rife in the *Sleepwalkers*.

When the trilogy attempts to complement the "irrationality" of the stories with the pure rationality of the theory of values—an idea Broch stated in many letters—a new problem appears: the theory cannot be abstracted from its enunciation, otherwise the place of its production (*Setzung*) would be a blind spot in the theory of the *Setzung* of value positions. If, as Kurt Gödel has demonstrated, each system has to allow for a point of undecidability and incompleteness, then the *Sleepwalkers* must allow for a degree of sleepwalking in the theory itself. There can be no closure without Nuchem's irresponsible laughter, which may betray the culmination of his seriousness.

Broch's theory of the "narrator as idea" (developed in his reading of Joyce when explaining that "one cannot simply place an object under a lightbeam and describe it, but the subject of representation, hence the 'narrator as idea,' and no less language, with which the object of representation is described, are part of the means of representation")[19] has often been commented on but always with the assumption that this new "idea" would not attack the point of view of the totality needed to denounce the "disintegration of values."

My contention is somewhat different, since I would argue that the general "somnambulism" cuts across all the layers of rationality and irrationality, creating a sort of theoretical unrest that also posits a trembling boundary between modernism and postmodernism. We would have to examine the *Death of Virgil*, Broch's response to Kafka's work (Virgil's decision to burn his poem has some historical foundation and also alludes to Kakfa's famous testamentary demand that Brod should burn all his unfinished pieces), and his critical response to *Finnegans Wake*, in order to understand the complex splicing of lyricism and theory by which he planned to solve this problem. The solution, in fact, needed to rely on the creation of a new language, or a language of the limits, with huge sentences, newly coined words, and an obscurity that seems at odds with the main explicit theme: the lack of justification of any work of art in comparison to the urgency of moral and political commitment. Broch's paradoxical "negative aesthetics" appears to be loaded with strange contradictions, which also account for the general disorganization of his later years in exile, when he seemed to be working frantically in the hope of a synthesis that his manifold endeavors could only destroy or indefinitely postpone.

Similarly, Bertrand Müller's awareness of the failure of his philosophical synthesis corresponds to the subjective conclusion that no system can close itself off, can suture its enunciative apparatus. Bertrand Müller is indeed a reincarnation of Bertrand, who emerges as the negation of romantic values, simply because he embodies aestheticism, which is defined as "evil" in the first system of values explored by the trilogy, romanticism. We cannot forget that the first "theoretical" statement provided in the *Sleepwalkers* is directly ascribed to Bertrand and sounds very close to Bertrand Müller's later musings. After just a dozen pages of straightforward narrative, we find the following aside:

> On the theme of the military uniform Bertrand could have supplied some
> such theory as this:
> Once upon a time it was the Church alone that was exalted as judge over
> mankind, and every layman knew that he was a sinner. Nowadays it is the
> layman who has to judge his fellow-sinner if all values are not to fall into
> anarchy, and instead of weeping with him, brother must say to brother: "You
> have done wrong." . . . And because, when the secular exalts itself as the
> absolute, the result is always romanticism, so the real and characteristic ro-
> manticism of that age was the cult of the uniform. (S, 20)

Only through the intervention of this point of view does the novel justify its own subtitle of "Romanticism." This is again the point of view that judges without condemning a Hugenau associated with a new modernity, a modern-ist matter-of-factness, a wish to abolish all the ancient and spurious values.

In this movement, modernism is indeed a crime; it is criminal for it gener-ates the worst evils (fascism, mass hysteria, totalitarianism). Modernism corre-sponds to the culmination of the atomization of values, and its philosophical equivalent is logical positivism. Such a modernism will finally have to be re-deemed, because a world entirely free of values is a contradiction in terms for Broch. The redeeming moment is always subjective, context- and value-bound, and it always entails deep personal suffering.

This defines the plight of the philosopher as "novelist in spite of himself" — this misleading catchphrase of Brochian criticism has been coined by Hannah Arendt, who perhaps paid too much attention to the way Broch would de-scribe his lifelong ambivalence toward literature. This refers not just to Broch himself but also to one of his characters, who, like him, is seen hesitating between two worlds and two beliefs, always uncertain and suffering, because he must question *and* redeem a process that tortures the questioner and finally questions the foundation of his beliefs. Bertrand Müller speaks for Broch and for us all when he appears as one among the company of sleepwalkers.

Sleepwalking entails that we act without knowing the reason or the logic of our action. The philosopher as sleepwalking rationalist becomes a mere ghost of a hidden rationality that can never be fully perceived. Yet this blindness is not complete, for in the midst of the trance, a flickering light may appear. Like Dante or Virgil, the sleeper only wakes up to a new pain testifying to hard-won discernment. Thus, the philosopher voices his doubts:

> I said to myself: "You are a fool, you are a Platonist, you believe that in com-
> prehending the world, you can shape it and raise yourself in freedom to
> Godhood. Can you not see that you are bleeding yourself to death?"
> I answered myself: "Yes, I am bleeding to death." (S, 559)

SEVEN

Beckett and the Ghosts of Departed Quantities

In one of the strangest and densest passages of Wilfred Bion's novel, *Memoir of the Future*, the author, a famous psychoanalyst of the Kleinian school, struggles with two imaginary projections of himself, Mycroft and Myself, who are engaged in a dialogue with Sherlock Holmes and Dr. Watson. Mycroft, who defends his right to speak and insists that the author should go back to sleep or to some form of nonexistence, makes an impassioned plea for the reality of fictional beings. These he calls "ghosts," noting that the Greeks believed in ghosts, as "independent of anatomy yet with a visible counterpart": "They spoke of them frequently and as if they had no shadow."[1] The curious way Bion the author allows himself to be replaced by characters who appear more real than their creator evokes Flann O'Brien's *At Swim-Two-Birds*[2] or, in Bion's words, the fate of poor "spiritualistic Conan Doyle" driven off the stage by Sherlock Holmes (*MF*, 95). Mycroft's discourse recalls some of Bion's theses, suggesting that we need to build abstract systems in order to "learn from experience."

> MYCROFT Leave the long words out of it. They are useful only for mystification and dominance. We can use constructions and verbal transformations of objects derived from what were in origin part of the sensuous domain. For example, that poor fellow, though he knew better, struggled to transform his religious rubbish into what he called "opticks." Quite erroneous and limited insofar as he was successful. Berkeley had no difficulty; even labouring with the equipment of religious training he could detect the infinitesimal increments and the part they could play in postponing the detection of a fallacy for at least a century. (*MF*, 94)

The reference to the "poor fellow" will remain cryptic unless we remember that in *Transformations*, a book that provides a conceptual grid with which to systematize the analyses of *Learning from Experience* and *Elements of Pyscho-Analysis*, Bion directly quotes the polemical remark with which Bishop George Berkeley sought to destroy Isaac Newton's *Opticks*.

In the following passage, taken from a treatise aptly entitled the *Analyst* (1734), Berkeley attacks Newton's theory of "fluxions" (instrumental in defining differential calculus) as suffering from a vicious circularity:

> Whatever therefore is got by such exponents and proportions is to be ascribed to fluxions: which must therefore be previously understood. And what are these fluxions? The velocities of evanescent increments. And what are these same evanescent increments? They are neither finite quantities, nor quantities infinitely small, nor yet nothing. May we not call them the ghosts of departed quantities?[3]

Berkeley acknowledges the truth of Newton's results in so far as differential calculus is "true," but questions the method by which he has invented it. As Bion notes, both Newton and Berkeley deny the "ghosts" of vanished matter, Newton because he believes in the validity of his method, Berkeley because Newton uses the difference between qualities and quantities as a conceptual wedge by which he can separate series of perceived impressions in his idealist rewriting of empiricism (as we have seen in chapter 1).

In a later passage from *Memoir of the Future*, Myself discusses once more the controversy between Newton and Berkeley: "You refer to Berkeley's attack on the Analyst in Newton's formulation of the 'ghosts' of increments? I have always been impressed by the language in which Berkeley clothed his attack. It is the language Freud might have used to describe a theory of anal eroticism" (*MF*, 193). If this explanation remains a little enigmatic, a further reference brings more light. This time, the speaker is P.A. (for Psycho-Analyst):

> P.A. Berkeley made fun of these objects whichever way they were growing less or more; even the object that did not exist, the object so small that it was the ghost of a departed increment, or what I describe as the increment of a "ghost" coming into being according to the laws of change whether crescent or decay. All this is easier to formulate if it is talk about the decay or growth of a corporeal object, or a use of the language appropriate to corporeal objects for a purpose for which it was not intended — incorporeal objects, thoughts, minds, personalities.
> ROLAND Has this talk got anything to do with our present state or is it a substitute for it, just to take up time?
> P.A. It may be a "nothing" out of which something comes; the increment of a "ghost of a departed increment," or the disappearing, declining something which is destined to disappear — or both. (*MF*, 315)

I should probably account for the presence of these quotations in a chapter purporting to examine Samuel Beckett's works: by plunging in medias res in Bion's labyrinthine texts, I imply some connection between the Irish writer and Bion, who was Beckett's analyst in the mid-thirties, at the time of the writing of *Murphy*.[4] My contention is that a hidden correspondence between the theses of the two writers can be discerned, especially as they are both concerned with "ghosts" and the question of the positivity of "nothing."

By a strange coincidence, Bion's novels, written after many difficult and technical studies of psychoanalysis, seem to follow in the steps of the neurotic young Irishman he had sought to cure in London. Bion's trilogy, *The Dream* (1975), *The Past Presented* (1977), and *The Dawn of Oblivion* (1979, the year of Bion's death) can be seen as a third trilogy, following Beckett's two narrative sequences of the 1950s and 1980s.[5] In order to explore the cryptic links between these works, I would like to situate the psychiatric background of Beckett's early work against his main philosophical theses, before returning to Bion's theories.

Whenever Beckett evokes his first creative period in later works, he seems to call up a moment of naive storytelling, a preanalytic time when it was still possible to believe in novels. When Moran is told to leave his house and look for Molloy, he muses on the real nature of his previous missions, all duly performed at the request of the mysterious Youdi: those whom Moran has helped or worked for are described tantalizingly as his "patients":

> I lost interest in my patients, once I had finished with them. I may even truthfully say I never saw one of them again, subsequently, not a single one. No conclusions need be drawn from this. Oh the stories I could tell you if it were easy. What a rabble in my head, what a gallery of moribunds. Murphy, Watt, Yerck, Mercier and all the others. I would never have believed that—yes, I believe it willingly. Stories, stories. I have not been able to tell them. I shall not be able to tell this one.[6]

The French term for rabble in the original version is *tourbe*, suggesting more than a troubled and troublesome crowd, since it points to the specific Irish "turf" of bogs. This suggests the "matter" of a resisting imaginary mass, from which individual ectoplasms detach themselves to perform a few little tricks before being summoned back to the dark crucible in which all the forms are generated. Moran initiates the series of self-conscious narrators who crop up regularly in Beckett's fictions, invent a few names including their own, and spin out yarns in order to forget their own sufferings.

Murphy (1938) is perhaps Beckett's only "novel," in the sense that it still pretends to depict a plot, to present characters who act in a more or less normal way. The verbal pyrotechnics of *Dream of Fair to Middling Women* (1932) or *More Pricks than Kicks* (1934) had prevented any stable characterization that would not immediately dissolve into post-Joycean linguistic games. Moreover, *Watt* (1942–44), his last fiction to be written in English—before a much later return to his mother tongue—works toward a total exhaustion of all the possibilities of narrative patterns. The three moments of the first trilogy are all haunted by the disappearance of the subject as narrator, who is literally replaced by the stories he narrates to pass the time.

Murphy owes its centrality not just to an interesting compromise between experimentation and classical structures but also to its theme: the handling of the "nothing" through fiction. *Murphy* is both a philosophical novel and a psychic exploration that uses psychiatry, psychology, and psychoanalysis to promote its exploration of a constitutive but frightening void in the soul. The narrator of *Molloy* (1950) briefly evokes his past fascination with the scientific discourses informing the fiction of *Murphy*, moving from a fascination for astrology to a questioning of institutional psychiatry in the second part of the novel, when the hero is a warden in a mental home:

> Yes, I once took an interest in astronomy, I don't deny it. Then it was geology that killed a few years for me. The next pain in the balls was anthropology and the other disciplines, such as psychiatry, that are connected with it, disconnected, then connected again, according to the latest discoveries. What I liked in anthropology was its inexhaustible faculty of negation, its relentless definition of man, as though he were no better than God, in terms of what he is not. (*MO*, 38)

Murphy also explores all the psychiatric and theological analogies in order to empty the term "man" of the ideological fullness we mistakenly attribute to it. As a character, Murphy's main role seems to embody the radical possibilities of negation of such a critical "anthropology."

Much has been made of the pun on the Greek *morphe*[7] which is grafted to one of the most common Irish names (we may recall how the two boys who play truant in Joyce's story, "An Encounter," decide to call themselves Murphy and Smith, should they happen to be harassed by the pervert they have met).[8] The submerged Morphe enables Beckett to connect the god of sleep, trance, and half-death with the philosophically loaded interrogation of *form*. The problematic of "form" as morpho-logy is introduced very early in the novel, through

Neary's teachings. We are told that Murphy has studied philosophy or yoga (this is not totally clear) with Neary, a master in Cork, who holds that "all life is figure and ground."[9]

Neary applies his teachings to his own life, since he keeps falling in love with various women, apparently just to cling to a "face" that will keep William James's notion of a "big blooming buzzing confusion" at some distance. First, he is infatuated with Miss Dwyer, then with Miss Counihan, who, in order to create a Racinian or Proustian pattern of a quest for impossible objects, can only love Murphy. But first, Miss Dwyer's "face" is evoked rapturously as: "The one closed figure in the waste without form, and void!" (MU, 7). The irony is that Murphy cannot follow his master on this single point, for all this analysis remains "Greek" to him—as if his own Greek-Irish name was enough to prevent him from falling in love, while Neary's name tellingly distorts his "yearning":

> "The love that lifts up its eyes," said Neary; "being in torment; that craves for the tip of her little finger, dipped in lacquer, to cool its tongue—is foreign to you, Murphy, I take it."
>
> "Greek," said Murphy.
>
> "Or put it another way," said Neary; "the single, brilliant, organized, compact blotch in the tumult of heterogeneous stimulation."
>
> "Blotch is the word," said Murphy. (MU, 7)

Murphy has to reduce the "form" to a "blotch" because he cannot believe in a rational promotion of Greek forms. His world is too close to a fundamental irrationality, and he replaces the Greek world with an almost Jewish stress on exile and return. After Neary has defined life as the interaction of "figure and ground"—which should at least posit the basis for the perception of forms, if nothing more—Murphy adds: "But a wandering to find home" (MU, 6).

Murphy had come to see Neary in the first place because he was hoping that the philosopher could cure the "irrationality" of his heart. His heart is always bursting or slowing down its pace, "like Petrushka in his box" (MU, 6). Neary has invented a system based on what he calls "Apmonia," a word neatly combining "harmony" as written in Greek letters (the ro looks like a "p") with "apnoea" since it is based on the regulation of the breath. But whether he calls it "Apmonia," "Isonomy" or "Attunement," he cannot "blend the opposites in Murphy's heart" (MU, 6).

Thus, from the start, Neary is presented as a sort of parodic Hegelian philosopher who can mimic in a strange body language the three stages of dialectics, showing his despair with his clenched hands, passing from "negation" to "sublation" (*MU*, 7). Neary is also a Pythagorean who believes in numbers and who alludes to Hippasos's fate in a discussion with another disciple, after Murphy has left and become a new object of desire for all the other characters. A rather drunk Neary explains his sad predicament to Wylie and concludes:

"But betray me," said Neary, "and you go the way of Hippasos."
"The Akousmatic, I presume," said Wylie. "His retribution slips my mind."
"Drowned in a puddle," said Neary, "for having divulged the incommensurability of side and diagonal."
"So perish all babblers," said Wylie.
"And the construction of the regular dodeca—hic—dodecahedron," said Neary. (*MU*, 31)

The term "irrationality" applies to feelings—metaphorized by a "heart" that possesses reasons unknown to reason, as Pascal said—and to mathematics, in a bold link close to Broch's theory of the irreducible irrationality of man.

Hippasos was a minor follower of Pythagoras, whose claim to fame derives only from his sad fate, since he is rumored to have been either stoned to death or drowned by a mob for having introduced irrational numbers. These had become necessary when calculating the relative values of the side and diagonal in the square from which one can build a rectangular triangle. His name reappears in a later essay, written in French, in which Beckett develops his idea of the fundamental irrationality of man (an idea shared by Broch when he speaks of the "irreducible irrationality" of humanity). This French text, written in 1938—the year of the long delayed publication of *Murphy*—is called "The Two Needs" (*Les deux besoins*) and begins with a pun on *deux boeufs* (two oxen) and *deux besoins*, which is taken from a song in Gustave Flaubert's *Sentimental Education*.[10] This rather cryptic and dense text contains Beckett's earliest systematic statement about the function of art. Art is apprehended anthropologically, in connection with the way human subjects are structured by desire.

The figure Beckett uses to illustrate this idea is the dodecahedron, a sort of star of David, with two identical triangles superimposed upon each other and pointing in opposite directions. The first triangle is called ABC and corresponds to the "need one needs," defining the realm of wants; the second triangle is called DEF and represents "the need to need," or unquenchable desire. In an almost Lacanian demonstration, Beckett proceeds to define desire as the subtraction of need from demand, but he uses the abstract grid he has sketched, exactly as Bion does in his metapsychological essays. The capitalized letters represent the summits of the two triangles, the lower case letters their points of intersection: "Need to need (DEF) and need one needs (ABC), consciousness of the need to need (ab) and consciousness of the need one needs—the need one *needed*, stemming from the chaos of wishing to see (Aab) and entering into the nothingness of having seen (Dde), producing and ending creative autology (abcdef)" (*DIS*, 56). The last part of the sentence alludes to the central function of art according to Beckett: the artist sees and makes other people see the impasse of a "monadic" desire that would satisfy itself too easily with "little needs." The main need of humanity is to need something, and art is produced at the intersection between needs and wants. "Side and diagonal, the two needs, the two essences, the being which is need and the necessity of being in need, hell of unreason from which rises the whitehot blank scream [*cri à blanc*], the series of pure questions, the work of art [*l'oeuvre*]" (*DIS*, 56).

Hippasos thus emerges as the first artist, the protomartyr of an awesome truth systematically repressed by society:

> Regular, too regular dodecahedron, according to the dimensions of which the unfortunate Almighty would have *considered* arranging the four elements, Pythagoras's signature, a divine figure whose construction depends upon an irrational number, namely the incommensurability of side with diagonal, subject without number and personality. Isn't it because he had betrayed this dark secret that Hippasos perished prematurely, lynched by a crowd of furious, bloodthirsty, and naive adepts in a public sewer? He was neither a fascist nor a communist. (*DIS*, 56)

Murphy is Hippasos's logical heir, and it is fitting that his death should be as undignified: already burnt in a gas explosion, his ashes will finally be disseminated on the dirty floor of a London pub, in a striking parallel to the desperate ending of Céline's *Journey to the End of the Night* (1932).

Beckett's admission of humanity's central irrationality allows for the centrality of art. Despite the cynicism and despair evident in the "Two Needs," the essay concludes on a paradoxical *ars poetica*—in spite of every difficulty. Since scientific or theological discourses are no longer valid (he adds: "Thank God and Poincaré"!), Beckett merely describes the site of art, giving voice and form to humanity's otherwise inaudible scream of despair and going beyond the facile antinomies of mind and matter.

Beckett staunchly identifies art with truth. This is a position from which he has not moved in his postwar texts. It has only become increasingly difficult to articulate the truth of such an irrational rationality. "It progresses through yesses and nos like shell detonators, until truth explodes. Another one. Irreversible. The dead and the wounded will testify" (*DIS*, 57).

We are reminded of Murphy's "eternal tautology": "Yes or No?" (*MU*, 27), when he remains skeptical in front of Neary's attempts at synthesis. The parodic side of *Murphy* does not spare the "hero" but debunks all the pretensions of reason to self-foundation and salvation. Like Neary, all the other characters in the novel keep running after Murphy, who seems important only because he is not running after anything. The authorial voice takes pains to distinguish between Murphy and the others: "All the puppets in this book whinge sooner or later, except Murphy, who is not a puppet" (*MU*, 71).

Neary's diagnosis of Murphy is not to be dismissed easily: for him, Murphy's inability to control his heart stems from an inability to love, and this derives from his being divided in two. Neary tells Murphy: "I should say your conarium has shrunk to nothing" (*MU*, 8), by which he means that, deprived of the pineal gland Descartes thought indispensable to a felicitous coordination of mind and matter, or of body and soul, Murphy cannot bridge the gap between his bodily impulses and the pleasure he derives from his mind. Neary later alludes more rudely to Murphy as a "schizoidal spasmophile," which seems even closer to truth. The two terms nicely connect the psychic level with the somatic basis and correspond to the major symptoms Beckett displayed when he spent years doing nothing in Dublin, before and after his father's death in 1933.

The heart, more than the conarium, represents the point of connection between body and soul: some kind of "love" (of self, God, or others) seems necessary for a harmonious post-Cartesian existence. In the early thirties, Beckett retreated into himself to the point of autistic isolation, in what he called his "baroque solipsism," but he was also consistently troubled by heart poundings and near seizures that woke him up at night, sweating and screaming (in clear imitation of his father's fatal heartstroke).[11] These symptoms, coupled with a few others, including urinary disorders and anal cysts, led him to accept the idea of undergoing psychoanalytical treatment in London. This treatment with Bion lasted roughly two years, from 1934 to 1935. This was also the time of his affair with the woman who turns up in *First Love* (written in 1945). *Murphy* seems to derive from the conflation of the two experiences: a "first love" with a woman who is a prostitute and the experience of undergoing psychoanalysis.

For, as if to prove Neary wrong, Murphy appears capable of love (or desire at least). Celia may not be the love of his life but he desperately *needs* her. When Celia comes to his room to free him from his overturned rocking chair, since a strange "heart attack" (*MU*, 21) has replaced the gradual calm he had felt when rocking himself to sleep at the end of chapter 1, Murphy, who has been compared to a crucified Christ, finally opens his eyes and discovers her face: "The beloved features emerging from chaos were the face against the big blooming buzzing confusion of which Neary had spoken so highly. . . . It was the short circuit so earnestly desired by Neary, the glare of pursuit and flight extinguished" (*MU*, 21).

One of the ironies of the novel is that Neary will in fact have articulated the truth about love: in the end, Celia will fall out of love, having replaced Murphy on his famous "rocker" and experiencing a strange mourning for an unknown butler who has just committed suicide, while Murphy will prefer his own private nirvana or mental peace to the "short circuit" of love.

Murphy is indeed a philosophical novel that allegorizes Murphy's mind in order to show how the "nothing" can provide a stronger object of desire than the "something." Beckett's only direct statement about this early novel was made in a letter written in 1967 to Sighle Kennedy, then a research student preparing a thesis on *Murphy* (published as *Murphy's Bed*, as already mentioned), in which Beckett stresses the novel's irrationality and negativity. He first dissociates himself from the influence of his two former "masters," Proust and Joyce, an influence assumed to have been crucial by Kennedy, then explains that the real point of departure of any investigation into the novel's theme must be the "nothing." The "nothing" appears through both Democritus's famous "Nothing is more real than nothing" and Geulincx's statement, "*Ubi nihil vales, nihil elis*" (You will not want anything where you are worth nothing).[12] Beckett thus writes: "If I were in the unenviable position of having to study my work, my points of departure would be the 'Naught is more real' . . . and the 'Ubi nihil vales' . . . both already in *Murphy* and neither very rational" (*DIS*, 113). The stress on the "nothing" as a fundamental object of the unconscious was also one of Bion's major discoveries in the thirties. Bion, Beckett's psychoanalyst, is apparently never far from the Hegelian Neary who seems to believe in the centrality of desire.

Why should Beckett have situated Neary in Cork, before having him follow Murphy to London? Bion came from India, where he was born, which may trigger the association of Neary with an Indian sacred river: his training has been obtained somewhere "north of the Nerbudda" (*MU*, 6). One might imagine a respectful allusion to Joyce's father, who came from Cork, as *Portrait of the Artist* makes clear, but a more relevant hint is provided when we are told that Miss Counihan gives Neary an appointment "at the grave of Father Prout [F. S. Mahony] in Shandon Churchyard"—which, allegedly, is the only place in Cork "where fresh air, privacy, and immunity from assault were reconciled" (*MU*, 32).

Beckett alludes here to a famous Irish wit, Francis S. Mahony, who signed "Father Prout" to his numerous poems, parodies, and songs, among which is the minor masterpiece known as "The Bells of Shandon." This poem, like many others, was attributed to Greek or Latin originals adapted into English by Mahony and his former student, Frank Stack Murphy, whose name he would write in Greek, presenting him as "an obscure Greek poet, Stakkos Morphides."[13] The parodic Morphides-Mahony couple anticipates the philosophical Murphy-Neary couple. Neary's psychoanalytical diagnosis of Murphy could appear to be motivated by an understandable jealousy (Murphy is his successful rival for Miss Counihan's heart), but the mere existence of the couple points out the need for a rival: if life is only figure and ground, as he repeats, then the "face" of the beloved will not only illuminate the surrounding chaos but also have to choose between at least two persons.

Neary, who does not share Murphy's predilection for breakups (for Murphy, "the rationale of social contacts" is the "*plaisir de rompre*" [*MU*, 31]), is thus astonished when Miss Dwyer accedes to his wishes: "No sooner had Miss Dwyer, despairing of recommending herself to Flight-Lieutenant Elliman, made Neary as happy as a man could desire, than she became one with the ground against which she had figured so prettily. Neary wrote to Herr Kurt Koffka demanding an immediate explanation. He had not yet received an answer" (*MU*, 31). Neary is thus presented as a baffled partisan of gestalt psychology.

Kurt Koffka had just published his *Principles of Gestalt Psychology* (1935) in London at the time Beckett was struggling with *Murphy*. The name of his namesake hero may have been provided by a book that was the standard textbook on contemporary psychology in England, Gardner Murphy's *Historical Introduction to Modern Psychology*.[14] The superposition of the two names can be construed either as an oblique proof of Beckett's interest in modern psychology or as a happy coincidence, attributed to the stars of the horoscope.

Gardner Murphy's monumental compendium begins with a summary of Descartes's thesis, taken as the basis of modern psychology, and ends with a postface written by a colleague, Heinrich Klürer, on the recent developments in German psychology. The treatise's progression is thus the equivalent of Beckett's real life trajectory, from a fascination for Descartes at the time of the *Whoroscope* poem, to his melancholy travels to Germany first inspired by Peggy Sinclair, then by a desire to know more about modern art, meanwhile anxiously waiting for *Murphy*'s publication.[15]

For Gardner Murphy, Descartes's dualism radically separating the mind from the body sparked the major debate of psychology: how can the mind and body influence each other? If the theory of the conarium is not viable scientifically, Descartes's rationalist cogency forces subsequent psychologists to opt either for dualism or monism. Anglo-Saxon associationists and German Wundtians, whose theories had reigned until the beginning of the twentieth century, could not, according to Murphy and Klürer, move beyond the sphere of dualism.

Külpe's original experimental psychology started as a critique of associationnism. When he founded the Würzburg school, he linked the series of associations of ideas with unconscious determinations. Külpe, Marbe, Watt, and Ach worked from experiments aimed at showing how subjects easily adapt to the context of the experiment and then develop verbal association techniques. They also used association testing to measure the intensity of the verbal reaction when a word is given as a stimulus.[16] Their results seem to militate for the theory of a "thought without images" that Stout had already advanced as a hypothesis around 1896. These linguistic experiments parallel the technique invented by Jung at the same time, in the first years of the century, with a series of free-floating word associations that betray unconscious associative processes. Ach finally classified individual types according to "determining tendencies." His idea was to ask embarrassing questions, then to have the subject check all the mental possibilities offered at the time of the response.

Thus, the overall importance of the Würzburg school lies in the proximity of empirical psychology to psychiatry and to a nascent psychoanalysis; the school also took part in the controversy surrounding "unconscious thought" or "thought without images." The posterity of the Würzburg school lies in a new *Denkpsychologie*, close to Husserlian phenomenology, and also in the lineaments of the gestalt psychology invented by Koffka and Köhler. Koffka and Köhler also criticize what they see as traces of dualism in the Würzburg school and its belief in an opposition between organic processes and psychological laws. This discussion should provide a context for some of the scenes of *Murphy*, in which the names of these theoreticians appear.

The main scene is the moment when we are told how Murphy manages every day to drink two cups of tea while only paying for one. The scene is described with the precision of a scientific experiment. Murphy catches the attention of the waitress, then says:

"Bring me," in the voice of an usher resolved to order the chef's special selection for a school outing. He paused after this preparatory signal to let the fore-period develop, that first of three moments of reaction, in which, according to the Külpe school, the major torments of response are undergone. Then he applied the stimulus proper.

"A cup of tea and a packet of assorted biscuits." Twopence the tea, two-pence the biscuits, a perfectly balanced meal.

As though suddenly aware of the great magical ability, or it might have been the surgical quality, the waitress murmured, before the eddies of the main-period drifted away: "Vera to you, dear." This was not a caress.

Murphy had some faith in the Külpe school. Marbe and Bühler might be deceived, even Watt was only human, but how could Ach be wrong? (*MU*, 49)

Ach is the most reliable psychologist because of the rigor with which he would throw totally disjointed and absurd fragments of sentences to his patients in order to measure precisely the difference between associative forces and deter-mining tendencies. This technique will indeed recur in chapter 3 of *Watt* (the name of a psychologist, again), when language begins to collapse as Watt is locked up in an asylum.

Murphy's inhuman attitude—he has to resist the waitress's seduction—is enhanced by the "surgical" quality that Neary and Wylie had already acknowl-edged in him. He still has to mount another experiment if he wishes to cheat the restaurant. Having gulped down the first cup of tea, he eructates, com-plaining that the tea is Indian not Chinese as he had asked. Given a fresh cup of tea, Murphy then asks for a refill and some milk.

"I am most fearfully sorry," he said, "Vera, to give you all this trouble, but do you think it would be possible to have this filled with hot?"

Vera showing signs of bridling, Murphy uttered winningly the sesame.

"I know I am a great nuisance, but they have been too generous with the cowjuice."

Generous and cowjuice were the keywords here. No waitress could hold out against their mingled overtones of gratitude and mammary organs. (*MU*, 50–51)

We can see how Murphy deliberately plays on the unconscious register in or-der to swindle the caterer of a few pennies, "a triumph of tactics in the face of the most fearful odds" (*MU*, 50). His near starvation or unwilling anorexia transforms the psychological experiment into a protracted fight with the very logic of capitalism, on the one hand (Vera is "a willing bit of sweated labour, incapable of betraying the slogan of her slavers, that since customer or sucker was paying for his gutrot ten times what it cost to produce and five times what it cost to fling in his face, it was only reasonable to defer to his complaints up to but not exceeding fifty per cent of his exploitation" [MU, 50]), while staging a direct confrontation with the maternal principle, on the other.

The fact that the waitress is named Vera inscribes her in the long series of feminine characters whose names end in "a," from Smeraldina, Thelma, and Alba in More Pricks than Kicks to the Celia of Murphy, and links her with a "truth" that is nonetheless humiliated and exploited. The truth her name seems to contain can be interpreted in Kleinian or Bionian terms as the primitive link established between truth and the "good object" or "good breast." For Bion, for instance, if the relation between the infant and mother is lacking in truth, there is a premature weaning or starvation: "This internal object starves its host of all understanding that is made available. In analysis such a patient seems unable to gain from his environment and therefore from his analyst. The consequences for the development of a capacity for thinking are serious; I shall describe only one, namely precocious development of consciousness."[17]

Bion's fascinating "Theory of Thinking" opens with an analysis of what happens when a mother loses her capacity for reverie and patience, thus creating a sort of perverse couple with her infant. The starvation of truth attacks the thinking process, which Bion normally explains in terms identical to those describing the digestion of healthy food: for him, thinking can only take place if "beta elements" (inchoate impressions, early sense data, raw feelings of loss and anger) are transformed into alpha elements, which are the conditions for the mental such as it deploys itself in dreaming, memorizing, and thinking thoughts.[18]

Bion's theory of schizophrenia supposes that schizophrenic patients have not had "experienced mothers." Their mothers, deprived of any capacity for reverie, could not help the infant transform its inchoate experiences, early feelings, and impressions into real thoughts. What remains as Bion's distinctive contribution to the Kleinian school, namely this neo-Kantian grid of abstract a priori categories that provides the condition for normal and pathological thinking, finally leads to a notion of "thoughts without a thinker."

Bion's paper "On Linking" looks at patients who wish to cut all links, in particular the link between themselves and the analyst. They will tend to attack language and thinking to achieve this end: "For a proper understanding of the situation when attacks on linking are being delivered it is useful to postulate thoughts that have no thinker."[19] Bion's argument compares thinking with the concept of infinity:

> Thoughts exist without a thinker. The idea of infinitude is prior to any idea of the finite. The finite is "won from the dark and formless infinite." Restat-

ing this more concretely the human personality is aware of infinity, the "oce-
anic feeling." It becomes aware of limitation, presumably through physical
and mental experience of itself and the sense of frustration.[20]

This can also describe Murphy's own plight, when he hesitates between a sur-
render to the infinite he has discovered in himself and the acceptance of a
sense of limitation.

If we return to the scene with Vera, we can understand why Murphy trusts
the Würzburg school, whose dualism can derive more easily from his Carte-
sianism, and attempts to move from this dualism to a psychoanalytic approach.
This will correspond to the evolution of his thought, as we shall see later. By
contrast, we may see why Neary is closer to gestalt psychology. Koffka and
Köhler believe in an essential unity of the forms of matter and spirit—the crucial term is of course "form." They call this "isomorphism," and Köhler for
instance explains that he founds his system on this concept.[21] Isomorphism
surfaces again in *Murphy* as Neary's "Isonomy" (*MU*, 6), as we have seen. For
gestalt psychology, there is no fundamental difference between the organization of magnetized steel dust in the neat pattern created by the magnet and
the structural schemes organizing humanity's perception of the world. Our
perception mimics its underlying somatic processes; there is merely a difference of scale between the molar masses and the molecular atomic groupings.[22]

The Würzburg school is faulted for not having gone far enough in the critique of associationism: Külpe and his disciples suppose blind associative forces,
on the one hand, and mental forces dispensing order to such a chaos, on the
other. The "tendencies" supposed to guarantee the specificity of individuals
appear as a sort of deus ex machina that cannot be accepted: it still adheres to
the Cartesian vision of a mechanical body inhabited by a strange ghost, the
soul.[23] Koffka's and Köhler's radical monism looks more toward Hegel's philosophy of nature, in which the deployment of shapes betrays the workings of
an organizing spirit, than toward Descartes's dualism.

Neary will consequently unify Hegelian and gestaltian features. But as we
have seen, Neary's "sublations" are short-lived and not very satisfactory precisely because the synthesis he expects has to occur in the field of perception.
Neary's drama is the drama of human desire that abolishes its object as soon as
it is satisfied. If the object structures the field of perception, are we condemned
to the alternative: either keep yearning blindly, in the hope of a redeeming
"face," or open our eyes and discover an abyss of nothingness?

Wylie seems closer to the truth when he tells Neary that there is no palliation: "'I greatly fear,' said Wylie, 'that the syndrome known as life is too diffuse
to admit palliation. For every symptom that is eased, another is made worse.

The horse leech's daughter is a closed system. Her quantum of wantum cannot vary'" (*MU*, 36). The biblical reference to Proverbs 30:15 suggests an image of eternal want, of never being satisfied: want is a quantity that can never change since the world is a "closed system."

The second law of thermodynamics could only introduce entropy or death by the slow exhaustion of all energy. One might prefer Berkeley's solution of radical idealism, but this is denounced by Neary as a deliberate blindness. Berkeley, called the "young Fellow of Trinity College," has, according to Wylie, found a remedy for another disease than the one he wished to cure ("'He thought relief in insulin . . . and cured himself of diabetes,'" says Wylie). Neary concurs: "'I don't wonder at Berkeley. . . . He had no alternative. A defense mechanism. Immaterialize or bust. The sleep of sheer terror. Compare the oppossum'" (*MU*, 36). This sketches one of the options for Murphy: immaterialize *and* bust, after he has undergone an experience of radical regression.

From this discussion, Neary understands that "the possession . . . of angel Counihan will create an aching void to the same amount":

> "What I make on the swings of Miss Counihan," said Neary, "if I understand you, I lose on the roundabouts of the non-Miss Counihan." . . . "There is no non-Miss Counihan," said Neary.
> "There will be," said Wylie. (*MU*, 37)

In this exchange, Wylie's position is explicitly compared to Murphy's. If Miss Counhinan is Neary's "only symptom," Wylie knows that she will be replaced by another symptom of the same type. This endless discussion derives from the fact that the monism of gestalt psychology misses one crucial element in perception, which is confirmed by all those ambiguous figures and drawings that can be interpreted in two ways (a rabbit or a man, a young woman's face or an old woman's face): perception is also structured by desire; the figure is detached from its ground not merely because it follows some pattern but because it is seen by a desiring subject. The figure of perception cannot but become a loved face, embraced by desire.

Desire cannot fit easily into the schematism of isomorphic forms precisely because it distorts the field, changes time and space in conformity with its wishes, abolishes itself, and is reborn immediately with another fleeting face. The philosophical issue then becomes whether it is possible to unify perceptions and unconscious wishes in one single field. Murphy's radicalism, on the other hand, similar to Berkeley's gesture, refuses to unify the field of "life," cuts all links between bodies and minds, and prefers the void to the fullness of the face. One of the recurrent questions posed by Koffka in his *Principles* is "why we see things and not the holes between them."[24] Murphy's "surgical quality" prefers at times to see the holes between things: this deprives him of the need to invent a face that will divide chaos against itself.

If Neary is so afraid of chaos that he is prepared to sacrifice everything — position, fortune, social consideration — in his desiring quest, which lasts as long as the loved object refuses itself, Murphy's position on this point is more ambivalent. He has been expelled from his imaginary completude, symbolized by his finding a pure mental pleasure in rocking himself into a sort of trance ("such pleasure that pleasure was not the word" [MU, 6]) once he has met Celia and has a taste of real love. Unhappily, real love brings the pressure of real life problems: Celia is a prostitute who, like Nadja, cannot go on making money by selling her body as before, although Murphy, "liberal to a fault," would neither force her nor condemn the practice (his "look of filthy intelligence" is after all a tribute to her salable beauty! [MU, 15]). Celia is a woman in love who expects her companion to work and make a decent living. This sends Murphy against his will into a quest for a job.

But because this "job" has become the main object of Celia's desire (she and Murphy have fought long enough about it), Wylie's dialectical law applies: as soon as Murphy has found the position that could allow them to live according to her wishes, Celia loses interest. When Murphy triumphantly tells her that he has at last found "*her* job" (MU, 80), he cannot elicit any response, for Celia is lost in some "impersonal rapture" that corresponds to her mourning the Old Boy. Murphy responds by telling a silly joke in a hysterical way and then leaves her for good, deciding to live in his garret at the hospital. He thus hits upon the only acceptable compromise to his division: since he cannot live alone in a rocking chair without creating some catastrophe, since he cannot live with a woman who believes that one is what one does (MU, 25), he will live among people who are all locked up within their cells and their selves. Already living "out of the world," he discovers the "small world" of deliberate confinement and explores it with rapture. In the padded cells, he discovers concrete monads, his "own little dungeon in Spain" (MU, 102), and in the secluded lives of those who are "immured in mind," he finds kindred spirits.

The strange happiness that Celia has discovered when slipping into the penumbra of rhythmical rocking is now offered to Murphy once more. The hospital is both a refuge and the end of his exile, because the inmates resist the dialectics of desire and possession, living an autarky that secures total freedom. Beckett does not conclude on a happy ending in which Murphy would stay happily as a model warden among the psychotics. Instead, a disquieting encounter with a schizophrenic will lead to his untimely death.

At first sight, the schizophrenic Endon (from the Greek *endo*, meaning "inside," punned in the familiar Beckett oxymoron, "[the] end?—[go] on!") provides an ideal version of the state Murphy is still striving to attain. Murphy, who knows he could only consummate his "life's strike" by a "slap-up psychosis" (*MU*, 104), identifies so closely with Endon that he feels a strange homoerotic attraction for him, which is even called "love" and seems devoid of any physicality: "It seemed to Murphy that he was bound to Mr. Endon, not by the tab only, but by a love of the purest kind, exempt from the big world's precocious ejaculations of thought, word and deed" (*MU*, 104).

The replacement of Celia with Mr. Endon will prove to be Murphy's deepest error and his final undoing. Murphy still labors under the delusion that he has found a "friend" ("Mr. Endon would have been less than Mr. Endon if he had known what it was to have a friend; and Murphy more than Murphy if he had not hoped against his better judgment that his feeling for Mr. Endon was in some small degree reciprocated" [*MU*, 135]). In fact, for Mr. Endon, Murphy only evokes the pleasant activity of chess playing, while Murphy imagines that some tenuous personal link has been created by their endless games. Therefore, the final game exemplifies the schizophrenic's lack of human connection with a vengeance: whereas Murphy is ready to sacrifice all his pawns so as to drag Endon out of his reserve, Endon only moves his pawns in a circular fashion, before having them return to their original positions.

The result of the psychotic game is a sort of trance during which Murphy swoons, head falling on the chessboard, while Endon, left free to roam in the hospital, drifts around the corridors pushing buttons and switches at random, having fun with a "hypomanic" he sets bouncing in his cell "like a bluebottle in a jar" (*MU*, 139). Murphy's trance, evoked in terms that smack of gestalt psychology, opens onto a deeper abyss:

> But little by little his eyes were captured by the brilliant swallow-tail of Mr. Endon's arms and legs, purple, scarlet, black and glitter, till they saw nothing else, and that in a short time only was a vivid blur, Neary's big blooming buzzing confusion or ground, mercifully free of figure. . . . Mr. Endon's finery persisted for a little in an afterimage scarcely inferior to the original. Then this also faded and Murphy began to see nothing, that colourlessness which is such a rare postnatal treat, being the absence (to abuse a nice distinction) not of *percipere* but of *percipi*. (*MU*, 138)

The reduction of Mr. Endon's body to a *fascinum* that induces a sort of hypnosis is relayed by its being just an afterimage that also fades and allows an insight into an equivalent of prenatal bliss. Not being perceived by Mr. Endon, Murphy discovers in one sensuous ecstasy the pure nothing that Democritus saw as the keystone of his atomistic philosophy. Murphy discovers "the positive peace that comes when the somethings give way, or perhaps simply add up, to the Nothing, than which in the guffaw of the Abderite naught is more real."

It seems that Beckett's hero has managed to reach the third zone of his mind, as it is described in chapter 6. We are told how Murphy's mind has its "treasures" and how they are divided into three layers. The first zone is light, the second light, and the third dark; the first zone corresponds to "forms with parallel" in real life, the second zone to "forms without parallel" or pure contemplation, and the third zone is defined as "a flux of forms, a perpetual coming together and falling asunder of forms" (*MU*, 65). The dark third zone connects the mind with a pure irrationality, since it is also called "Matrix of surds" (*MU*, 66), an irrationality that provides a way to freedom, while still being couched in the language of forms: "But the dark [contained] neither elements nor states, nothing but forms becoming and crumbling into the fragments of a new becoming without love or hate or any intelligible principle of change. Here there was nothing but commotion and the pure forms of commotion. Here he was not free, but a mote in the dark of absolute freedom" (*MU*, 66).

It is thus quite fitting to find that the same expression recurs to depict Murphy's release from "perceivedness" (to use Beckett's language in *Film*)[25] when he slips out of Mr. Endon's consciousness. Having regained consciousness, Murphy puts a catatonic Mr. Endon to bed and stares at his eyes that seem fixed on another nothing. He approaches so close that he and Mr. Endon seem ready for a "butterfly kiss" (*MU*, 140), and he finally articulates the words that Mr. Endon would never utter. They are presented as a little poem:

"the last at last seen of him
himself unseen by him
and of himself" (*MU*, 140)

The three lines, so evocative of Beckett's later "fizzles" and short epigrams, are translated three times. First, "The last Mr. Murphy saw of Mr. Endon was Mr. Murphy unseen by Mr. Endon. This was also the last Murphy saw of Murphy." Then, "The relation between Mr. Murphy and Mr. Endon could not have been better summed up by the former's sorrow at seeing himself in the latter's immunity from seeing anything but himself." And then finally, "Mr. Murphy is a speck in Mr. Endon's unseen." This glosses the fact that Murphy has seen, in Mr. Endon's cornea, "horribly reduced, obscured and distorted, his own image" (*MU*, 140).

The mental ectasies Murphy could apparently produce at will when he lived in the third zone of his mind and was a "mote in the dark of absolute freedom" are quite different from this new discovery. Murphy has reached this radical "immunity" (the term reappears in *Film* when Beckett calculates the "angle of immunity" from the camera's look) from the pain of being seen, but this creates a feeling of more acute discomfort, for which the term "sorrow" is too weak. The discovery generates a sort of panic that forces Murphy to run from the scene, strip off his clothes, and lie panting on the ground. He then tries to conjure up images but only produces fragments that call up mutilation and castration:

> When he was naked he lay down in a tuft of soaking tuffets and tried to get a picture of Celia. In vain. Of his mother. In vain. Of his father (for he was not illegitimate). In vain. It was usual for him to fail with his mother; and usual; though less usual, for him to fail with a woman. But never before had he failed with his father. He saw the clenched fists and rigid upturned face of the Child in a Giovanni Bellini Circumcision, waiting to feel the knife. He saw eyeballs being scraped, first any eyeballs, then Mr. Endon's. (*MU*, 141)

The ambiguous term of "failure" suggests a sexual impotence reaching universal proportions; the "fiasco" of Murphy's life is rendered as an impossibility to see loved faces at will, which is transformed into a general bankruptcy of the imaginary (to use Lacanian terms).

The imaginary realm thus reveals its gaping dehiscence, especially when confronted with the symbolic logic of maternity and paternity. Even the threat of the father's castration appears unable to restructure this rout of images. All this sounds like a schizophrenic delirium, a moment of crisis that could bring about a positive resolution at the end of a psychoanalytic session or could lead to murder and savage aggression. The passage continues by describing how Murphy's reel of images unwinds itself madly:

> He tried with the men, women, children and animals that belong to worse stories than this. In vain in all cases. He could not get a picture in his mind of any creature he had met, animal or human. Scraps of bodies, of landscapes, hands, eyes, lines and colours evoking nothing, rose and climbed out of sight before him, as though reeled upward off a spool level with his throat. It was his experience that this should be stopped, whenever possible, before the deeper coils were reached. (*MU*, 141)

This extreme experience of seeing the multiplicity of disordered images as a "wound of thought" has also been evoked by a writer who wrote a first novel at about the same time as *Murphy*, Maurice Blanchot. In *Thomas the Obscure*, the hero walks at night in a wood after having gone swimming in the sea and entertained ideas of suicide:

> Soon the night seemed to him gloomier and more terrible than any night, as if it had in fact issued from a wound of thought which had ceased to think, of thought taken ironically as object by something other than thought. It was night itself. Images which constituted its darkness inundated him. He saw nothing, and, far from being distressed, he made this absence of vision the culmination of his sight. Useless for seeing, his eye took on extraordinary proportions, developed beyond measure, and, stretching out on the horizon, let the night penetrate its center in order to receive the day from it.[26]

Blanchot's narrative transforms this temporary cecity into a paradoxical illumination through blindness, closer to a negative theology or mystical account of the "night of the soul." Murphy cannot bear to arrive at the "deeper coils": this repulsion, this frenzied agony is very curious when we think of this place as the "matrix of surds" in which one can reach "a point in the ceaseless unconditioned generation and passing away of line" (*MU*, 66).

Murphy regains some composure when he is able to rock in his garret, and he decides to leave the hospital for good, "back to Brewery road, to Celia, serenade, nocturne, albada" (*MU*, 141)—all these terms refer back to the sexual bliss he had known with Celia. But the rhythmical rocking he engages in leads to his death, whose nature remains unclear: is it a suicide or just an accident when someone else mistakenly opens the gas pipe? The text remains deliberately vague:

> Most things under the moon got slower and slower and then stopped, a rock got faster and faster and then stopped. Soon his body would be quiet, soon he would be free.
>
> The gas went on in the wc, excellent gas, superfine chaos.
>
> Soon his body was quiet. (*MU*, 142)

The shared etymology of "chaos" and "gas" accounts for such an ultimate dispersion of the self. Beckett does not identify this "quietness" with death, but this is our last picture of Murphy alive.

I wish to stress the heterogeneity of Beckett's two models of the mind: The first model, found in chapter 6, elaborates on the philosophical model of a post-Cartesian contemplation of the infinite, which is treated as the endless multiplication of forms; chaos is positive and brings peace. The second model (when Murphy cannot stop the reel of images created by his dismay at not being seen by Mr. Endon) has moved away from the Berkeleyan idea of being as being perceived. It has been replaced by a psychoanalytical model, probably borrowed from Jung.

Deirdre Bair recounts how Bion took Beckett to a lecture by Jung and how Beckett felt he had been given the insight he needed to complete *Murphy*.[27] Even then, Jung could not have been totally unknown to Beckett, who surely read his paper on "Psychology and Literature," published in *transition* in 1930, an issue that also carried Beckett's poem "For Future Reference." Jung's talk was supported by a diagram with "the different spheres of the mind in gradually darkening colors, in circles of decreasing circumference, until the personal and collective unconscious was reached, shown as a black circle at the very heart of the drawing."[28] Jung concluded that when the individual sinks into this black hole at the center, he disappears and is "victimized" by it.

It is just such a "victimization" that Murphy wants to avoid when he runs away to the safety of his rocker. The anarchic proliferation of fragmented images corresponds to the savage irruption of the collective unconscious into the life of a subject who fails to master it by evoking private faces. This model finally returns to the opposition between figure and ground, but this time the buzzing confusion of the ground turns into a nightmarish ghoul and the face—be it that of Celia, the mother, or the father, "all the loved ones"—is but a frail rampart against the disruptive negativity of a pure "night of the soul."

Thus, the only model that could reconcile Murphy's philosophical dualism and a psychological or psychoanalytical monism, based on desire and the unconscious, would be Bion's "theory of thinking." Bion may not have been able to communicate his thoughts to the reluctant patient who used to count the number of sessions and grumble that therapy led to nothing. It was precisely with Bion's help that Beckett was able to start thinking with "nothing," transforming the experience of an ineffable horror conveyed by disjointed and threatening images into a "thought without a subject"; such an anonymous process bridges the gap between the Würzburgian concept of "thinking without images" and a philosophical model of a divided consciousness that appears closer to Husserlian phenomenology, with the radical inflection provided by Blanchot.

When Thomas, a Murphy who survives the death of his beloved Anne and feels himself at one with the universe, sees the "nothing" with his blind eye, he penetrates beyond sight to the source of vision itself: "And so, through this void, it was sight and the object of sight which mingled together. Not only did this eye which saw nothing apprehend something, it apprehended the cause of its vision. It saw as object that which prevented it from seeing. Its own glance entered into it as an image, just when this glance seemed the death of all image."[29]

In the same way, Bion keeps praising the function of truth, which he calls "O," and opposes it to knowledge ("K"). O can only be reached if one suspends memory, desire, and even understanding. One can only approach O by a systematic annulment of K, which recalls the mystical *via negativa* (Bion invariably quotes Saint John of the Cross at this point).[30] O emerges as a lack of forms, a lack in forms, since knowledge bears on "phenomena" and never the "thing-in-itself," to follow the Kantian language favored by Bion. The dialectic of "other-people-seen-by-me" or "me-seen-by-other-people" still confirms the pattern of forms. As Bion reminds us:

> It is possible through phenomena to be reminded of the "form." It is possible through "incarnation" to be united with a part, the incarnate part, of the Godhead. It is possible through hyperbole for the individual to deal with the real individual. Is it possible through psycho-analytic interpretation to effect a transition from knowing the phenomena of the real self to being the real self?[31]

The analyst can only achieve this through a negativity that should release the mother's reverie in him. Bion's stress on the analyst's Keatsian "negative capability" is best expressed by a quotation from Freud's letter to Lou Andreas Salomé: "I know that in writing I have to blind myself artificially in order to focus all the light on one dark spot."[32] The death of the *morphe* permits a salutary mourning of the mother, coupled with a creative reverie, in a blinding and illuminating process which draws the blinds, as it were, on too much rationality.

Murphy's death is therefore neither tragic—it does not follow from a decree sent by the gods, since his horoscope had not announced it; it occurs as a benign "after dinner sleep," a modest and unaccountable disappearance between two lines or two paragraphs—nor reduced to a mere trifle. Murphy's demise confirms the inevitable death of forms and becomes necessary if the "nothing" is allowed to lead back to truth. Such is Murphy's legacy to Celia, in the novel's melancholy close. This death is nevertheless "absurd" but in the positive sense: it cannot be reduced logically to either an accident or a suicide—and in that sense, the novel remains open-ended—but it frees the psyche from the stark haunting of a vampiric Other, while letting truth speak in this same place.

The mourning process indeed generates the "matrix of surds" that Murphy saw at the end of his mind's tunnel. Beckett insists in a letter to McGreevy that Murphy's death was a sort of anticlimax, had to remain "subdued" while the novel proceeded "coolly" for a few pages. This corresponds to our own subjective detachment from the hero's plight. Beckett speaks of the "mixture of compassion, patience, mockery and 'tat twam asi'" he has given to him, adding, "with the sympathy going so far and no further (then losing patience)."[33] When readers lose patience, like the author, they "kick against the pricks" and rebel against a form that is condemned because it has too long served to perpetuate illusions. One of these fictions is that death marks off a clear limit, that it can put an end to the thoughts that keep buzzing in us. Not so true, at least if we trust Molloy:

> Perhaps there is no whole, before you're dead. An opiate for the life of the dead, that should be easy. What am I waiting for then, to exorcise mine? It's coming, it's coming. I hear from here the howl resolving all, even if it is not mine. Meanwhile there's no use knowing you are gone, you are not, you are writhing yet, the hair is growing, the nails are growing, the entrails emptying, all the morticians are dead. Someone has drawn the blinds, you perhaps. Not the faintest sound. Where are the famous flies? Yes, there is no denying it, any longer, it is not you who are dead, but all the others. So you get up and go to your mother, who thinks she is alive. (MO, 27)

Shades of the Color Gray

The light: faint, omnipresent. No visible source. As if all luminous. Faintly luminous.
No shadow. (*Pause.*) The colour grey if you wish, shades of the colour grey. (*Pause.*)
Forgive my stating the obvious.
The Voice of "Ghost Trio," in Beckett's *Complete Dramatic Works*

Beckett's later works have rightly been called "ghostly."[1] For Beckett, ghosts are
encrypted words emerging from the deepest layers of the unconscious, words
that sketch the dim contours of blurred images. The "crypt" described by
Abraham and Torok is the site of half-verbal, half-visual spooks that keep returning despite any attempt at control from the rational centers. Thus, the
"ghost" has to be described by a voice that reiterates its insistent drone in the
"skull" and identifies the specter by its color. In Beckett's works, the word
"ghostly" always calls up a particular color, not just the white of Gothic shrouds,
but gray, a color that mediates imperceptibly between black and white, light
and darkness.

This colorless color, the shade of a shade, which finally dominates in the
experimental films and plays for television of Beckett's later years, visibly embodies the prenatal penumbra that Murphy found so tempting in the asylum's
padded cells:

> The pads surpassed by far all he had ever been able to imagine in the way of
> indoor bowers of bliss. The three dimensions, slightly concave, were so ex-
> quisitely proportioned that the absence of the fourth was scarcely felt. The
> tender luminous oyster-gray of the pneumatic upholstery, cushioning every
> square inch of ceiling, walls, floor and door, lent colour to the truth, that
> one was a prisoner of air. The temperature was such that only total nudity
> could do it justice. No system of ventilation appeared to dispel the illusion
> of respirable vacuum. (*MU*, 103)

The absence of the fourth dimension suggests two related meanings: time has
stopped in the "windowless monad," which exemplifies both the mind's absolute freedom and its total isolation and ultimate impotence. We are also aware

that the fourth side of the cell's square has to remain open, at least by means of a shuttered judas that allows for inspection. The inhabitants of the asylum can be branded as inmates because they are seen from time to time by a warden.

The issue of the Berkeleyan "not being seen" (*non percipi*) acquires another dimension in this context. For the crucial oscillation between a closed square seen from above as in *Quad*, which embodies a view of humanity as endless repetition seen *sub specie aeternitatis*, and the illusionistic perspective on three sides of a rectangular room seen from one side, left free for a camera representing a human eye always avid for more details, describes the main aesthetic choice in Beckett's later television plays, as Deleuze has noted in his excellent postface to the television plays.[2] Deleuze describes Beckett's desire to "depotentialize" everything, to reach an absolute neutrality that he identifies with the overwhelming thematic domination of ghosts and specters.

While adhering to the idea that Beckett's late fiction stems from a desire to "exhaust" the world and language, thus qualifying as a "literature of exhaustion," Deleuze lists the four ways available to Beckett when he decides to "exhaust the possible":

1. generating exhaustive series of things;
2. drying up the fluxes of voices;
3. extenuating the potentialities of space;
4. dissipating the power of the image.[3]

The drying up of the linguistic flux relates to the three stages of his first Trilogy, which correspond to a logical development from *Watt*'s serial explorations to the almost muted whisper of a subject who refuses to be identified with his "I." Beckett himself stressed the fact that he felt trapped by his own development: "*Malone* grew out of *Molloy*, *The Unnamable* out of *Malone*, but afterwards—and for a long time—I wasn't at all sure what I had left to say."[4] Carla Locatelli describes such a process as close to a Husserlian "reduction" of words and the world.[5]

An investigation of the parallel exhaustion of voices and images can thus take *Texts for Nothing* as a point of departure.[6] These texts are clearly written in the wake of the *Unnamable*: they explore the famous "impasse" in which Beckett found himself; they are "for nothing" in the sense that they promote the "naught" or void with which Murphy was still embarrassed to the level of ghostly textuality—a textuality that describes itself in the making. Like the narrator of the *Unnamable*, the narrator of these texts hears voices or sees images from his past but continues speaking despite his having reaching a point of impossibility: "Suddenly, no, at last, long last, I couldn't any more, I couldn't go on. Someone said, You can't stay here. I couldn't stay there and I couldn't go on" (TN, 75). We recognize a familiar predicament: the division of the self into body and soul leaves the "I" dangling in the middle, uncertain of its capacity of synthesis or reunion. In fact, instead of a reunion, it is a pluralization of the narrative agency that can be observed here:

> I should turn away from it all, away from the body, away from the head, let them work it out between them, let them cease, I can't, I would have to cease. Ah yes, we seem to be more than one, all deaf, not even, gathered together for life. Another said, or the same, or the first, they all have the same voice, the same ideas, All you had to do was stay at Home. (TN, 75–76)

The voices resounding inside the narrator's mind are also described as images, as ghosts or ghouls that haunt the being who says "I." The haunting process prolongs a technique Joyce would have called "epiphanic" but which is here reduced to "apparitions."

No one can tell whether these apparitions are pure hallucinations or authentic memories. The only sure thing is that they happen and that, between these returns, the speaking voice must find something to chatter about: "How are the intervals filled between these apparitions?" (TN, 101). Then the "I" wonders how many hours he can go on before being engulfed by silence, for it is the possibility of pure silence that is excluded. What remains is the necessity of taking stock of all the traces still crowding the closed space of the skull:

> Ah to know for sure, to know that this thing has no end, this thing, this thing, this farrago of silence and words, of silence that is not silence and barely murmured words. Or to know it's life still, a form of life, ordained to end, as others ended and will end, till life ends, in all its forms. Words, mine was never more than that, than this pell-mell babel of silence and words, my viewless form described as ended, or to come, or still in progress, depending on the words, the moments, long may it last in that singular way. Apparitions, keepers, what childishness, and ghouls, to think I said ghouls, do I as much as I know what they are, of course I don't. (TN, 104)

What the Trilogy kept naming, in order to provide minimal identities (as when for instance the narrator of the *Unnamable* invents a Mahood) in this case remains "unnamable" precisely because the speaking subject realizes he or she is constituted by words: "With what words shall I name my unnamable words?" (TN, 105).

Another passage describes this process in terms of a proliferation of ghosts who appear both as the speaking subject and an outside:

> It's a game, it's getting to be a game, I'm going to rise and go, if it's not me it will be someone, a phantom, long live all our phantoms, those of the dead, those of the living and those of those who are not born. I'll follow him, with my sealed eyes, he needs no door, needs no thought, to issue from this imaginary head, mingle with air and earth and dissolve, little by little, in exile. Now I'm haunted, let them go, one by one, let the last desert me and leave me empty, empty and silent. (*TN*, 98)

Beckett's virtuosity is nowhere more apparent than in his playing with a vortex of whirling positions in a "game" that never allows any rest for the voice. For, if at times the voice produces the ghosts, at times it is spoken and created by them. The ghost becomes a concept pointing to the lack of identity of the self:

> It's they murmur my name, speak to me of me, speak of a me, let them go and speak of it to others, who will not believe them either, or who will believe them too. Theirs all the voices, like a rattling of chains in my head, rattling to me that I have a head. . . . But the phantoms come back, it's in vain they go abroad, mingle with the dying, they come back and slip into the coffin, no bigger than a matchbox, it's they have taught me all I know, about things above, and all I'm said to know about me, they want to create me, they want to make me. (*TN*, 98–99)

The haunted self is still presented as writing, even if he drops the quill at the end of the piece: "That's where the court [of the phantoms] sits this evening, in the depths of that vaulty night, that's where I am clerk and scribe, not understanding what I hear, not knowing what I write" (*TN*, 98).

The ghostly apparatus appears less mysterious if we assume that it metaphorizes the act of writing. Another passage of the same "text for nothing" confirms this. The narrator is still hoping to become deaf-mute:

> Then what a relief, what a relief to know I'm mute for ever, if only it didn't distress me. And deaf, it seems to me sometimes that deaf I'd be less distressed, at being mute, listen to that, what a relief not to have that on my conscience. Ah yes, I hear I have a kind of conscience, and on top of that a kind of sensibility, I trust the orator is not forgetting anything, and without ceasing to listen or drive the old quill I'm afflicted by them, I heard, it's noted. (*TN*, 96)

We realize that the trinity of the ear, eye, and writing hand still underpins the strange choreography of ghostly voices or images.

The ghosts define a supplement that prevents the "I" from being either deaf or blind, or even paralyzed. The twelfth text even suggests that they constitute a "trio," which is not too far from the later "Ghost Trio":

> and who's this speaking in me, and who's this disowning me, as though I had taken his place, usurped his life, . . . and who is this raving now, pah there are voices everywhere, ears everywhere, one who speaks saying, without ceasing to speak, Who's speaking? and one who hears, mute, uncomprehending. . . . And this other now, obviously, what's to be said of this latest other, with his babble of homeless mes and untenanted hims, this other without number or person whose abandoned being we haunt, nothing. There's a pretty three in one, and what a one, what a no one. (TN, 134)

In a very illuminating philosophical commentary of Beckett's works, Alain Badiou takes this stratification of the three selves seriously and distinguishes three levels. First, there is the linguistic subject of enunciation:[7] he is the "one who speaks" and who suffers from the terror of solipsism, thus insisting upon identifying the voice's origin. Second, there is the passive subject who hears, the reverse side of the subject of enunciation. The third level is the subject supporting the question of identification, the agency that, through enunciation and passivity, insists upon the question of being and who, for this end, is ready to submit himself to endless torture.[8]

It is as if Beckett radicalized Eliot's idea of the monadic self as depicted at the end of the *Waste Land* in terms borrowed from Bradley's neo-Hegelian system. Beckett would have merely decided to superimpose the self locked in a prison and "confirming the prison" simply because he "thinks of the key" with the experience of exhausted explorers who, after they have reached the limits of their strength, keep hallucinating an extra person. This extra "third person" dramatizes a ghostly Christ walking next to his baffled disciples who fail to recognize him:

> Who is the third who walks always beside you?
> When I count, there are only you and I together
> But when I look ahead up the white road
> There is always another one walking beside you
> Gliding wrapt in a brown mantle, hooded
> I do not know whether a man or a woman
> —But who is that on the other side of you?[9]

Beckett would thus force us to modify our views of a "monologue": a monologue is not only a dialogue with oneself, it always entails three persons—at
least!

Badiou links this with the problems bequeathed by the Cartesian cogito. If
the evil genie can intervene to dupe me while belonging to my unconscious,
the only stable point of identity is not my thought but my voice—a voice that
proves that I am "ego" only as long as I can repeat "ego." Starting from the way
Lacan reformulates Descartes's sentence as cogito: "*ergo sum*" (I think and say:
"therefore I am"), Badiou stresses the links between the ghost and the cogito.
The ghostly dialogization of the divided self calls up the wish of Murphy or of
the main character in *Film* to invert the postulates of the cogito. The Berkeleyan
maxim of "*esse est percipi*" is used as a last ironic transformation of Cartesian
essentialism:

> It is the argument of the *Cogito*, with the ironical nuance that the quest for
> non-being is substituted to the quest for truth, and that, by an inversion of
> values, the "inescapability of self-perception" which is for Descartes the first
> victory leading to certainty, appears here as a failure. The failure of what, to
> be precise? What fails is the extension to the Whole, which includes the
> subject, of the general form of being, which is the Void. The *Cogito* stops
> this extension: there is a someone whose being cannot not exist, and it is the
> subject of the *Cogito*.[10]

Indeed, the complex logical operation that allows Beckett to simplify his
Film to the utmost, reducing it to some pure scheme of vision, is founded on a
similar triangulation. The notes that explain the argument of the film begin
with a general thesis that will be exemplified by old Buster Keaton, in flight
from the camera's gaze and from any sort of glance:

> Esse est percipi.
>   All extraneous perception suppressed, animal, human, divine, self-per-
> ception maintains in being.
>   Search of non-being in flight from extraneous perception breaking down
> in inescapability of self-perception.[11]

In order to exemplify this abstract axiom in a concrete way, the notes suppose a division in the protagonist between the object (O) and the eye (E). The
object is in flight from perception, the eye, which is in fact the real hero of the
movie, is in pursuit. As it would have been difficult to attribute an inquisitive

and predatory attitude to what is after all the condition of a film, the presence of a camera, Beckett has to imagine a subterfuge:

> Until end of film O is perceived by E from behind and at an angle not exceeding 45°. Convention: O enters *percipi* = experiences anguish of perceivedness, only when this angle is exceeded.

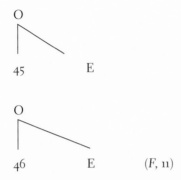

(*F*, 11)

The "camera eye" tries not to be seen in the strange pursuit that makes it follow the man, and when the angle is exceeded in the first sequence, Buster Keaton, who has been storming along "in comic foundered precipitancy," is discovered by the camera. The result is a sort of acute pain that makes him halt and turn toward the wall. Then the camera reduces the angle, which suddenly releases him (*F*, 14–15).

Alan Schneider's account of the shooting of *Film* indicates how contradictory and misleading Beckett's indications are: the basic convention of the angle can work when there is a wall that functions as a background (this is again the idea of the ground out of which a figure is carved), but this remains a very artificial situation. Besides, the shooting of the first sequence achieved exactly what Beckett wanted, but at the cost of a more radical undecidability: in the movie itself, Keaton seems to be paralyzed when the camera closes in on him, thus at the angle of 45°, and he is freed when the camera allows for an oblique angle, in other words, when it comes closer to the wall and lets him hurry off to the right-hand side. The problem is that, as soon as the character is close enough and not panned against the wall that serves as the left-hand side of the angle, no viewer can really distinguish between an angle of 45° and an angle of 90°, which corresponds to a full frontal shot—let alone between an angle of 45° and 46°!

The result of these hidden calculations would be something like this:

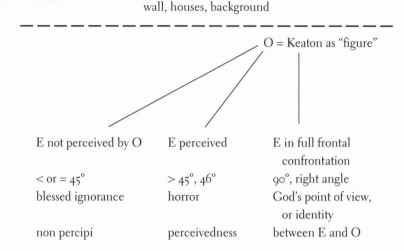

wall, houses, background

O = Keaton as "figure"

E not perceived by O	E perceived	E in full frontal confrontation
< or = 45°	> 45°, 46°	90°, right angle
blessed ignorance	horror	God's point of view, or identity
non percipi	perceivedness	between E and O

Even if Beckett writes that "no truth value attaches to the above, regarded as of merely structural and dramatic convenience" (*F*, 11), the parallels between this scheme and the "quadrangle" of *Quad*, which is divided by two diagonals, are obvious:

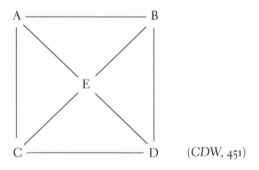

(*CDW*, 451)

The meeting point of the diagonals in E is described as a "danger zone" that has to be avoided by a series of "deviations" (*CDW*, 453). This allows for a slight degree of freedom in the mechanical movements of the four players. What could be a better staging of the need to avoid the dark core, the third zone of Murphy's unconscious? The players repeat the same steps, endlessly retracing their *bolgias* in hell, but show their humanity by this dehiscence, a step aside that somehow recovers the missing salutary "grace."

Thus, *Quad* and *Film* engage with Hippasos's problem: how to be rational with the irrationality of the unconscious? The hypotenuse of the right angle provides the beginning of a solution since it is the point of divergence between rationality (the square) and irrational or tangential numbers. Although the director Schneider writes about the shooting of *Film:* "And I suddenly decided that my early academic training in physics and geometry was finally going to pay off in my directorial career" (*F*, 65), he finally admits to having been daunted by technical problems: "We were fortunate to persuade Kaufman and Meyers that Beckett had not lost his mind in confining those camera angles so rigidly" (*F*, 68). The result, never far from a real catastrophe, with a great part of the footage totally unexploitable ("Cursing and sweating and wondering why, we shot more 180-degree and 360-degree pans than in a dozen Westerns; the apparently simple little film was not so simple, technically as well as philosophically" [*F*, 78]), is successful only in the sense that Beckett's rationale manages to question the trappings of the entire cinematographic apparatus.

The main idea behind the "plot," which climaxes when Keaton has finally got rid of the dog, cat, and goldfish, has covered the mirror, torn all the photographs that kept some traces of his past, and is ready to sleep or face death, only to discover that he is still seeing himself, is given away in Beckett's note: "It will not be clear until the end of film that pursuing perceiver is not extraneous, but self" (*F*, 11). Thus, we have to admit that the first panning movement that follows Keaton along the wall is already perceived by E. The suspense of the movie is the delayed recognition that O = E! As Schneider writes, the problem is more complex than that posed by a shift between a subjective and an objective camera: "What was required was not merely a subjective camera and an objective camera, but actually two different 'visions' of reality: one, that of the perceiving 'eye' (E) constantly observing the object (the script was once titled *The Eye*), and one, that of the object (O) observing his environment" (*F*, 65).

Such a change in perspective is hardly clear to the audience, and the director had to use the hackneyed technique of blurred shots in two instances to signal the difference between E's and O's points of view: when Keaton jostles a woman with a pet monkey and a lorgnon, she is seen briefly in a blurred shot that marks it as seen by O, in other words, Keaton in flight. At the end, when Keaton wakes up from his trance in the rocking chair, he discovers E, that is, himself! The commentary is very explicit: "Cut to E, of whom this very first image (face only, against ground of tattered wall). It is O's face (with patch) but with very different expression, impossible to describe, neither severity nor benignity, but rather acute *intentness*" (*F*, 47). This is again expressed by a blurred shot of Keaton's face, with the same patch on the eye, who thus appears as the source of the pursuit, as the moral conscience that cannot be avoided by the mere suppression of all exterior images.

These technical difficulties are not in themselves insuperable, but the embedding of the two visions can rarely be perceived by a viewer who has not read Beckett's notes, and moreover leads to a stilted style derived from the fact that Schneider took pains to identify the camera eye with Keaton's point of view ("Most of the time I didn't even have to choose the camera's position or angle; we just put it at eye level directly behind Buster and stuck there with him" [*F*, 78]). Therefore, the actor's presence had to be carefully erased: for Beckett, Keaton as O is only an eye, and the technique of a loose subjective camera, in which one sees the actor from behind, and then objects as he or she sees them, is avoided. Keaton would grumble that his face, which had been "his livelihood all these years," was being avoided: "In fact, when even a fraction of profile did get in, as it often did, we immediately did another take" (ibid.).

Nevertheless, the stilted style is the element that saves the film from total opacity: the technique mimics Keaton's deadpan humor and finally creates a unity of means, in which style and objects, wry humor and metaphysical anguish, lack of sound (except for a telling "shhh!"), and black-and-white atmosphere converge toward a recreation of a previous era of moviemaking. Indeed, the scene takes place around 1929, which recalls the time of Keaton's productive years but also suggests an atemporal "mother's room" in which a Molloy could have written his pages. Beckett had written: "This obviously cannot be O's room. It may be supposed it is his mother's room, which he has not visited for many years and is now to occupy momentarily, to look after the pets, until she comes out of hospital. This has no bearing on the film and need not be elucidated" (*F*, 59).

The main weakness of *Film* is not that the result should be lacking in deep emotion or even in entertaining slapstick comedy, but that these funny or moving elements are perceived directly, without any need of the complex calculations aimed at a triangulation or doubling of the gaze. Most of the "angles" are lost on the audience, they seem a mere scaffolding, an Oulipian constraint, only useful for defamiliarizing the medium of the film. By comparison, it is far from the technical mastery of the later experiments for television. Beckett may have learned from his not entirely successful encounter with Buster Keaton, or he may have found a more congenial medium when working with the relatively poor quality of the television image. It seems less perverse to impoverish the medium when dealing with the "ill seen" of the cathodic pixels. Beckett's constant maturation process derives from his obsessively rigorous probing of images through words and of words through images. *Ill Seen Ill Said* provides an exacting meditation on the very failure of the reconciliation of O and E; the double pejorative "ill" not only puts verbal series and visual series on a par but also refuses to confirm the negative cogito that begins and concludes *Film* with *esse est percipi.*

Like the two other companion pieces in the second trilogy, *Ill Seen Ill Said* retains a strong performative character—as we are meant to "imagine" with the narrator of *Company,* here we must not only see but meditate on the condition of possibility of any vision. The text hesitates between the status of minimalist poetry and rough notes sketching a possible second *Film.*

The "object" of the vision in this case is an old woman about whom we know very little, for she is presented in a lunar landscape, coming and going between sheep and stones, surrounded by twelve guardians. She seems half paralyzed because of age and never really sleeps, fascinated by Venus whom she observes from her lonely cabin. "Careful" is heard as the key injunction here, since we are made aware that the simple act of watching is close to an aggression, a voyeuristic rape; thus the investigation progresses through scrupulous qualifications, suspicious questions, and reticent answers.

> [23] The cabin. Its situation. Careful. On. At the inexistent centre of a formless place. Rather more circular than otherwise finally. Flat to be sure. . . .
> How come a cabin in such a place? How came? Careful. Before replying that in the far past at the time of its building there was clover growing to its very walls. Implying furthermore that she is the culprit. And from it as from an evil core that what is the wrong word the evil spread. . . . Question answered. . . . Flowers? Careful. Alone the odd crocus still at lambing time.
> . . . Are they always the same? Do they see her? Enough.[12]

This dialogic and methodical prudence supposes an "imaginary stranger" (*ISIS,* 61) who would discover the scene and an authorial voice who can tell about the "far past." The old woman's unnamable mourning dominates most scenes: "[25] The long white hair stares in a fan. Above and about the impassive face. Stares as if shocked still by some ancient horror. Or by its continuance. Or by another. That leaves the face stone-cold. Silence at the eye of the scream. Which say? Ill say. Both. All three. Question answered" (*ISIS,* 73). Knowledge is often withheld, and most scenes remain quite mysterious. Has the woman been married and then abandoned? Is she dying slowly? Is she a figure of rebirth? Why is she so fascinated by the moon, stars, and especially Venus?

"[2] Chalkstones of striking effect in the light of the moon. Let it be in opposition when the skies are clear. Quick then under the spell of Venus quick to the other window to see the other marvel rise. How whiter and whiter as it climbs it whitens more and more the stones" (*ISIS*, 58–59).

The cosmology sketched in these fragments is deliberately paradoxical, since the night scenes are illuminated, and the day scenes are quite dim. "Suddenly it is evening. Or dawn" (*ISIS*, 66). Such a hesitation stems undoubtedly from the classical example used by all logicians after Gottlob Frege and Bertrand Russell when discussing the opposition between "meaning" and "referring" (Frege's *Sinn* and *Bedeutung*). The shepherd's star that appears in the sky at both dawn and evening is the planet Venus, which can be called variably "morning star" or "evening star" while keeping the same reference. These varying names thus all "ill say" what can be glimpsed, half-seen or ill seen, in this ghostly light, with a deteriorating vocabulary.

The opening words indicate the old woman's attitude of defiance, for, although she is being watched from all sides, she feels a bond with the moon and stars and resents the intrusion of the sun (she is a feminine version of Murphy, who sits out of the sun, "as though he were free" [*MU*, 5]): "[1] From where she lies she sees Venus rise. On. From where she lies when the skies are clear she sees Venus rise followed by the sun. Then she rails at the source of all life. On. At evening when the skies are clear she savours its star's revenge. At the other window" (*ISIS*, 57). The cycle of the seasons, the four cardinal points, the passing of time from day to night and night to day are insisted upon, producing a curiously minimalist allegory.

In a fascinating article, Monique Nagem has pointed to interesting similarities between *Ill Seen Ill Said* and Mallarmé's aborted *Igitur*.[13] In both texts, the presence of Hecate as the goddess of the moon provides an image of sterility that preserves the virginity of Herodiade, the feminine embodiment of the Mallarméan pure idea, that is to say, the radical negativity of the mind thinking itself. Hecate's flower is the crocus, and she describes a circle which is that of the zero or the infinite. The counterpart of this mythological presence is punned into the abbreviation used by Beckett for the English version: ISIS.[14] The initials produce another female ghost, the ghost of the loving sister who moves around, searching among the stones for the dismembered parts of Osiris. A tomb is evoked several times among the sheep and stones. Besides, the old woman herself seems to have cut off the middle finger of her left hand, in a moment of "panic":

> It is now the left hand lacks its third finger. A swelling no doubt—a swelling no doubt of the knuckle between first and second phalanges preventing one

panic day withdrawal of the ring. The kind called keeper. . . . Who is to
blame? Or what? They? The eye? The missing finger? The keeper? The cry?
What cry? All five. All six. And the rest. All. All to blame. All. (*ISIS*, 76)

Corresponding to the unimaginable past panic, the narrative is at times caught
up in eddies of dread and frenzy. One such occurrence is triggered by the wish
to "close" the eye and stop the narrative prematurely:

On to the next. Next figment. Close it for good this filthy eye of flesh. What
forbids? Careful.
[28] Such—such fiasco that folly takes a hand. Such bits and scraps. Seen
no matter how and said as seen. Dread of black. Of white. Of void. Let her
vanish. And the rest. For good. And the sun. Last rays. And the moon. And
Venus. Nothing left but black sky. White earth. Or inversely. No more sky or
earth. Finished high and low. Nothing but black and white. Everywhere no
matter where. But black. Void. Nothing else. Contemplate that. Not another
world. Home at last. Gently gently.
[29] Panic past pass on. The hands. Seen from above. (*ISIS*, 74–75)

The unutterable "I" of *Not-I* has not been split into an "eye" and a female
presence, whose interaction maintains an ambivalent dialogue. The eye's vision can be blurred, as in *Film* ("Long this image till suddenly it blurs" [*ISIS*,
66]) or lost in a treacherous and dazzling haze (88). This "eye of flesh" "returns to the scene of its betrayals" (72); it "breathes" or "makes haste," then
"gluts itself" when its vision is swallowed in a kind of black hole, which is
expressed by the nearly oxymoronic phrase of "black blanks": "[59] Ample time
none the less a few seconds for the iris to be lacking. Wholly. As if engulfed by
the pupil. And for the sclerotic not to say the white to appear reduced by half.
Already that much less at least but at what cost. Soon to be foreseen two black
blanks. Fit ventholes of the soul that jakes" (*ISIS*, 95–96).
    Despite the irruption of absolute blackness into the iris, the eye perceives
the feminine presence as an exhausted totality that still preserves its manifold
attributes: it is alive and dead, nature and soul, fertility (the pastures) and sterility (the stones), eternal goddess and dying old crone.
    As Frazer noted in his classic study of Adonis, Isis, and Osiris, Isis came to
be identified as a marine deity and thus with the "Star of the Sea" invoked by
sailors: "On this hypothesis Sirius, the bright star of Isis, which on July morn-
ings rises from the glassy waves of the eastern Mediterranean, a harbinger of
halcyon weather to mariners, was the true *Stella Maris*, 'the Star of the Sea.'"[15]
Even if *Ill Seen Ill Said* apparently takes place on "one April afternoon" (95)
and gestures toward the end of a journey rather than placing itself under the

auspices of a journey's beginning ("Sweet foretaste of the joy at journey's end," [94]), it is indeed the ambivalent meaning of a "Farewell" that can be deduced from this text—in spirit not very far from Eliot's *Dry Salvages*, in which Arjuna's invocation of the "time of death" that is "every moment" ("Not fare well, / But fare forward, voyagers") immediately precedes the Virgin's "perpetual angelus."[16]

The stuttering iteration of the verb "to be" in the third person, shows that the fateful "is" must be repeated endlessly but also badly: the "is" is ill said because it is ill seen, ill seen because it is ill said. The hesitant "Is-Is" could represent Beckett's retranslating of Stein's "A rose is a rose is a rose." What Beckett states becomes something like "A rose is illseen a rose is illsaid a rose."[17] In a similar key, the last moving fragment of *Ill Seen Ill Said* rewrites in ten lines the three pages of melancholic lyricism with which Joyce concludes the monologue of dying Anna Livia Plurabelle in *Finnegans Wake*—a text whose dense coinings, strange portmanteau words, and overdetermined polyglotisms seem to be emulated by *Worstward Ho*.

> [61] For the last time at last for to end yet again what the wrong word? Than revoked. No but slowly dispelled a little very little like the last wisps of day when the curtain closes. Of itself by slow millimeters of drawn by a phantom hand. Farewell to farewell. Then in that perfect dark foreknell darling sound pip for end begun. First last moment. Grant only enough remain to devour all. Moment by glutton moment. Sky earth the whole kit and boodle. Not another crumb of carrion left. Lick chops and basta. No. One moment more. One last grace to breathe that void. Know happiness. (*ISIS*, 96–97)

The "phantom hand" that half betrays itself here not only draws attention to the crucial role of a fading "arranger" or conjurer seen slowly drawing the curtain but also signals a sort of reversal: as voice and eye move toward their fusion and dissolution, it seems that they strive not only to converge but also to keep as much of the "final instants" as possible. A paradoxical positivity is granted to life in extremis: the happiness of living, of seeing and breathing are asserted precisely at the (imaginary) moment of its fading away for good.

A similar significant reversal of the "ghost theme" is found in Beckett's late television pieces. Commenting on the difference between *Eh Joe* (written in 1965, televised in 1966), in which the narrator is victimized by the voice of moral conscience that forces him to "imagine" the ghost of the woman who had committed suicide, and the two television plays produced ten years later by the British Broadcasting Corporation (BBC), *Ghost Trio* (written in 1975, televised in 1977) and *. . . but the clouds . . .* (written in 1976, televised in 1977), Katharine Worth writes: "The protagonist no longer shrinks from his ghosts but on the contrary seeks them out. These plays focus with the same unremitting intensity which in *Eh Joe* was applied to a state of dread, on the opposite state—of longing for some remembered being to appear. The word 'appear' acquires a mystical resonance."[18] Indeed, these companion pieces are similarly haunted by the return of ghosts: in *Ghost Trio*, a male figure is seen in a room listening to a cassette recorder, while a female voice repeats that he "will think he hears her" (*CDW*, 410–11). The music heard is the Largo of Beethoven's Fifth Piano Trio, called "The Ghost," and its function is to create the gaps or holes in language that language is unable to manifest.

Beckett's musical ghost surges and fades as the host of the desired "nothing"—as another passage from the German letter of 1937 makes clear:

Is there any reason why that terrible materiality of the word surface should not be capable of being dissolved, like for example the sound surface, torn by enormous pauses, of Beethoven's Seventh Symphony, so that through whole pages we can perceive nothing but a path of sounds suspended in giddy heights, linking unfathomable abysses of silence? An answer is requested. (*DIS*, 172)

At the end of *Ghost Trio*, a young boy dressed in black oilskins glistening with rain appears at the door, shakes his head twice, and leaves: is this a sign that the woman will not come, is he a messenger or someone who has rung the wrong bell? Is he just suggesting a little more patience? Beckett's . . . *but the clouds* . . . also insists on the positive "apparition," because when the male figure begs for "her" to appear, the female shape really appears and three times murmurs snatches of verse, the last lines of Yeats's "Tower," the lines in which the poet seems to prepare for his own death, accepting this death as a natural phenomenon.

We realize that these final apparitions are thus as much intertextual and literary as visual or auditory hallucinations, they depend on the discourse that rehearses ("Let us now run through it again," [*CDW*, 421]) four different modalities of apparition, ranging from a glimpse to a lingering vision accompanied with the recitation and including the failure of the exhortation. The most common case is, as Beckett confides, the "case nought," when nothing happened: "When I begged in vain, deep down into the dead of the night, until I wearied, and ceased, and busied myself with something else, more . . . rewarding, such as . . . such as . . . cube roots, for example, or with nothing, busied myself with nothing, that MINE, until the time break, with break of day, to issue forth again" (*CDW*, 421). The apparition introduces a pure supplement, brings a rare gift of the gods to a poor lonely character who has mastered the various combinations of irrational numbers or the different uses of the nothing. From the "mine" of nothingness to the "deepening shades" that conclude Yeats's poem and the play, we have gone through the stages of a poetic annulment, which hovers ambiguously between the rational and the mystical, in a delicate blending of the pastoral and the spectral.

The last examples I wish to discuss vary slightly the ghostly colors we have just encountered, from *Footfalls* (1975), in which the ghost of the mother is evoked through the same old gray ("The semblance. Faint, though by no means invisible, in a certain light. (*Pause.*) Given the right light. (*Pause.*) Grey rather than white, a pale shade of grey" [*CDW*, 402]), to the strange garb of the narrator of a *Piece of Monologue* (1979) who appears all in white to explain that "Birth was the death of him" (*CDW*, 425). He seems to have gone through the same experiences as the character of *Film*, since he too tried to get rid of all images: "Backs away to edge of light and stands facing blank wall. Covered with pictures once. Pictures of . . . he all but said of loved ones. Unframed. Unglazed. Pinned to the wall with drawing pins. All shapes and sizes. Down one after another. Gone. Torn them to shreds and scattered" (*CDW*, 426). The endless monologue full of gaps and ellipses of a narrator tormented by an impending yet impossible end appears as a last avatar in the long series of spectral speakers that goes from the *Unnamable* to *Worstward Ho*.

The speaker, like all the others, seems to have emerged from a mourning process now identified with life, even if he avoids the crucial admission that he misses the "loved ones" who are gone. Just as the protagonist of *Not-I* cannot utter "I," the soliloquizing ghost of himself obsessed by the "one matter" of the fateful interaction of life and death ("The dead and gone. The dying and going. From the word go. The word begone") recites what literally is a *re-hearse*: the funeral procession, or the reiteration of a "hearsay" through which the subject believes he or she can "hear-se" (meaning hear the self speaking to itself). "Nothing stirring. Faintly stirring. Thirty thousand nights of ghosts beyond. Beyond that black beyond. Ghost light. Ghost nights. Ghost rooms. Ghost graves. Ghost . . . he all but said ghost loved ones" (*CDW*, 429). The last words have to fail: as the light, they are described as "unutterably faint." When words and music have been sufficiently eroded, the ghost then proves his or her benign nature. It is the curious dream apparition of *Nacht und Träume* (1982) that suggests ethereal and angelic comfort; the feminine figure brings a cup and gently wipes the male character's brow before fading away.

These silent images are the last vestiges of a clash between opposite colors, all symbols of life and death, birth and agony, reduced to the tension between black and white. The return of the "shade" is the sole triumph of the linguistic image recovered for the "catastrophe." This defines the place of the ghost, both in and out of language, walking the tightrope of dreams, advancing gingerly between the "Real and—how ill say its contrary? The counterpoison" (*ISIS*, 82). Although this should point to wordless images, the missaid words of Beckett's last texts still manage to convey the cyclical return that haunts our language as well as our imaginary worlds in a mesmerizing diminuendo: "Less. Less seen. Less seeing. Less seen and seeing when with words than when not. When somehow than when nohow. Stare by words dimmed. Shades dimmed. Void dimmed. Dim dimmed. All there as when no words. As when nohow. Only all dimmed. Till blank again. No words again. Nohow again" (*Worstward Ho*, 123).

Uncoupling Modernism

For we moderns have nothing of our own. We only become worth notice by filling ourselves to overflowing with foreign customs, arts, philosophies, religions and sciences: we are wandering encyclopedias, as an ancient Greek who had strayed into our time would probably call us.

You can only explain the past by what is highest in the present.

NIETZSCHE, "The Use and Abuse of History"

These two epigraphs by Nietzsche[1] should provoke, by their tension, a sort of wonder: we may have nothing of our own, we merely inherit a chaotic and overburdening culture, yet our present position must provide the only point of view available from which to take stock of this cumbersome mass. Moreover, the first sentence seems to have been taken all too literally by Joyce, who accordingly transforms Bloom into an ancient Greek and then pours whole encyclopedias into the hitherto limited frame of the Victorian novel.

The clash between these two declarations would also account for the paradoxical logics of Eliot's famous article, "Tradition and the Individual Talent," especially when Eliot describes the "historical sense" as involving "a perception, not only of the pastness of the past, but of its presence" and yielding in typically Baudelairian fashion "a sense of the timeless as well as of the temporal, and of the timeless and of the temporal together."

Nietzsche's invectives against the "antiquarian" mentality of his fellow Germans could find a more direct equivalent in Gertrude Stein's straightforward statement: "You can be a museum or you can be modern, but you can't be both." Yet much of what we call "modernism" consists precisely in the attempt to eat the cultural cake and *be* it (that is, embody its most radical potentialities), or to keep postulating an ideal museum—from Homer to the present, according to Eliot or Pound—a synthetic and mobile museum in which the modernist will appoint himself as sole curator. This double postulation no doubt raises the stakes for the artist, increases the responsibilities and the "great labor" awaiting whoever wishes to "make it all new," despite a paralyzing awareness of secondarity. Any would-be "author" will return to the medieval dilemma:

under what conditions can he or she "add" (*augere*) to the already constituted tradition? The "author" will have to turn into a *modernist* museum curator.

Thus, following Nietzsche's lead, I shall try to be both genealogical and taxonomic in an effort to map out different uses of the term "modernism." I shall stress convergence rather than statistical occurrences and sketch an historical context that remains alert to differential values and intensities. The main difficulty lies in mediating between broad and sweeping generalizations—well exemplified in a spate of books and articles devoted to a definition of modernism[2]—and the study of individual authors, each of whom tends to generate a new critical industry. Now that Joyce and Pound scholars are taking inventory of their stocks and prepublication materials, we are witnessing the rise of new cultural concentrations such as the Woolf, Stein, and H.D. branches.

Since this chapter cannot hope to emulate their cumulative thrust, I would like to suggest a slightly different approach encompassing the collective impetus of avant-garde groups and movements, without bypassing individual trajectories or anecdotal histories. Following the hint provided by Wayne Koestenbaum's suggestive book, *Double Talk: The Erotics of Male Literary Collaboration*,[3] but with a slightly different emphasis, I shall attempt to approach modernism through the concept of "literary couple." This term, which I shall not limit to male partners or to gay or lesbian relationships (although they will also figure in it), insists on the collaborative effort of two writers or artists as crucial to any avant-garde project, from the famous joint labors of Wordsworth and Coleridge in the first publication of the *Lyrical Ballads* to the shared authorship of *Les Champs magnétiques* by Breton and Soupault, from Pound and Eliot's collective editing of the *Waste Land* to the *Survey of Modernist Poetry* jointly written by Robert Graves and Laura Riding.

The actual number of literary collaborations would be overwhelming: I have selected a few examples from a cultural history whose landmarks have shaped our sense of "modernity." It seems vital to begin with Rimbaud's concept of the "modern" not just because he went "further" than, say, Baudelaire or Mallarmé, but because the term "modernism" was used for the first time, with its full meaning, by Verlaine in reaction to Rimbaud's writings. I would thus like to sketch not a history of modernity but an archaeology of modernism understood as a literary concept. This is why it seemed so important to problematize the issue of the "end"—the decline or failure—of modernism.

What Adorno, Bürger, and Ross see as the outcome of a long crisis had been prepared by writers and artists who were all interested in actively preparing such a demise. I shall thus examine how Graves and Riding, apparently intent on presenting modernism in its broadest sense, in fact attempt to bury it, to close off modernism as an active movement. In order to achieve this cunning sleight of hand, they have to identify the termination of modernism with what they see as its inception—namely, with the works of Gertrude Stein. A study of Stein's peculiar "couplings" and "uncouplings" will then be necessary to throw a different light on this issue.

Moreover, I have limited my investigation to just four "couples" not only for historical reasons but also because this seems to exhaust the possibilities of sexual permutation: I thus shall deal with a male homosexual couple (Rimbaud and Verlaine), a female homosexual couple (Stein and Alice Toklas), a heterosexual couple linking two writers who had been lovers (Graves and Riding), and a male couple uniting two writers whose heterosexuality may be questionable but who were, for better or worse, both married (Pound and Eliot). I attempt to broaden the scope of a purely "male" collaboration and stress the central agency of femininity in modernism—a femininity that need not, as the Verlaine case will show, be ascribed only to women.

Furthermore, my title signals that I shall focus on the "uncoupling" of these couples. This is because the fundamental gain of literary collaboration is derived as much from tensions and disconnections as from an incremental association. If the physics definition of "couple"—a "pair of forces of equal magnitude, acting in parallel but opposite directions, capable of causing rotation but not translation"—can apply as well in the literary domain, then all couples will appear to have already "uncoupled" themselves: uncoupling suggests disconnections or "dissociations," to use a term Pound borrowed from Remy de Gourmont,[4] and calls forth an idea of paired concepts or agencies working together but also against each other.

The halo of unwritten potentialities generated by these couplings and uncouplings corresponds to what I shall describe as its "ghosts." More real than phantom pregnancies, such uncouplings systematize a sort of hysterization as described by Freud—that is, the effect of two antagonistic sexual tendencies bound together and vying with each other in a struggle for domination (*DT*, 17-42). If it is obvious that any collaboration thrives as much on antithesis as on agreement, it belongs to the specificity of modernism to have systematized internal tensions in a series of "antimasks," a term launched by Yeats in order to describe the drift of a whole historical epoch rather than his personal ambivalence. The notion of uncoupling would add to Pound's *personae*, these masks through which he speaks, like Odysseus, in order to resurrect dead authors, thus bringing "blood to the ghosts," the idea of antipersonae, as even more powerful and productive. The archetypal modernist gesture of summoning dead souls from a vast cultural past cannot be achieved without some bloodletting. After all, Odysseus must fight against countless shades while he guards over the "bloody beaver" (Pound's Canto 1) that will lure Tiresias, who will allow him to hear the truth about his homecoming.

In a different context, Edward Said has noted in his revised introduction to *Beginnings* that the originality of modernism had been to replace a concern for *filiation* with a desire to set up new *affiliations*.[5] Undoubtedly less concerned by Bloom's "anxiety of influence" than by the desire to launch a "new age" and "new language" valid for all (and all ages, too), modernism repeats the Freudian tale of how the sons, united by the murder of the (Victorian or Georgian) father, feel guilt and remorse at his demise. Even when Pound claims Browning as his spiritual mentor and "father" (*"Und überhaupt ich stamm aus Browning. Pourquoi nier son père?"*),[6] it is in a retrospective letter that already surveys the past and reviews movements such as symbolism, imagism, or vorticism from a different (Italian, protofascist) vantage point. In the same way, despite Eliot's strong personal identification with Jules Laforgue, the French poet appears more as a "brother," the shadow of a *"hypocrite lecteur, mon semblable, mon frère,"* than as a real or symbolic father. The dialectics of affiliation supposes the domination of a group mentality that finds its cohesion in a strange heterodox orthodoxy, reaching back to more ancient models so as to erase the remnants of an inferior bourgeois culture while radically transforming the present.

Neither Pound's and Eliot's countermodels, such as the Georgian poets but also Mallarmé (until Eliot rediscovers him quite late), nor their favorite heroes (Dante, which is quite understandable, or the Gautier of *Émaux et Camées*, which is less predictable) could account for the overall impact of their combined energies. But when they start ventriloquizing through them, or against them, in communion or in antiphonal counterpoint, then the whirl of modernism can start spinning, displacing or translating in a different idiom the purely "modern."

As I mentioned in the introduction, the real originator of the term "modernity" is not so much Chateaubriand, who used it for the first time in his *Memoirs* in order to suggest the lack of aesthetic sense of the present age, as it is Baudelaire, who in *Painter of Modern Life* launches the concept of a beauty of modernity, thus defining a protomodernism as an alliance between the eternal and the circumstantial. Beauty is made up of two halves; art must eternalize the present, situate the here and now in a niche of time that will be accessible to further generations.[7] Baudelaire's modernity supposes the exaltation of the pure present in its most "fashionable" aspects and bases the rejection of the past on an awareness that history has emerged as the dominant science of the nineteenth century. A "painter of modern life," such as Constantin Guys, strives toward a fusion of the transitory (in his rapid Parisian sketches) and an atemporal norm of absolute beauty. The task of someone like Guys is indeed "heroic," for Baudelaire speaks of the "heroism of modern life" when he describes how the painter focuses on ephemeral objects, on "scenes" of everyday life, through a rapid technique adapted to immediate recording, yet remaining attentive to the canons of eternal art. Guys's *minor* art (he would probably be forgotten if Baudelaire had not cited him as an example of modernity) acknowledges transcendent beauty in the midst of present day vulgarity, much as Stephen Dedalus can find epiphanies in nearly every corner of Dublin's dull brown streets. This aesthetic of the absolute contingent still cannot offer access to what we typically call modernism, close as it is to Baudelaire's metaphysical view of the horrors of the flesh, of desire, and even of transcendence, and germane as it is to Joyce's epiphanic "poetics of disappearance."[8]

Two close friends, who also happened to take Baudelaire for a "god" or a "seer"—even if the younger was to remark in a famous letter that his medium was too "artistic," his much praised forms too "mean" (*mesquine*)[9]—created the concept of modernism by their stimulating collaboration. This term appears for the first time with the sense of a poetological concept in a letter written by Verlaine in September 1872, just after he had left Paris (and his wife) to live in London with Rimbaud. To his Parisian friends he writes his first impressions of the then world capital:

> London is less melancholy than its reputation; it is true that one must be a searcher like me in order to discover its distractions; I have found many. . . . No matter, this incredible town is very well, black as a crow and noisy as a duck, prudish although *all the vices are here for sale*, eternally drunk despite ridiculous *bills* on alcoholism, immense, although at bottom nothing but a confused collection of clamouring, rival, ugly and flat little towns; without *any monuments at all*, except its interminable docks (which anyway are sufficient for me and my more and more *modernist* poetics).[10]

I want to stress the place and time: the "Revolution of Poetic Language," to use Julia Kristeva's words,[11] takes shape in a city that, in contrast to the Paris of the Second Empire, was seen by Verlaine and Rimbaud somewhat as Duchamp and Picabia saw New York during World War I: the concrete embodiment of bold and stark modernity. The lack of monuments reflects the functionality of a city geared toward industrial and capitalist production. The scope on which this activity is visible—endless docks revealing trade and imperialism on an enormous scale that almost renders them sublime—predestines London for its role as birthplace of international modernism. Moreover, another French artist couple had preceded them in London: Monet and Pissaro had visited England together in 1870, returning to Paris full of "impressions" of London whose pictorial equivalents were used when they launched together the first artistic revolution of the nineteenth century, impressionism.

Modernism thus belongs fundamentally to the nineteenth century, a century that can be called the century of revolutions, bracketed as it is by the French and Russian Revolutions. As a global cultural manifestation, modernism stands for the cumulative outcome of all the "isms" that had succeeded one another since 1871, and London was the only place that could permit its epiphany.

Verlaine's letter also mentions a few poems from *Romances sans paroles:* his collection, drafted and composed as a volume in 1872, was published in 1874, the year of "Impression," the first collective exhibition of impressionist paintings in Paris. For Verlaine in 1872, however, the endlessness of the London docks provides a *sufficient* basis for an apprehension of modernity that transforms itself—translates itself—into a whole *poetics.* Verlaine is right when he alludes to his personal "poetic art," for he was obsessed by the need to generalize from his own practice (stressing, for example, the advantage of odd [*impair*] lines in French verse). Verlaine's modernism can be described above all as his reaction to a sort of poetic rape by a younger and fiercer writer.

As is well known, Verlaine had left Paris with Rimbaud in July 1872. They stayed together for a year, until the Brussels incident of July 1873 when Verlaine shot Rimbaud, wounding him slightly in the hand. When they first met, Verlaine was the already admired author of the *Poèmes saturniens* (1866) and *Fêtes galantes* (1869). Rimbaud was barely seventeen and had not written his *Illuminations* or a *Season in Hell.* But Rimbaud's letters already expose a revolutionary approach to language moving far beyond Verlaine's.

In the letter where Verlaine refers to his "modernist" poetics, he mentions two fragments of "Birds in the Night" as well as other poems for *Romances sans paroles.* This corresponds to the group of poems he worked on first in Belgium, then in England, with Rimbaud as main addressee and critical adviser. Most of them have English titles, such as "Birds in the Night," "Green," "Spleen," "Streets," "Child Wife," "Beams," and "A Poor Young Shepherd." They introduce a new note into Verlaine's subtle poetry. It is hardly coincidental that Joyce admired them and knew by heart "Spleen" (quoted in chapter 5). The apparent simplicity of "Spleen," its deceptive and untranslatable musicality, are to be admired and may be the best embodiment of Verlaine's "modernism."[12]

Another of Verlaine's poems of this period ("*Ariettes oubliées*") is also justly famous; moreover, part 3 quotes a line from a lost poem by Rimbaud:

> It rains gently on the town.
>   ARTHUR RIMBAUD
> It weeps in my heart
> as it rains on the town.
> What languorous hurt
> thus pierces my heart?
> . . . .
> It's far the worst pain
> not to know why,
> without lover or disdain
> my heart has such pain. (*SP*, 262)

Here, one can witness the curious fecundation of a poet by another poet that also involves direct sexual contact, with their share of perversity (Verlaine had been cut in the legs and back during some games invented by Rimbaud). Verlaine's cringing, whining returns to his estranged wife could not lead the younger man to respect his moral integrity. Verlaine had been more than seduced, almost "raped" ("corrupted" by the younger man, as his wife would say!), and forced to "translate" himself into poetic exile by Rimbaud's radical gesture.

Rimbaud's influence can be felt in most of the poems in *Romances sans paroles*, which nevertheless remain undoubtedly Verlainian. A new simplicity, directness, and musicality emerge from the collection, whose proofs were corrected in the Mons prison. Yet these poems are by no means revolutionary. Verlaine is still working in an idiom of the self, investigating new forms with which to evoke his changing moods, whereas Rimbaud strives toward an "objective" form, far from the recurrent sentimentality, or even self-indulgence, of his friend. Moreover, Rimbaud's project aims at a fundamental upheaval of all values: his project needs the invention of a new language. However, it is precisely because the radicality of the attempt cannot be expressed in purely aesthetic terms that Rimbaud does not call this "modernism" but only the "modern." Verlaine's suggestive musicality probably paved the way for Mallarmé's more daring experiments, but without Rimbaud's dogged desire to break with all past conventions, modernism would never have reached its real roots—Pound acknowledged this when he declared that the whole of French poetry could be summed up by the names of two untamed "rebels," François Villon and Rimbaud.

Rimbaud uses the word "modern" twice in his *Illuminations*, always in connection with a vast metropolis that closely resembles London. Indeed, the vision of "Cities" opens with a futuristic spectacle in which the modern is allied with barbarity, whereas the classical world is merely preserved in an antiquarian fashion: "The official acropolis outdoes the most colossal conceptions of modern barbarity. . . . They have reproduced, in singularly outrageous taste, all the classical marvels of architecture. I go to exhibitions of painting in places twenty times vaster than Hampton Court" (*CP*, 261, modified).

In a similar mood, in "Promontory" he describes mysterious "Temples lit up by the return of the processions [note the 'classical' vocabulary: *Des fanums qu'éclaire la rentrée des théories*]; immense view of the defenses of modern coasts" (*CP*, 277). The modern is caught up in a movement that brings all the decorative riches of the world before the astonished gaze of the beholder. The most enigmatic occurrence of "modern" is found in the last section of a *Season in Hell* in "Farewell," with the famous sentence: *"Il faut être absolument moderne"* (One must be absolutely modern). This statement is often taken as the key to Rimbaud's poetic autobiography and read as a positive injunction. I would like to plead for more caution and suggest that its status is properly undecidable, since the context evokes the return of autumn, the loss of an "eternal sun," and a downward movement toward the enormous city full of fire and mud. If this modernity is indeed associated with the metropolis, its value is not necessarily positive. For beyond the promise of a purified vision at dawn, the last paragraph also denounces the lie of "couples": "I can laugh at the false loves, and strike shame into those lying couples—I have seen the hell of women down there—and it will now be permitted to me *to possess truth in a soul and a body*" (*CP*, 346).

Rimbaud's Promethean wish to view the poet as "the thief of fire" who will invent a new language is expressed in letters antedating the experience of the London cohabitation. It is clear that until 1872, Rimbaud the "Seer" remains a romantic and is only radicalizing the poetic credo and political passion of someone like Shelley. After the moment of "coupling," the process of "uncoupling" releases all the verbal energies the couple had hatched and creates a whirl of ambivalent declarations that can no longer be taken at face value.

The famous phrase "True life is lacking. We are not in the world," often quoted to illustrate Rimbaud's desire to change the world, is in fact spoken by a character resembling Verlaine in a dramatization of their former relationship. The passage is titled "Foolish Virgin" and subtitled "The Infernal Bride-groom." It announces a confession ("Let us hear the confession of a compan-ion in hell") that goes to the end, with its attendant quotation marks, until the text abruptly concludes on: "A queer couple!" The transparent veil allows Verlaine to present an indictment of Rimbaud who is equated by the whining, timid voice as a demon albeit almost a child. This vertiginous dialogism goes as far as to have this speech quote the satanic voice in a pastiche of the begin-ning of a *Season in Hell* ("'I am of a far-off race'" [*CP*, 320], which recalls "Bad Blood"). It is in this troubling interplay of frames within frames that Rimbaud finally embeds his revolutionary postulation of "secrets for *transforming life*" (*CP*, 322). The modernity of the presentation is so staggering that most com-mentators are still baffled by these cryptic and intense verbal nuggets continu-ally revolving around each other. I would be wary of calling this "modernis-tic"—it is, at any rate, a far cry from Rimbaud's early romanticism—since this comes closer to a radical sense of "modernity."

In the section of *Illuminations* called "Tramps," Rimbaud again evokes his time with Verlaine: they are presented as two tramps, two ill-matched accom-plices looking for quite dissimilar objectives in their wanderings. Again, the "poor brother" is afraid of prison, complains, and has horrible nightmares while his friend jeers and taunts: this time, it is the Verlaine-persona who is dubbed "satanic scholar": "I would reply by jeering at this satanic scholar, and would end by going to the window. I would create, beyond the countryside crossed by stretches of unusual music, specters of the nocturnal luxury to come." This latter striking phrase (*les fantômes du futur luxe nocturne*) could describe what I earlier called "ghosts" born of the curious couplings and uncouplings of these literary pairs of divergent visionaries. The vision is almost parodic, just a "vaguely hygienic diversion" before sleep, but it keeps the utopia alive; the poet needs this imaginary outlet as a stepping-stone on the way to sunlike splendor since he wishes to restore his companion to "his original state as child of the sun," and he presents himself as "impatient to find the place and the formula" (*CP*, 262). This fragment immediately precedes the vision of the modern and bar-baric cities quoted earlier.

It is no coincidence that London should have been the place where a sec-ond male foreign couple—two Americans this time—met and launched what we have now come to call "high modernism." Pound came first, not directly from the East Coast, but via Venice, where he had his first collection of poems printed. The story of how Pound managed to influence and then control some of the most innovative artistic channels (through a strategy that entailed con-trolling a few magazines and convincing key figures such as Yeats that they should become more radically "modern") has been well documented. I wish to point out that, even if Pound learned to mediate between two salons, between the Yeats coterie and the Ford group—thus blending fin-de-siècle aestheticism with a postimpressionism that had chosen prose as a more flexible and straightforward medium—he systematically insisted on discovering the "new" among his compatriots. This is how he introduced his Philadelphian friend Hilda Doolittle to Harriett Monroe, the editor of the Chicago-based magazine *Poetry*: "I've had luck again, and am sending you some *modern* stuff by an American. I say modern, for it is in the laconic speech of the Imagistes, even if the subject is classic. . . . Objective—no slither; direct—no excessive use of adjectives, no metaphors that won't permit examination. It's straight talk, straight as the Greeks!" (*SL*, 11). As in Rimbaud's *Illuminations*, the modern resides as much in a happy coexistence with classic themes as in a simplification of language. This language is direct, economical, hard, resilient, objective, musical, inventive, serious—all the qualities Pound was busy extolling before a rather bewildered English audience still accustomed to the poetic diction of a Tennyson or of the young Yeats.

A similar compliment is paid to Eliot two years later, when Pound again "discovers" him: "He is the only American I know of who has made what I can call adequate preparation for writing. He has actually trained himself *and* modernized himself *on his own*" (*SL*, 40). This was written just after Eliot had shown Pound "The Love Song of J. Alfred Prufrock," which initiated a fruitful collaboration. If Pound seems to realize that there is not much he can teach Eliot (Eliot would at the same time express reservations, saying for instance that Pound's verse was "touchingly incompetent"), he has at least provided him with a mirror in which Eliot could become conscious of his own modernity.

This led to the collaborative fervor of the *Blast* enterprise, in which the energies of Wyndham Lewis, Henri Gaudier-Brzeska, Pound, and Eliot were combined for one year. As Lewis later remarked, a lot of that activity corresponded to a prewar frenzy: he notes in *Blasting and Bombardiering* that "all this organized disturbance was Art behaving as if it were Politics," adding that he could later see how "it may in fact have been politics."[13] The main outcome of this collaboration was the publication of the *Waste Land*.

We can note that Pound attempted to play an active editorial role with Joyce during the serial publication of *Ulysses*, a role that Joyce consistently repulsed.[14] This places Joyce in a category apart, while Pound could congratulate Eliot and himself on the "birth" of the *Waste Land*: "Eliot's *Waste Land* is I think the justification of the 'movement,' of our modern experiment, since 1900"

(SL, 180). Again, the term "modern" inscribes the poem in a category later generalized as "modernism."

The peculiar "obstetrics" to which the manuscript of the poem was subjected has often been discussed. It is generally agreed that Pound's cuts transformed a chaotic mass of poetry into a precise, aggressively modern masterpiece. Koestenbaum contends that the poem was "feminine" in its original form but transformed radically by Pound's assertive masculinity. We might indeed be tempted to see in this productive coediting of a great poem the shift away from a bisexuality that left open many potentialities to "masculine" values mistakenly identified with the essence of high modernism. Moreover, Eliot's prose poem "Hysteria" already points toward such a femininized pathologia. Koestenbaum writes: "Eliot's poem—semiotic, negative, riddled with absences—is 'feminine' not because women always sound like The Waste Land, but because, in 1922, its style might have seemed more recognizably a hysterical woman's than a male poet's" (DT, 113). He adds curiously: "Hysteria is a disturbance in language, and the very word 'hysteria' marks it as a woman's affliction"—which seems to imply that there is no male hysteria! Such an etymological fundamentalism is strange in a critic who wishes to reread modernism from the point of view of gay discourse. Koestenbaum's predilection for the anus starts from an understandable rehabilitation but leads him into absurdities at times (as when he sees the fatefully repressed organ in Eliot's identification with a "broken Coriol-anus" or when he reads a double inscription of "anus" in the way Pound dates a letter "24 Saturnus, An 1") (DT, 122, 137). Whereas I am entirely ready to see the enigma of bisexuality as one of the most intriguing subplots of the Waste Land, I think that the attempt to "queer" Eliot and Pound's collaboration leads to a series of misreadings.

The most crucial case in point is Pound's rather bawdy letter written to celebrate the "birth" of the poem. This well-known piece of male bantering had been expurgated in D. D. Paige's edition of Pound's letters and was only published in full in the first volume of Eliot's Letters of T. S. Eliot.[15] In the letter, Pound assumes the function of a midwife or rather "sage homme," a masculinization of the French sage-femme (midwife): "These are the Poems of Eliot / By the Uranian Muse begot; / A Man their mother was, / A Muse their Sire." The letter leaves no doubt as to the role Pound has chosen: he is only the midwife ("Ezra performed the caesarean operation") and not the impregnator of his friend. From the suppressed lines in which Pound speaks of his own masturbatory activity, Koestenbaum finds an argument for his having actually "fathered" the poem. In fact, Pound merely laments his own impotence, or the fact that his masturbatory writing has prevented him from producing really *modern* creations, such as *Ulysses* or the *Waste Land*:

> E. P. hopeless and unhelped
> Enthroned in the marmorean skies
> His verse omits realities,
> Angelic hands with mother of pearl
> Retouch the strapping servant girl,
>
> . . . .
>
> Balls and balls and balls again
> Can not touch his fellow men.
> His foaming and abundant cream
> Has coated his world. The coat of a dream;
> Or say that the upjut of sperm
> Has rendered his sense pachyderm.[16]

The ironic self-portrait is quite in the mode of Mauberley's derision. What is deprecated is Pound's too easy recourse to an onanistic "dangerous supple-ment"—which apparently takes "strapping servant girls" as libidinal objects rather than, say, Eliot's anus. This is why I cannot agree with Koestenbaum's conclusion: "Pound, Eliot's male muse, is the sire of *The Waste Land*" (*DT*, 121). Koestenbaum superimposes two scenes: the scene described in the June 1921 postscript to Pound's translation of the *Natural Philosophy of Love* by Remy de Gourmont, in which Pound sees himself as an overactive phallus fertilizing the passive vulva of London, and the many traces of femininity left in Eliot's *Waste Land*. But Koestenbaum forgets that one of the major consequences of Pound's excisions was to make it much more of a London poem than it had been originally. Pound has not deleted the "femininity" of the poem: he has "framed" it, as it were, within a mythical discourse that is less "male" or "phallocratic" than neutral. Such is the effect of the famous beginning of the poem ("April is the cruelest month"), which leaves the voice anonymous, the "we" asexual and floating in the void, until we hear it modulate into Marie Larisch's familiar confidences.[17]

In view of these complex issues, I would emphasize instead the disjunctive nature of Eliot and Pound's collaboration and stress that the blind spots in their joint parturition left what I again would like to call textual ghosts. It is true that Pound drastically modified the draft given to him. He reduced it by half, deleted the long opening describing a night out in Boston ("He Do the Police in Different Voices"), suppressed the hesitations, the autobiographical tone, and some of the pastiches of classical genres, and hence changed the polyphonic texture or tessitura of the poem. Pound also tried to eliminate all the reminiscences of "Prufrock," as Koestenbaum aptly notes: "Eliot's wobbliness was made flesh in Prufrock, echoes of which Pound sought to cut" (*DT*, 127), but while he was impatient with Tiresias as a central figure (Pound originally felt the same misguided distaste for Leopold Bloom who, according to him, unduly supplanted Stephen Dedalus), going so far as to write: "make up / yr. mind / you Tiresias / if you know / know damn well / or / else you / dont" [*sic*] in the margin,[18] he never persuaded Eliot to change anything substantially in the characterization of the blind and bisexual seer.

Strangely enough, what annoys Pound also annoys Koestenbaum, who would prefer to see Eliot "come out," as it were, rather than hide in ambiguities and ambivalences. Yet it is precisely these hesitations (as later *Finnegans Wake* will be written in a systematically undecidable language) that make up the irreducible force of its modernist poetry. This corresponds to the fact that modernism as such, despite Hugh Kenner's insistence, cannot be reduced so easily and univocally to a phallocratic stance. In a way, this would lead us to admit that high modernism, too, is "softer" than we thought and also closer to Verlaine than to Rimbaud.

If Tiresias is the most important figure of the poem, as Eliot's central note clearly states, is it not because he embodies a hysterical bisexuality of which Eliot was dreaming at the time? This fantasy cannot be reduced to the clearcut opposites suggested by Koestenbaum: "Through Tiresias, Eliot describes (from the inside) an epoch we might call The Age of Inversion, when heterosexuality was in the process of being undermined and traduced by its eerie opposite" (*DT*, 128). If indeed the Tiresias paradigm provides Eliot with another "epoch," it is less a dream of inversion than of ecstatic fusion, a dream expressed in the deleted poem, "The Death of Saint Narcissus":

> First he was sure that he had been a tree
> Twisting its branches among each other
> And tangling its roots among each other.
>
> Then he knew that he had been a fish
> With slippery white belly held tight in his own fingers,
> Writhing in his own clutch, his ancient beauty
> Caught fast in the pink tips of his new beauty.
>
> Then he had been a young girl
> Caught in the woods by a drunken old man

Knowing at the end the taste of her own whiteness
The horror of her own smoothness,
And he felt drunken and old.[19]

Here, Eliot rewrites Nietzsche's praise of dancers in *Thus Spake Zarathustra* through a myth of metempsychosis that borrows from Empedocles' famous distych according to which the Greek philosopher had once been "a boy and a girl, a bush, a bird and a fish,"[20] and from Buddha's own transformations: these ascetic "rapes" were to lead him to the way of absolute compassion. The rape of a passive girl by an old man whose taste lingers bitterly in the speaker's memories, the Buddhist acquiescence to universal metamorphosis, the Keatsian rapture at selflessness—all this sums up what Pound intensely dislikes. This compendium of Eastern mysticism and Western "negative capability" has remained to this date a textual ghost (now and then added to Eliot's collected works as a curious appendix), outside of the canon constituted by Pound. This shows a different Eliot, closer to Flaubert when he could identify utterly with Emma Bovary and the setting of her love scenes.[21]

The joint attempt by Pound and Eliot to provide a justification for the "modern movement" by publishing at last a modernist masterpiece derives from the very high claims they had made for themselves. All this looks a little like a wholesale takeover bid, a tender offer on European culture, seen as whole from two conflicting and half-imaginary opposites: Eastern mysticism on the one hand (Pound rewrites Eliot's more metaphysical drift in his Chinese idiom) and the American pseudo-wilderness on the other. In a letter to his British friend, Mary Hutchinson, Eliot makes a revealing admission, just as he announces his essay on "Tradition" as forthcoming. He concludes a discussion of the different meanings of "culture" and "civilization" on a more personal note: "But remember that I am a *metic*—a foreigner, and that I *want* to understand you, and all the background and tradition of you. I shall try to be frank—because the attempt is so very much worthwhile with you—it is very difficult with me—both by inheritance and because of my suspicious and cowardly disposition. But I may simply prove to be a savage."[22] In this mildly flirtatious tone, Eliot conflates images of barbarism and strong moral values inherited from his family, thus discovering the best word to introduce himself (in every sense): a *metic*, that is, an alien who has been admitted into the city (as in Athens), who has been granted certain rights and pays taxes but cannot have full citizenship or access to the most intimate mysteries.

The metic, both inside and outside, is thus defined from within the polis, which also accounts for the thematic centrality of the city as metropolis in the

Waste Land: Oedipus's Thebes, Augustine's Carthage, and Baudelaire's Paris are superimposed upon a London where the city provides a fulcrum for international capitalism. Indeed, the suppressed passage beginning with "He Do the Police in Different Voices" looks back to Dickens's London with the subtle allusion to Betty Higden's praise of Sloppy in *Our Mutual Friend:* Sloppy manages to recreate different policemen's voices when he reads to her, thanks to his wonderful mimetic abilities. Here, "police" rhymes ironically with polis, while metic leads to a "mimetic" who remains well hidden in the "world's metropolis" (as Mr. Podsnap says). The ending of the *Waste Land* finally releases all the voices that had been kept more or less separate and creates a bewildering vortex of hysterical polyphony. This is also a dominant feature in Pound's *Cantos:* we keep hearing individual voices whose interaction creates an epic through counterpoint. However, this similarity should not blind us to a crucial divergence—which shall oblige me to examine a last "uncoupling."

If Pound and Eliot agree that "tradition" supposes an "historical sense" that sees the presence of the past as well as its pastness (since "It is dawn at Jerusalem while midnight hovers above the Pillars of Hercules. All ages are contemporaneous," as the preface to the *Spirit of Romance* momentously states), then they would not translate the Greek concept of polis in exactly the same way. Though both are indeed metics in the British Empire, they opt for different strategies of assimilation and adaptation. Pound always sees the polis in its original Greek meaning, as a religious and political context determined by local polytheism and the domination of a few brilliant minds. Eliot, on the other hand, follows the conclusions of his investigation into European roots and therefore revives linguistic energies dormant in Virgil, Augustine, and Dante. He translates the polis into the "City" (of God or men), that is, into Augustine's *civitas.* As Emile Benveniste has shown, polis cannot be translated into civitas without some distortion.[23] In the Greek mind, polis is a concept that predetermines the definition of the citizen as *polites.* One is a citizen because one partakes of the abstract concept of the polis, a linguistic radical divided between sameness and otherness, belonging and rejection. In the Latin mentality, the adjective *civis* comes first, the radical is anterior to the derivation of civitas (meaning "city" in the sense of a group of people living together, and not *Urbs,* reserved for Rome, the "capital"). In the Latin model, actual people as citizens help derive the concept: thus, civitas refers to a community understood as a mutuality, a collection of mutual obligations.

Eliot's choice of a quote from *Our Mutual Friend* to highlight the polyphonic nature of urban discourse out of which contemporary civility must emerge is hardly accidental. Nor was Pound's erasure of the same motif random. Pound's historical point of departure is the American Revolution, seen as the birth of the modern idea of the just state and "volitionist" politics; Eliot consistently returns to the English Revolution as the main "catastrophe" of the modern world. According to Eliot, the introduction of the new parliamentary democracy triggered all its attendant negative side effects: the loss of central-ized values and the "dissociation of sensibility," which had weakened British culture since the seventeenth century. Thus, Pound is ready to acclaim the "Tovarishes" of the Soviet Revolution in his first cantos, while Eliot condemns the uprising as chaotic, atheistic and "drunken" (through a German quotation taken from Hesse) in the notes to the *Waste Land.*

Pound's specific mode of hysterization leads him to play the eccentric, to leave the confines of the Empire, and to embrace Mussolini as a symbolic father, out of sheer ignorance of his regime's true nature—all the while insist-ing that he was fighting against ignorance! Eliot, who knew better, and maybe knew too much, chose the opposite strategy, becoming more British than the British after 1927 and his conversion to Anglo-Catholicism and devising a new and quite personal game of hide-and-seek with high culture.

The literary "ghost" produced by such a disjunction must be found in the way Eliot's success in British and American culture served to acclimatize mod-ernism as a purely intellectual adventure—a "betrayal" that was deeply lamented by William Carlos Williams. The "monsters" Eliot was led to suppress indeed concerned sexuality as well as politics, as Koestenbaum suggests, but his atti-tude led to dissimilar enabling or disabling strategies if we compare him with Pound who, at least, never really tried to hide his peculiar monsters. These finally brought about the sublimation of modernism into academic enshrin-ing, while at the same time Eliot himself had embraced the values of a revis-ited classicism. The real ghost generated by the coupling/uncoupling collabo-ration between Pound and Eliot was in fact just a word: the term "modernism," which could then be thrown as a sop to the academics of the entire world.

Indeed, one of the most remarkable features of the word "modernism" is that it was not bandied about by the actual artists, writers, and "agitators" who en-livened the rather stifling literary life of London in the late 1910s and early 1920s. The word was used in New York by James Waldo Fawcett when he launched in 1919 a new magazine whose ambition was to be "Radical in Policy; international in scope. Devoted to the common cause of toiling people. Op-posed to Compromise; pledged to truth."[24] Never has a prospectus been so misleading: symptomatically, the soon abortive New York review attempted to cater to everybody and failed to attract an audience. The publication was so mediocre that even its contributors—including Hart Crane, who published a few poems in it—were disgusted with it. It did not survive beyond its first and only issue and is not mentioned in most surveys of American modernism.

A similar syncretism had earlier been noted in the announcements for *Blast*, which purported to discuss "Cubism, Futurism, Imagism and all the vital forms of modern art" in 1914. Modernism always betrays a collective effort but in a different sense from the collective spirit implied by the cubist, futurist, or imagist groups: these "movements" can all be dated, related to one or a few cities, and names can be provided. Modernism remains a vaguer and more abstract notion that derives its impetus from the lumping together of all the "isms" of a given period that believes it discovers the "modern." Like philosophy for Hegel, modernism as a concept always intervenes at the end of a process of creation or gestation; one could speak of the "owl of modernism" along with the "owl of Minerva" that takes its flight at dusk.

To understand the full value of this classifying urge, we can turn toward the third couple I wish to examine: Robert Graves and Laura Jackson Riding. I shall focus on the moment of their collaboration resulting in the publication of a *Survey of Modernist Poetry* in 1927. This interesting heterosexual couple was transnational. Riding was already known in America before she came to England. She was associated as early as 1923 with the "Fugitives," a literary group active in Nashville, Tennessee, that included John Crowe Ransom, Robert Penn Warren, and Allen Tate. They belonged more to a southern literary renaissance than to modernism proper but had elected Eliot as one of their mentors. In this context, Riding's poetry was soon to be hailed "metaphysical" and thought to belong fully to the seventeenth-century tradition praised by Eliot in his essays.

After having received the Fugitives' prize in 1924, Riding left for London, where she was expected by her already devout admirer, Robert Graves. She followed him, his wife, and their four children to Cairo, where she started "haunting" him by seeing "ghosts" everywhere.[25] This "strange trinity" then returned to London; due to Riding's and Graves's strained financial circumstances, Virginia and Leonard Woolf agreed to publish her first collection of poetry, *The Close Chaplet*, while another joint project was launched. After his successful *On English Poetry* (1922), Graves decided to present the modern poets to a broader British audience: he enlisted Eliot's contribution for what was first called *Untraditional Elements of Poetry*. Riding quickly superseded Eliot, and the volume that had meanwhile been renamed *Modernist Poetry Explained to the Plain Man* was finally published in November 1927 under the title of a *Survey of Modernist Poetry*.

Riding soon dominated the English novelist and poet, whose feminist wife (a mother of four children, she was also a very close friend of Riding) proved of little weight in the face of their "mystical" collaboration, which lasted from 1925 to 1940. Their relationship was often entangled in sentimental triangles, one of which involved Geoffrey Phibbs, an admirer of Riding, then of Graves's wife; Phibbs suddenly switched allegiances, returned to his wife, and deserted Riding. This resulted in a dramatic suicide attempt in April 1929, when first Riding jumped out of the window after Phibbs had just left, Graves and his wife being present in the room. She uttered a terse "Goodbye, chaps" and jumped from the fourth story, soon followed by Graves, who only jumped from the third story and was hardly injured. After painful surgery, Riding was able to walk again, but remained celibate the next ten years, although she had assembled around her a court of devotees who followed her (and Graves) to Deyà, a village in Majorca (an island already hallowed by the stay of Stein and Toklas during the war).

When she and Graves left England for Majorca, they stopped in Bilignin for a few weeks in October 1929, where they were housed by Gertrude Stein and Alice Toklas, who allowed them to recuperate. The Majorca years belong to a different story, while "modernism" calls up a ghostlier past; Riding was able for a few years to play the role of absolute muse and goddess, a "white goddess" slavishly adored by Graves.

Another interesting aspect of Riding's life was her final renunciation of poetry upon returning to America and marrying her second husband, Schuyler Jackson. Her last poetic publication is thus her monumental *Collected Poems* (1938). For Riding, history had ended around 1929, after she had risked her life and entered into the realm of the transcendent: only the absolute mattered from then on, with the need to define a language adequate for the expression of truth.

The central thesis of a *Survey of Modernist Poetry* is likewise rather ahistorical, distinguishing between an "eternal modernism" and a purely fashionable one: "The vulgar meaning of modernism, especially when the word is employed as a term of critical condemnation or by the poets themselves as a literary affectation, is modern-ness, a keeping-up in poetry with the pace of civilization and intellectual history."[26] Their negative use of the term is restricted to critics or poets who only follow a movement or program: these are the two recurrent butts of Graves and Riding's critique (one chapter is tellingly entitled "Modernist Poetry and Dead Movements"). They posit an ideal reader, that hypothetical "plain reader" who is cultured enough to read Shakespeare but feels daunted by Pound or Cummings. But critics underestimate the intelligence of "plain readers" (*SMP*, 102) and force-feed them. They see difficulty as the consequence of an ethics of language or the outcome of personal accuracy in perception. The *Survey* is very helpful in that it provides fresh readings of poems and teaches how to write in the manner of Cummings, who provides one of many examples of practical criticism.

It rapidly becomes apparent that modernism is defined in terms of an attempt to fuse form and content, not in terms of programs or movements (the authors have only ironic remarks for imagism). Wherever this fusion takes place, real modernism is reached. The influence of Eliot's theory of the "objective correlative" is certainly present but generalized in an effort to erase any distinction between technique and meaning. Impressionism is acknowledged as the first "modernist" movement or, more precisely, "one of the earliest manifestations of the general modernist tendency to overcome the distinction between subject-matter and form" (*SMP*, 42).

The literary axiology that can be deduced from these principles is at times striking: Pound, Williams, H.D., Aldington, even Yeats are all debunked, and the plain reader is used as a limit to formal audacity. The plain reader will thus be expected to favor Frost over H.D., while Pound's provocatively short poem:

PAPYRUS
Spring. . . . . . .
Too long. . . . . .
Gongula. . . . . .

is given as an example of obscurity that will frighten away the plain reader (*SMP*, 218). Riding and Graves refuse to play the game of learned annotations (they do not bother to ascertain whether the poem is—as it is indeed—a quotation from a real Sappho papyrus) and unhesitantly call this charlatanry. The three real "modernist" poets are T. S. Eliot (they throw in a few barbs, denouncing "vanities" and too great a "sophistication"), E. E. Cummings, and . . . Laura Riding (the last two pages quote from her poems without naming her)!

Riding and Graves are very pointed when they note that anti-Semitism seems to be a dominant feature among modernist writers, and that irony is rare, apart from a few poems by Eliot. Only Cummings and Riding thus seem to have achieved a perfect identity of consciousness and language: the techniques that have been invented are the artist's path toward truth, which readers can take as soon as they acknowledge the beauty and strength of the experience. In a similar fashion, if the poet has to resist the temptation to become a critic who writes to fulfill his own manifestos, modern poetry has to rely on a sense of inner justification: "Modern poetry . . . is groping for some principle of self-determination to be applied to the making of the poem—not lack of government, but government from within" (SMP, 47).

This principle is demonstrated concretely in one of the most fascinating and self-contained chapters, "William Shakespeare and E. E. Cummings: A Study in Original Punctuation and Spelling," which contextualizes the vexed issue of the alleged obscurity and difficulty of modernist poetry. The chapter shows that if we could read Shakespeare's sonnets in the original text as printed, with all the visual puns and echoes, the new ambiguities introduced by the f's and s's that look alike, they would not be different from a short piece by Cummings. This chapter alone was to have a tremendous influence on William Empson, motivating him to write *Seven Types of Ambiguity* and anticipating the whole school of New Criticism. This entirely duplicates the movement by which modernism will be sanctified in the name of Eliot, and the *Waste Land* discussed and taught in universities as the unique gateway to modernity.

Although this chapter was written by Graves alone (as he claimed later), it finds a poetic equivalent in a poem by Riding, entitled "Tale of Modernity." It opposes in a striking allegorical fashion a Shakespeare obsessed by lust ("Shakespeare knew Lust by day, / With raw unsleeping eye. / And he cried, 'All but Truth I see, / Therefore Truth is, for Lust alone I see'") to a strange "Bishop Modernity" who cannot believe in Christ or sexuality ("Bishop Modernity plucked out his heart. / No agony could prove him Christ. / No lust could speak him honest Shakespeare. / A greedy frost filled where had been a heart"). Then Bishop Modernity decrees that the moon (identified with truth or femininity) is an illusion: petrified, it falls and becomes one with a text ("Never had time been futured so, / All reckoning on one fast page"). I shall quote the fourth and last part in its entirety because it suggests that Riding and Graves also managed to give birth to a strange "ghost" through their productive collaboration:

Bishop Modernity in the fatal chapel watched
And end-of-time intoned as the Red Mass
Of man's drinking of the blood of man:
In quenched immunity he looked on her

Who from the fallen moon scattered the altar
With thin rays of challenged presence—
The sun put out there, and the lamps of time
Smoking black consternation to new desire.

Then did that devilish chase begin:
Bishop Modernity's heart plucked out
In old desire flew round against and toward her—
And he but shackled mind, to pulpit locked.

Which stirred up Shakespeare from listening tomb,
Who broke the lie and seized the maid, crying,
"Thou Bishop Double-Nothing, chase thy soul—
Till then she's ghost with me thy ghostly whole!"[27]

Shakespeare, although dead, appears more modern than modernity itself, and he sends back pure mind and impotent desire, as the two sides of the same coin, to the void. Like an awakened Count Dracula, he preys on "her" who becomes a ghost as she becomes one with him. The moon will then be hidden again, and desire will learn to cope with "challenged presence" without transforming this quest into a gospel or ideology. This cryptic poem indeed announces Dylan Thomas's intricate metaphysical and sexual musings and cannot be reduced to a straightforward meaning. However, the "ghost of Shakespeare" that is conjured up haunts a modernity unable to erase its ancient longings.

In a similar vein, Riding reminisces on her fateful decision to commit suicide and commemorates the date not of her jump through the window (1929), but of the joint redaction of their *Survey* (1927) in the poem entitled "In Nineteen Twenty-Seven." This fragment illuminates Riding's identification with a ghost:

Then, where was I, of this time and my own
A double ripeness and perplexity?
Fresh year of my time, desire,

Late year of my age, renunciation—
Ill-mated pair, debating if the window
Is worth leaping out of, and by whom.

If this is ghostly?
And in what living knowledge
Do the dressed skeletons walk upright?
They memorize their doings and lace the year
Into their shoes each morning,
Groping their faulty way,
These citizens of habit, by green and pink

In gardens and smiles in shops and offices;
Are no more real than this. (*RCP*, 123)

It is indispensable to understand from which subjective point of view Riding
and Graves can posit the annihilation of chaotic everyday time as the most
powerful wish underlying modernism (modernism in the positive sense). The
personal radiance, the unremitting intelligence, the absolute devotion to truth
and poetry, which all those who flocked to Deyà could feel in Laura Riding,
found its basis in an overarching belief that reality has little consistency (as
André Breton expressed it in his "Introduction to the Discourse on the Paucity
of Reality")[28] and that time can stop:

> The calendar and clock have stopped,
> But does the year run down in time?
>
> . . . .
>
> But I, charmed body of myself,
> Am struck with certainty, stop in the street,
> Cry "Now"—and in despair seize love,
> A short despair, soon over.
> For by now all is history. (*RCP*, 124)

The ambiguous "all is history" may mean that the crisis is over or that the
outcome of the despair is a domination of history: as the *Survey* confirms, the
modernists indeed belong to a "lost generation."

Interestingly, the *Survey* ends not only on the self-serving commendation of
Riding's poems but with forceful praise of Gertrude Stein's work: from somewhat guarded comments on her "barbarism" ("Gertrude Stein is perhaps the
only artisan of language who has ever succeeded in practicing scientific barbarism literally" [*SMP*, 274]) and her utter lack of originality ("She exercised
perfect discipline over her creative faculties, and she was able to do this because she was completely without originality" [*SMP*, 280]), the *Survey* places
her safely at the center of real (that is, transcending merely "historical") modernism. The main reason for this centrality resides in Stein's invention of a
writing devoid of any history. In fact, it seems that Stein has achieved all at
once what Riding has been painfully groping toward in her poetry, realizing
all the potentialities of a creation that remains eternally here and now.

There are two central theses regarding Gertrude Stein suggested in the
Survey's conclusion. The first is that for her, "Time does not vary, only the
sense of time" (*SMP*, 281). Eliot also endorses this notion as he moves from his
"historical sense" to the *Four Quartets*. As the *Survey* says: "Beauty has no his-

tory, according to Miss Stein, nor has time: only the time-sense has a history" (*SMP*, 282), or again: "All beauty is equally final" (ibid.). This justifies in Graves and Riding's eyes the systematic use of repetition in Stein's works, which "has the effect of breaking down the possible historical sense still inherent in the words" (*SMP*, 285).

Thus, they see no difference, no evolution in the style of Gertrude Stein and believe that she still writes in 1926 as she wrote in 1906. To further illustrate this point, they quote from *Composition as Explanation*—which had just been published by the Woolfs' Hogarth Press in 1926: "Beginning again and again and again explaining composition and time is a natural thing. It is understood by this time that everything is the same except composition and time, composition and the time of the composition and the time in the composition" (*SMP*, 285).

Their second thesis on Stein is more constructive than metaphysical: "The theme is to be inferred from the composition" (*SMP*, 284). "The composition is final because it is 'a more and more continuous present including more and more using of everything and continuing more and more beginning and beginning and beginning'" (*SMP*, 284). But the reverse of this thesis is equally true: "The composition has a theme because it has no theme" (*SMP*, 286). Pure language is being recreated in Stein's word litanies, which illustrate the essentially timeless aspect of real modernism. The *Survey* concludes with full praise for Stein's "courage, clarity, sincerity, simplicity": "She has created a human mean in language, a mathematical equation of ordinariness which leaves one with a tender respect for that changing and unchanging slowness that is humanity and Gertrude Stein" (*SMP*, 287).

This encomium postulates a paradoxical domination of modernism by a woman writer (Laura Riding, as a feminist, was always prone to combatting phallocratic bias) who figures both at the origins of "historical modernism"— her first experimental writings were produced at a time when Pound was still immersed in archaism and fin-de-siècle affectation, and when Joyce was slowly transforming his juvenile autobiography into *Portrait of the Artist as a Young Man*—and at its conclusion: for the main objective of the *Survey* is to overcome purely historical modernism and to generalize the concept so much that it will be finally identified with "good and true writing."

The same element of "collaboration" can be seen in the strong relationship between Gertrude Stein and Alice Toklas, even if Toklas did not write. Their relatively slow courtship began in 1908, when Alice Toklas typed the huge manuscript of the *Making of the Americans*. The pleasure she found in this apparently dreary task was closer to some feminine *jouissance* as Lisa Ruddick has aptly demonstrated.[29] Toklas said of this period: "It was like living history. . . . I hoped it would go on for ever."[30] We should not forget that Stein "seduced" Toklas when she showed her the drafts of the novel, whose inception goes back to her student days, and which opens so dramatically with an Oedipal scene. This is how Stein imagines Toklas remembering the event:

> It was during this summer that Gertrude Stein began her great book, The Making of Americans. It began with an old daily theme that she had written when at Radcliffe,
> "Once an angry man dragged his father along the ground through his own orchard. 'Stop!' cried the groaning old man at last. 'Stop! I did not drag my father beyond this tree.'" And it was to be the history of a family. It was a history of a family but by the time I came to Paris it was getting to be a history of all human beings, all who ever were or could be living.[31]

The mention of Radcliffe College, where Stein studied with William James (before being failed in obstetrics at Johns Hopkins), calls up the first couple that provided the adolescent Gertrude with emotional stability, the couple she formed for a while with her brother Leo. As she recalls, after Leo discovered the dead body of their father, "then our life without father began. A very pleasant one" (GA, 48). Indeed, a systematic archaeology of modernism would have to tease out all the implications of the slow falling apart of this first fatherless couple who had been united by a common love for modern art, while distinguishing between purely personal factors (such as the gradual introduction of Alice Toklas into the household at rue de Fleurus, where she took over Leo's unused studio) and ideological discussions. Leo could not follow Gertrude's daring experiments with language, thinking that she knew no grammar, any more than he could understand Picasso's new departures.

The "uncoupling" of Leo and Gertrude Stein may have been primarily due to their protracted and bitter discussion of the worth of Picasso's *Demoiselles d'Avignon*, much more than to the introduction of a new "wife" into their "family." Yet only Alice Toklas was ready to embrace the whole extent of these novelties without hedging. This exchange, at the outcome of which a female couple replaced the brother-sister pairing, is crucial not only if one is to distinguish between cubism and modernism but also to evaluate the complex linkages between the "modern movement" of literature and fauvism, cubism, and, later, surrealism in painting (not Stein's favorite, of course).[32] Stein had no doubts about being the "genius," who could acknowledge the presence of only one other "genius" and in a different field: Picasso. At the same time, she had chanced upon someone who would be satisfied with being the "genius's wife," a little like Fernande, one of Picasso's wives, described so well in "her" *Autobiography*. After 1908, a second couple emerges, first as literary collaborators, then as lovers and finally as husband and wife. The "uncoupling" of this fourth vignette would describe how Leo and Gertrude Stein discovered the link between sexuality and modernity—in their different modernities, for sure. The only "ghost" this chiasmic uncoupling and recoupling may be said to have produced is thus not too far from a Joycean "Holy Ghost": it resides in the very belief in genius—a belief that upheld both Stein and Joyce throughout their careers. When she met Stein for the first time, Toklas heard bells ringing (she heard then again only twice, in the presence of Picasso and Whitehead): this was less love at first sight than instant genius-spotting, absolute awe in front of the "goddess" who encompassed all experiences of life (GA, 117–19). If Stein had indeed no qualms in presenting herself as a genius, it is also because she knew the quantity of moral courage it had taken her to become one: "It takes a lot of time to be a genius, you have to sit around so much doing nothing, really doing nothing."[33]

The epicene term "genius" enabled her to see herself as more male than female and indeed already contains all those loaded terms that hesitate between lesbian eroticism in a muted key and an experimental cubist dislocation of syntax and vocabulary. Genius is not far from cow in the famous sentence: "My Wife Has a Cow" ("to have a cow" meant to experience orgasm in the little language used by Gertrude and Alice). William Gass has written very perceptively on the intense eroticism of *Tender Buttons* and of most of Stein's apparently abstract and nonrepresentational pieces.[34] This oblique, yet transparent style of writing produces sexual euphemism as a verbal matrix that generates endless substitutions. Like Joyce in *Finnegans Wake*, Stein manages to say always two things (or more) at once, while creating a strange verbal music. The repetitive compositional urge is coupled with an instinctive recoil from anything that looks like "patriarchy" (Pound and William Carlos Williams did not escape unscathed, whereas Ernest Hemingway fared a little better). While Stein could quip about fathers: "It is funny the two things most men are proudest of is of the things that any man can do and doing does in the same way, that is being drunk and being the father of their son,"[35] she would not idealize married life: "There is no such thing as being good to your wife," she wrote.[36]

Stein had married the ideal wife, a devotedly monogamous partner who would care for her, help her write, and finally help her speak in a different voice—her own. Thus, after having had the intuition of an "eternal present" that would also be the dominant mode of *Finnegans Wake*, she could move from the oblique self-portrayal of herself through her "wife" and finally write *Everybody's Autobiography*. At this point, we have surely gone beyond the confines of movements such as cubism, but we are probably closer to postmodernism than modernism. Let us reread the paragraph in which Toklas-alias-Stein recaptures the year when almost everything happened at once:

> This was the year 1907. Gertrude Stein was just seeing through the press *Three Lives* which she was having privately printed, and she was deep in *The Making of Americans*, her thousand page book. Picasso had just finished his portrait of her which nobody at that time liked except the painter and the painted and which is now so famous, and he had just begun his strange complicated picture of three women. Matisse had just finished his *Bonheur de Vivre*, his first big composition which gave him the name of fauve or a zoo. It was the moment Max Jacob has since called the heroic age of cubism.[37]

The fate of modernism could lie in the disjunction between Matisse the fauve and Picasso the cubist later turned neoclassicist. This is how Clement Greenberg interpreted the concept in the fifties, when he systematically applied it as a grid or measuring rod with which he could extol Stella, Rothko, and Pollock and dismiss Warhol, Rauschenberg, and the whole of pop art. His notion of modernism owes as much to Stein as to Kant, whom he is fond of quoting and who provides him with a historical standard by which he can link early cubism with American abstract expressionism. The criteria that he adduces to define modernism—the autonomy of art in an autotelic closure, the stress on pure flatness of the support, and concern for the unity of medium and meaning—are exactly those used by Graves and Riding to praise Stein (and their own) work.

But as Leo Steinberg has since demonstrated in his brilliant refutation, we may need *Other Criteria* to dispel the illusion that modernist art creates an absolute rupture with the past.[38] As Steinberg suggests, even the old masters knew how to "use art to call attention to art" and not merely conceal it in an attempt at producing a transparent window. In the same way as modernism cannot be reduced to a wish to repudiate the past—after all, it "invented" collage and montage and played with the proliferation of codes as much as it simplified the pictorial vocabulary—it can never totally dehistoricize itself. Those artists who were called postmodern, such as Rauschenberg and Warhol, only received that label because a few critics managed to impose a normative and limited concept of modernism.

Just as the "historical" publication of Stein's *Geography and Plays* in 1922—with Sherwood Anderson's enthusiastic introduction in which he predicts that Stein will write the new great American novel and has managed "an entire new recasting of life, in the city of words"[39]—put her achievement on a par with *Ulysses* and the *Waste Land*, it also inscribed history into the texture of the work. This holds true from the first "collaborative" pieces, such as "Ada" (in which a few sentences had been written by Alice Toklas, much as Vivien Eliot added one or two lines to the *Waste Land*),[40] to the last pieces, such as "Accents in Alsace," which recaptures the war experiences of the two women, and "The Psychology of Nations," one of Stein's clearest political statements. She starts with a humorous evocation of the way "boys" play with soldiers and soon find themselves fighting a war, and she ends on a concept of democracy ("The boy grows up and has a presidential election") connected to writing, through a pun on the French meaning of "permission" (leave) in the military sense and its suggestion of *imprimatur*. The last words of this piece have often been quoted, but I want to quote them again so as to link the "sense of an ending" of modernism with its recurrent beginning as "making it new":

> A boy who is the son of another has a memory of permission.
> By permission we mean print.
> By print.   Solution.
> Settle on another in your seats.
> Kisses do not make a king.
> Nor noises a mother.
> Benedictions come before presidents.
> Words mean more.
> I speak now of a man who is not a bother.
> How can he not bother.
> He is elected by me.
> When this you see remember me.
>   FINIS.[41]

While this cannot yet seal the "end" of modernism, it should help us problematize all attempts at declaring it dead or finished—or replaced by all varieties of postmodernisms. Stein was aware of this when she chose to let the biblical phrase echo again at the end of *Four Saints in Three Acts* (published in 1929; the leitmotiv also surfaces again unexpectedly in *Lifting Belly*): "When this you see you are all to me" turns into "When this you see remember me."[42]

Nothing could better express Stein's desperate need to create an audience, her audience, a need that was also crucial to Pound, Joyce, and especially Lewis.

Besides, the insistence of Graves and Riding on the "plain reader" corresponds to the same strategy: modernism is the art of a period dominated by journalism and advertising, as Apollinaire's *Zone* brilliantly demonstrates. If Mallarmé had been the first poet to measure the interaction of crowd and artist, of the "Book" and futile mundane scribblings, especially after he had published *La Dernière mode*, Joyce would acknowledge the fusion in *Ulysses* and then discover in it the possibility of creating a linguistic morass from which the amalgamative and transformative language of *Finnegans Wake* would emerge.

The forceful and systematic creation of an audience is founded on a clear definition of an ideal reader, who must of course be underwritten by real and empirical—if, at times, limited—readers. This is why Stein felt the need to use Toklas's voice in 1932, not so much in order to become an easy and accessible writer, as to orchestrate mirror effects that would attract a readership while recapitulating a period of intense creativity. This return to a historical chronicle depicting identifiable events presented in a more or less chronological manner did not signify the "death" of modernism, as some have said: it simply fell into a different category of text than her real "writings"—or her real "being-writing." It allowed the hitherto "unreadable" texts of the Stein canon to be read. If modernism cannot be reduced to the slow formation of a "captive audience" (we should never forget its wish to shock and startle, to "change" that audience by having a deep effect on it) the criterion provided by the growing audience, at least among critics and academics, confirms the ability of modernism to regenerate itself while remaining tangential to even more radical breaks and departures.

Stein's achievements with the help of Alice Toklas correspond to the "uncoupling" I described when opposing a Rimbaud boldly opting for the "impossible"—this is the subtitle of one of the last sections of a *Season in Hell* in which the poet wonders: "Why a modern world, if poisons like this [drink, tobacco, and all artificial paradises] are invented!," before rejecting Western rationality in its entirety (*CP*, 339)—to a Verlaine intent on creating an art of the possible. Yet even if the creation of an audience supposes a minimum of readability, one cannot subscribe to attempts such as Graves's and Riding's to use modernism as an "eternalizing concept": such recuperative strategies are too bland and obvious. If the term "modernism" is to retain its meaning as well as its force, it has to remain historical. However, insofar as the word encompasses a history of the present, and perhaps of what is "highest in the present," modernism can still be written in the mode of a "continuous present."

The "Moderns" and Their Ghosts

Some of the central figures of modernity have just passed across our screen. It remains, then, to determine in what sense these figures are spectral figures and through what instances of return these spirits become ghosts. I have tried to catch sight of the phantoms of theory in Freud's interpretation of the painting by Leonardo da Vinci. We have viewed the "phantom-vessel" of the surrealists looming on the horizon of the avant-gardes of yesterday and today. In imitation of these poetic phantoms, we have then plunged into the Barthesian spectrality of the would-be novelist posthumously tormented by a Proustian desire which, originating in various photographs, leads an involuntary memory to hallucination. We have made our way through the funerary processions held on the occasion of those various bereavements suffered by a modernity unable to forget the return of the repressed: the phantom of the dead infant recalling the spectral father, guilty by virtue of his exclusive knowledge of death; the phantom of pure language haunted by the ritual communion with truth; the phantom of the masses caught in the grasp of crepuscular fervor when they believe themselves the bearers of an historical mission.

Seemingly, a return toward Beckettian nihilism could allow us to advance forward in the exploration of such a vivid mourning. With Beckett, we learn to mourn the phantom of form and full meaning, while in his texts phantoms of a subjectivity in tatters—tempted by the prospect of ataraxia and autarchical survival independently of any image—multiply infinitely in the same movement of generalized returns illustrative of the postmodern, when the bits and scraps of citations drawn from historical modernism, from Baudelaire and Rimbaud to Apollinaire and Eliot form a vast polyphony of haunting obsession.

Has modernity, then, always been haunted? Yes, since a refutation of specters has always served as the very background for its formation. Two significant stages serve as points of reference in briefly outlining a history of these returns of the spectral figure so very persistent despite the repeated acts of distancing of which it was the object. Separated by an interval of almost two centuries, two debates intertwine around the belief in ghosts. The first sets Spinoza against Boxel; the second opposes Stirner to Marx.

In a letter of 1674, Boxel, the young and very naive law student, inquires of Spinoza whether he believes in ghosts. Even while expressing doubts as to their nature (are they "composed of a very thin and subtle matter," are they spirits, do they derive from the souls of the dead?),[1] Boxel appears quite certain on one point: the tales of ghosts are so numerous that they must encompass something of reality: "Though, as you must be aware, so many instances and stories of them are found throughout antiquity, that it would really be difficult either to deny or doubt them" (SCO, 376). From the start, we can discern an archetypal configuration: the ghost is a product of discourse for, if nobody or almost nobody has ever seen one with his own eyes, everybody is at least familiar with the widely circulated rumor.

The specter is a discursive being fabricated by the canard, by a diffused sort of hearsay that rests upon the crushing weight of the past. As is the case with any recourse to ancestral superstition, we are faced with a past that is not historical but immemorial, not modern but ancient. "Meanwhile, it is certain, that the ancients believed in them" (SCO, 375). Perhaps Boxel was less naive than he seemed and guessed in advance that Spinoza would not admit of ghosts: "As I am doubtful whether you admit their existence, I will proceed no further," he writes (SCO, 375), and yet proceeds! Indeed, the provocation seems especially crude: how could a Cartesian philosopher resist the pleasure of assailing such an adversary and, in killing the phantom, refrain from immediately clothing himself, as if by automatic response, in the fresh attire of the "modern"?

Spinoza does not immediately yield to such a provocation since he decides to view this seemingly absurd inquiry as an opportunity to mark out a path toward the truth with his young friend: "Although some might think it a bad omen, that ghosts are the cause of your writing to me, I, on the contrary, can discern a deeper meaning in the circumstance; I see that not only truths, but also things trifling and imaginary may be of use to me" (SCO, 376). Spinoza's customary prudence leads him to begin by requesting the hardly tangible evidence of the existence of ghosts. He asks Boxel to "select from the numerous stories which you have read, one or two of those least open to doubt, and most clearly demonstrating the existence of ghosts" (SCO, 377). But Spinoza's impatience finally grants free rein to a diatribe against the "children," "fools," and "madmen" who are enamored of puerilities that recall "the pastimes of children or fools" (SCO, 377).

Then, without even allowing Boxel time to produce any sort of evidence, Spinoza attributes the existence of ghosts to a very specific desire to tell stories:

> The desire which most men have to narrate things, not as they really happened, but as they wished them to happen, can be illustrated from the stories of ghosts and specters more easily than from others. The principal reason for this is, I believe, that such stories are only attested by the narrators, and thus a fabricator can add or suppress circumstances, as seems most convenient to him, without fear of anyone being able to contradict him. He composes them to suit special circumstances, in order to justify the fear he feels of dreams and phantoms, or else to confirm his courage, his credit or his opinion. (SCO, 377)

Would the debate come to an end before even having begun? Boxel commences his response by putting Spinoza on guard against a prejudice and quotes the proverb that says "a preconceived opinion hinders the pursuit of truth" (SCO, 378), but he grievously misses his objective when attempting to persuade his correspondent of the existence of such immaterial beings. Indeed, Boxel is first of all going to offer metaphysical arguments touching on the possibility of such existence (which "appertains to beauty and the perfection of the universe," and would tend to prove that the world was not created by chance [SCO, 378]), and then augment the number of bookish references. It seems that Boxel has misunderstood the cause of the resistance of Spinoza, whom he obviously takes for a "modernist": he attempts to convince Spinoza by demonstrating that the accounts derive not only from antiquity (Plutarch, Suetonius, and Pliny are cited) but also from the moderns of the sixteenth and seventeenth centuries: Melanchton, Cardano, Thyraeus, and Lavater are among the more or less immediate contemporaries who testify in favor of ghosts.

The quotation from Johann Lavater's essay on ghosts (which closes Boxel's letter) mingles skillfully—he supposes—the two types of "authorities": "He who is bold enough to gainsay so many witnesses, both ancient and modern, seems to me unworthy of credit" (SCO, 379). A few anecdotes coupled with the undeniable cumulative weight of authority should convince even a staunch rationalist such as Spinoza. However, formerly Boxel had inopportunely cited an anecdote mentioning night noises in a brewhouse—an account of hardly any discernible weight, which serves to expose Boxel's gullibility—and, even before, had made an apparently gratuitous remark: "Thus I think there are spirits of all sorts, but, perhaps, none of the female sex" (SCO, 378). It is here that Spinoza unleashes his skepticism by distinguishing between the stories that are told and those who tell them: "I confess that I am not a little amazed, not at the stories, but at those who narrate them. I wonder that men of talent and judgment should employ their readiness of speech, and abuse it in endeavoring to convince us of such trifles" (SCO, 380).

Confronted with Boxel's obstinate desire to preserve such childish illusions, Spinoza has only one effective weapon — irony:

> The distinction you drew, in admitting without hesitation spirits of the male sex, but doubting whether any female spirits exist, seems to me more like a fancy than a genuine doubt. If it were really your opinion, it would resemble the common imagination, that God is masculine, not feminine. I wonder that those, who have seen naked ghosts, have not cast their eyes on those parts of the person, which would remove all doubt; perhaps they were timid, or did not know of this distinction. (SCO, 380–81)

This strange and masterful mockery suggests in passing that God has no more of a sex than do ghosts. Boxel's embarrassed response on the question of the gender of ghosts consists in saying that he does not concede that such spirits can reproduce among themselves (SCO, 384). We know that Spinoza's *Ethics* defines timidity as the "desire to avoid a greater evil, which we dread, by undergoing a lesser veil" (SET, 182) but that if the evil feared is shame, then timidity becomes bashfulness, and if the fear of two evils is equivalent, so that the "man knows not which to choose, fear becomes *consternation*" (SET, 157). Thus, it seems that Spinoza here aims at the consternation of the adversary through these mordant remarks. They imply that the hoodwinked credulity of those who are too eager to listen to the sirens of their imagination rests upon a fundamental indifference. Not knowing how to distinguish between reality and fiction, the believers in ghosts are like children or madmen ignorant of sexual difference.

By contrast, Spinoza's rationalism aims at cutting into the very heart of beliefs and desires. Not that he would have defended a feminine portion of the human being that would be denied by the credulous. In fact, the philosopher's irony turns against those who lend an ear to the "old wives' tales" in order to weaken the authority of Democritus (SCO, 388). If one wishes to believe in specters, ghosts, and spirits, then why not confirm the gilded legend of the Christian saints?

> If you are inclined to believe such witnesses, what reason have you for denying the miracles of the Blessed Virgin and of all the saints ? These have been described by so many famous philosophers, theologians, and historians, that

I could produce at least a hundred such authorities for every one of the former. But I have gone further, my dear Sir, than I intended. (SCO, 388)

In this manner, the epistolary exchange ends with a final remark that, no doubt, is again not to Boxel's liking. Since his first letter, Spinoza had still retained some hope for the theory of ghosts provided that the term were better determined. He asserts that no "authority" had ever managed to convince him of the existence of ghosts and, if ghosts are so common, they should at least offer a stable topic of discussion:

> Yet it is evident, that in the case of a thing so clearly shown by experience we ought to know what it is; otherwise we shall have great difficulty in gathering from histories that ghosts exist. We only gather that something exists of nature unknown. If philosophers choose to call things which we do not know "ghosts," I shall not deny the existence of such, for there are an infinity of things, which I cannot make out. (SCO, 377)

Ghosts come to designate blind spots of knowledge, less like those superstitions, prejudices, and human fictions bound to the desire to believe in final causes denounced in the appendix to the first section of the *Ethics* (78–81) than those "miracles" that are natural manifestations surpassing human comprehension. These find their peculiar hermeneutical place when, as is explained by the treatise on theological and political authorities, we grasp that the ways of God are not at all distinguished from the laws of nature and that we can hope to gain with time a more complete and more scientific understanding of such phenomena.

Like Beckett, Spinoza refers to scripture just as easily as the "natural lights" to declare that the natural order cannot change and that, therefore, any dispute concerning the gender of angels or ghosts is futile. Nature cannot admit of miracles or fantastic phenomena because it always duplicates the same processes—there is never anything truly new under the sun, as the *Theologico-Political Treatise and Political Treatise* recalls when quoting Ecclesiastes 1:10: there never appears anything new in nature. An exhaustive contemplation of the laws of nature leads to God. Hence even a cursory examination of these same specters can lead back to God. Even though Spinoza opts for the more humorous route and decides not to remove Boxel from his mental confusion, it is his correspondent who does not furnish a single clear idea:

> If I had as clear an idea of ghosts as I have of a triangle or a circle, I should not in the least hesitate to affirm that they had been created by God; but as

the idea I possess of them is just like the ideas, which my imagination forms
of harpies, gryphons, hydras, &c., I cannot consider them as anything but
dreams, which differ from God as totally, as that which is not differs from
that which is. (SCO, 383)

Spinoza implies, then, in his following letter, that if ghosts existed, for them
God would also be a ghost (and if ghosts were women, their god would be a
god in the feminine mode): "I believe that, if a triangle could speak, it would
say, in like manner, that God is eminently triangular, while a circle would say
that the divine nature is eminently circular. Thus each would ascribe to God
its own attributes, would assume itself to be God, and look on everything else
as ill-shaped" (SCO, 386).

Such a remark assumes its full importance in the context of Beckett's
Murphy. When Beckett describes his hero's mind in chapter 6, the epigraph is
a parody of Spinoza: "*Amor intellectualis quo Murphy se ipsum amat*" (*MU*,
107). Beckett takes up the idea developed in the fifth section of the *Ethics*, in
proposition 36, according to which "the intellectual love of the mind towards
God is that very love of God whereby God loves Himself. . . . The intellectual
love of the mind towards God is part of the infinite love wherewith God loves
Himself" (*SET*, 264–65). That is very much Beckett's parodic strategy: fold
intellectual love back onto the Leibnizian monad, transform the definition of
divine love into an autonomy of the human intellect free to adore itself, and
link this fundamental desire to a psychotic paroxysm of the perception of an
irrevocable breach between the body and mind. Proposition 45 in "Of Human
Freedom," which states that "God loves himself with an infinite intellectual
love" (*SET*, 264), will apply, then, to Murphy, who embodies the figure deified
precisely because he is fascinated by the autistic of the psychiatric hospital.
"Murphy loves himself with an infinite intellectual love" in a mind that condemns the body to the vegetative survival of the psychotic. Such would be the
impasse of hyperrationalism, whose suicidal consequences Beckett ironically
recounts.

One historical detail is worth noting: like Spinoza, Beckett was once stabbed
in the street by a stranger. The difference between the two incidents, either of
which could have been fatal, is less political than rational: Spinoza was attacked because of his courageous support of the Witt brothers and their liberal
party, which led him to be the victim of intolerance and popular fanaticism.
Beckett, who ran into many other dangers during the German occupation of
Paris at the very moment when his Resistance network was broken up, had
several years earlier been assaulted by a total stranger bumped into on a side-

walk, a curious Parisian pimp who later declared not even to know why he had stabbed him. The same struggle of reason against intolerance persists, with a remarkable shift toward the fortuitous and the "absurd" (whose mathematical etymology must never be forgotten).

Indeed, it was between the Dutch seventeenth century, which saw the emergence of the first modern republic, and the nineteenth century that a radical displacement took place from God to humanity, now invested with a new responsibility. In fact, it seems as if the psychotic of Beckett strives to traverse this fissure separating the *Deus sive Natura* from modern humanism, offering the best parody of the cults of reason, humanity, or the supreme being that sprung forth with the revolutions.

In a certain fashion, then, Murphy parodies the man of Feuerbach and the ego of Stirner—those two secular versions of the Hegelian speculative system. Stirner effects a radical simplification of the system of the *Phenomenology of Spirit* (it is essentially for this that Marx reproaches him) by distinguishing between two great periods, that of the "ancients," or the world of ancient wisdom, and that of the "moderns," which he identifies with Christianity, an instance of the cult of the mind. "If the ancients have nothing to show but wisdom of the world, the moderns never did nor do make their way further than to theology."[2]

Theology is the resolute adversary of egoism that refuses to sacrifice personal interest to a great abstract idea. However, according to Stirner's definition, which takes up one of the fundamental intuitions of Feuerbach, theology is nothing but the belief in ghosts. Let us see how Stirner sets up the terms of his problematic:

> Have you ever seen a spirit? "No, not I, but my grandmother." Now, you see, it's just so with me too; I myself haven't seen any, but my grandmother had them running between her feet all sorts of ways, and out of confidence in our grandmother's honesty we believe in the existence of spirits.
>
> But had we no grandfathers then, and did they not shrug their shoulders every time our grandmothers told about their ghosts? Yes, those were unbelieving rationalists! . . . What else lies at the bottom of this warm faith in ghosts, if not the faith in "the existence of spiritual beings in general," and is not this latter itself disastrously unsettled if saucy men of the understanding may disturb the former? The Romanticists were quite conscious what a blow the very belief in God suffered by the laying aside of the belief in spirits or ghosts, and they tried to help us out of the baleful consequences. (*EO*, 42–43)

Stirner's point of departure is not fundamentally different from Spinoza's remarks. The traditional wisdom of old women must be opposed to the skepticism of mature men. Stirner more than energetically mimics that which is
whispered in contemporary ears by the "romantic" discourse of the so-called
moderns:

> "Spirits exist!" Look about in the world, and say for yourself whether a spirit
> does not gaze upon you out of everything. Out of the lovely little flower
> there speaks to you the spirit of the Creator, who has shaped it so wonder-
> fully. . . . The mountains may sink, the flowers fade, the world of stars fall in
> ruins, the men die—what matters the wreck of these visible bodies? The
> spirit, the "invisible spirit," abides internally! Yes, the whole world is haunted!
> Only is haunted? Nay, it itself "walks," it is uncanny through and through, it
> is the wandering seeming-body of a spirit, it is a spook. (EO, 43–44)

This phenomenological recreation of the romantic conscience of the "moderns"
requires the specific term of "ghost" or "specter" which alone permits a clear
distinction to be made between the reign of the modern intellect and the world
of the gods of antiquity.

> What else should a ghost be, then, than an apparent body, but real spirit?
> Well, the world is "empty," is "naught," is only glamorous "semblance"; its
> truth is the spirit alone; it is the seeming-body of a spirit. Look out near or
> far, a *ghostly* world surrounds you everywhere; you are always having "appa-
> ritions" or visions. Everything that appears to you is only the phantasm of an
> indwelling spirit, is a ghostly "apparition." . . . To you the whole world is
> spiritualized, and has become an enigmatical ghost; therefore do not won-
> der if you likewise find in yourself nothing but a spook. (EO, 44)

Everything has become spectral in this haunted modernity: Stirner's only response lies in a concentration, a severe reduction to the "ego"—that is, to a
transcendental egoism that will resist with all its strength the constraints of
abstract ideas. Unicity combats generality somewhat like the drive struggles
against the fictions of the Freudian superego. Accordingly, Stirner refuses to
admit that love is exercised in the name of an external value:

> If I cherish you because I hold you dear, because in you my heart finds
> nourishment, my need satisfaction, then it is not done for the sake of a higher
> essence whose hallowed body you are, not on account of my beholding in
> you a ghost; i.e., an appearing spirit, but from egoistic pleasure; you yourself
> with *your* essence are valuable to me, for your essence is not a higher one, is

not higher and more general than you, is unique like you yourself, because it is you.

But it is not only man that "haunts"; so does everything. The higher essence, the spirit, that walks in everything, is at the same time bound to nothing and only—"appears" in it. Ghosts in every corner! (*EO*, 54)

The ferocity of Marx and Engels's humor will find in Stirner a welcome butt when they examine the champions of German idealism: for them, Stirner figures as the absolute culmination of a ghostly ideology. In order to accuse him, Marx and Engels feign a tactical incomprehension of the critical importance of Stirner's analyses; consequently, they remain deaf to the ironic tone of this "phantasmagorical" evocation: "Without realizing it, Saint Max has so far done no more than give instruction in the art of spirit-seeing, by regarding the ancient and modern world as the 'pseudo-body of a spirit,' as a spectral phenomenon, and seeing in it only struggles of spirits. Now, however, he consciously and *ex professo* gives instruction in the art of ghost-seeing."[3]

Marx and Engels deride a Stirner who exclaims, "Yes, ghosts are teeming in the whole world," and then adds: "Only *in* it? *No*, the world itself is an apparition" (*GI*, 153). They prefer Hegel, whose exposition appears at least more rigorous because he demonstrated that the modern world had been despiritualized as much as it had been spiritualized. Hegel, above all, refuses the distinction instituted by Stirner between gods and ghosts. Marx and Engels write: "As against the world's despiritualisation in the Christian consciousness, the ancients, 'who saw gods everywhere,' can with equal justification be regarded as the spiritualisers of the world—a conception which our saintly dialectician rejects with the well-meaning warning: 'Gods, my dear modern man, are not spirits'" (*GI*, 47). Pious Max recognizes only the "*holy* spirit as spirit" (*GI*, 153).

To be sure, Stirner does not take pains to explain the history of Christianity through the "empirical conditions" and "industrial relations and relations of exchange" connected to a given form of society. Insofar as he goes no further than a vision of autonomous metamorphoses of the religious spirit understood as a series of "autodeterminations," he remains a prisoner of the very spirit he denounces. As Marx and Engels reassert, Stirner, by dint of crying "ghost," has effectively transformed himself and his entire conceptual world into a spectral phantasmagoria. At bottom, his "ghosts" are nothing but representations, general concepts, and ideas understood absolutely, independently of their material production.

Marx and Engels provide a list of ten major specters for Stirner and introduce it in a parodic way: "Then, we see the skies opening and the various kinds of spectres passing before us one after the other" (*GI*, 157):

Spectre N° 1: the *Supreme being,* God;

Spectre N° 2: *essence;*

Spectre N° 3: *vanity of the world;*

Spectre N° 4: *good and evil beings;*

Spectre N° 5: *the essence and its realm;*

Spectre N° 6: *essences;*

Spectre N° 7: the *God-Man,* Christ;

Spectre N° 8: *man* [Marx and Engels gleefully comment: "Here our bold writer is seized with immediate 'horror'—'he is terrified of himself,' he sees in every man a 'frightful spectre,' a 'sinister spectre' in which something 'stalks.'"];

Spectre N° 9: *the national spirit;*

Spectre N° 10: *everything.* (GI, 158–59)

Our two polemists conclude in an attack linking Stirner and Feuerbach: "And since Saint Max shares the belief of all critical speculative philosophers of modern times that thoughts, which have become independent, objectified thoughts—ghosts—have ruled the world and continue to rule it, and that all history up to now was the history of theology, nothing could be easier for him than to transform history into a history of ghosts" (GI, 160).

Certainly, there is no need to reenact the Marxist trial of idealism and ideology. It suffices to note that the analysis as a whole is referred back to the world of shadows from which it should never have detached itself: "The history of ghosts in Sancho [Stirner's nickname] has as its sole foundation, then, the belief in ghosts, traditional among speculative philosophers" (GI, 184).

There also remains the enigma of the curious relentlessness of Marx and Engels whose 350 pages of mocking remarks devoted to Stirner surpass by close to twenty pages the entire volume of the *Ego and His Own* and can be described as a rare feat of polemical overkill. They manage to quote almost all of Stirner's essay! (Marx and Engels are a little like Bouvard and Pécuchet when they try to go to the root of philosophical problems and fling at each other the epithets of "materialist" and "idealist" while quoting books they never really try to understand.) What seems at stake in this struggle for the reduction of ghosts is the staunch Marxist refusal to conceive of an idea without determination, a relation without relation, an "I" that only positions itself as "ego" or the "unique" in order to refute any positioning and hence disappear.

Marx and Engels reduce to a "magical incantation" the rhapsody on the term "unique," which concludes Stirner's treatise. They dub it "Solomon's Song of Songs or The Unique" (GI, 427) and only refer to its claim of being a "concept without determination" (GI, 448) for the purpose of mocking it. Stirner's "unique" becomes "the word which is simultaneously more and less than a word" (GI, 449). Sancho/Stirner has found as the object of his Quixotic quest a pure and empty word that plays the role of Christ the Redeemer—and redeems itself from any link with reality (GI, 449–50).

Yet the dialectic of an antidialectic devised by Stirner could be seen as heralding the intuitions of Nietzsche's last writings, Adorno's "negative dialectics," or Blanchot's neutral third person. The "I" only calls itself "ego" in order to transcend itself and vanish once again. It becomes a paradoxical foundation, a principle, a dialectical lever through the paradox of the enunciation of the "ego" by which all is inverted into nothing and vice versa. The famous final paragraph of the Ego and His Own confirms this:

> I am owner of my might, and I am so when I know myself as unique. In the Unique one, the owner himself returns into his creative nothing, of which he is born. Every higher essence above me, be it God, be it man, weakens the feeling of my uniqueness, and pales only before the sun of this consciousness. If I found my cause on myself [Sache], the unique one, then my concern rests on its transitory, mortal creator, who consumes himself, and I may say:
>
> I have founded my cause on nothing [Ich hab' Mein' Sach' auf Nichts gestellt].[4]

Is this merely, as the German Ideology maintains, a play on words, the absurd exploitation of a tautology that detaches itself from language in a mysterious and transcendent fashion? One may understand, however, how the derisive epithets of "Saint Max" and "Sancho" themselves need an enunciative montage without which the philosophical critique of Marx and Engels (surely not theoretical angels in this case!) could not work. They push the author who signs "Stirner" down among the intersecting plot schemes of two texts—the Bible and Don Quixote—both of which curiously play a driving dialectical role in the critical analysis of ideology in the course of which historical materialism takes shape. Indeed, the last word of the caustic review of Sancho/Stirner's thought is left to Cervantes.

I have no desire to rehabilitate "Saint Max," whose cult of the "unique" based upon a "nothing" might bespeak the Mallarméan desire for a ritual of the book rather than the historical anarchism that effectively claimed Stirner as a source of inspiration. The difference might be linked to the "ghosts" that Stirner continues to assail. These are truth, the king, law, the good, majesty, honor, the public welfare, order, the fatherland, and so on (*EO*, 54). The list could obviously go on infinitely and need not be limited to ten specters.

Marx saw in Stirner proof by incompetence and self-parody of the bankruptcy of the speculative system of German idealism. But it is also in a similar "unique" that "forgets itself in sweet self-oblivion"—a sentence from Stirner quoted against him by Marx and Engels at the close of the "Saint Max" section of the *German Ideology* (452)—that one might find the model for the Beckettian narrator in the *Unnamable* or the countless Jean Singuliers which populate the frenzied monologues of Valère Novarina.

Stirner is a writer who produces a work in order to extol the pleasure of a life perceived as the ego's autodelectation. Everything is ghost for the ego as unique, who is all and nothing at once and introduces nothingness into the world. This is an unassailable position, except if you convince the ego that it is just another ghost—which is what Marx and Engels, not without success, try to accomplish.

Another course could be that which is followed by Mallarmé when he decides to meditate almost exclusively on the labor of writing required simply to give shape to this "cause," to conduct this trial of the ego. That Mallarmé finally believed in a book that would condense the collective rite and cult attests to the inevitable reinscription in the social of such writing once it aims at assuming some consequence. The pages of the "Book" demonstrate not only that Mallarmé regarded the readings of the "Book" as an equivalent of the mass:

Reading.
12 people
    Redn. of
    Mass (f. 34)[5]

but also that he conceived of this mass as an "office" in which absence and lack were more important than the "real presence" of a substitute for the Eucharist:

The savior—we
all become him—
do the same thing-
    with

—he lacks
    the office.[6]

It is hardly accidental that the community reading of the "twelve" apostles had been forgotten for a half-century before reemerging in the last work of the only writer who attempted to take up the Mallarméan challenge: Joyce. Indeed, it is in *Finnegans Wake* that we systematically find the choir of the twelve drinkers in the pub of Chapelizod who contribute in such a dodecaphonic manner to the polyphonic texture of this Irish saga. Like Mallarmé, Joyce is also aware that, even if he "lacks the office," he must act as if he was endowed with such a charge in order to continue with the literary mass, that discreet rite in which readers and writers tend to coalesce.[7] Could the ghost of the "Book" be the last rational cult still possible in this fin de siècle when religion is making a foreseeable but terrifying return to the international stage?

Spinoza and Stirner would vie with one another in affirming that no religion can do without the belief in some sort of ghost. In fact, this is the view of Sade (who keeps apostrophizing Christ as "ghost"-in-chief), as well as Mallarmé and Joyce. What is, then, a ghost? As noted by Spinoza, this question cannot be dissociated from the question regarding the sex of ghosts. The question "what is a ghost?" could be untenable, the impossible interrogation par excellence, to the extent that it presupposes an enunciative mechanism from which it can never isolate itself. Depending on the tone in which it is uttered, we will obtain the assured reductions of triumphant rationalism or the tales of troubling events about which one is always already informed, without being exactly sure. And the suspense or the trembling of the voice will bring along a complicity that would be rejected in other contexts, and if this one is favorable, it will give rise to new tales (who does not have a grandmother who has heard about bizarre things?). Nobody will be able, then, to articulate the truth about the real nature of ghosts. They only exist in the "tales of good women" that are directed exclusively toward the imagination and designate the empty place of the dead's return to this world. These are the images that can appear or not appear, whether one feels oneself hallucinating or not, but which, as a first consequence, transform the subject of perception as well as the subject of narration into ghosts.

In fact, such could be the lesson drawn from the story of the ghost concealed by Hamlet: it is the appearance of the phantom that renders us phantasmal—us, that is, those to whom the apparition is addressed. The becoming-specter of Hamlet assumes a form exactly inverse to the act of bereavement that could not be carried out: Hamlet's delirium of procrastination is thus a form of haste, of hurry, as has been well demonstrated by Ella Sharpe.[8] Hamlet's lack of reaction, his untimely and inopportune deeds, everything in his comportment works to intensify the haste of the royal couple, the rush to move from the funerary rites to the marriage of the "adulterous" and "incestuous" lovers. The appearance of the phantom always originates in a gesture of mourning that cannot be performed; the interiorized side of such abortive bereavement is the hyperbolic melancholy that Hamlet himself exhibits.

In the same manner as Ella Sharpe or Jacques Lacan rereading Hamlet, the psychoanalysts Nicolas Abraham and Maria Torok analyze the function of the "ghost" in the subconscious, starting with the projections and introjections of a cadaver into the psyche caught up between mourning and melancholy. According to them, the phantom is a deceased figure buried in another person who can unwittingly make itself heard—like a "ventriloquist," a complete stranger in contrast to the "familiar stranger" of which Freud spoke in regard to the return of the repressed. This ghost appears through obscure words nonsemantically encoded: "The imaginings issuing from the presence of a stranger have nothing to do with fantasy strictly speaking. They neither preserve a topographical status quo nor announce a shift in it. Instead, by their gratuitousness in relation to the subject, they create the impression of surrealistic flights of fancy or of *oulipo*-like verbal feats."[9]

Such a theory of the phantom is equally applicable to both the polyglot verbal formations that make up the repertoire of the cryptonomic "Word Hoard" governing the unconscious verbal associations of the "Wolf-Man" as well as the phobias of children. In fact, Torok's study suggests that the ghost pursuing little Hans in his horse nightmares and his birth trauma refers back to no one else but Freud himself![10]

We are not, then, very surprised to observe that Beckett employs the same unconscious play on words as little Hans's pun on the birth and hole of castration when he decides, from 1937 onward, to work against the current of the modernism of Proust and Joyce. Beckett assigns to literature the task of "boring holes" in language and signs thereby the act of birth of a postmodernity conscious of the echoes linking *bohren/gebohren* to *bore/be born*. Freud writes of Hans's anxiety:

> It was not until later that it was possible to guess that this was a remolding of a *fantasy of procreation*, distorted by anxiety. The big bath of water, in which Hans imagined himself, was his mother's womb; the "borer," which his father had from the first recognized as a penis, owed its mention to its connection with "being born." The interpretation that we are obliged to give to the fantasy will of course sound very curious: "With your big penis you 'bored' me" (i.e., "gave birth to me") "and put me in my mother's womb." (*SE*, 10:128)

Beckett explains that he is looking to "discredit" language and that, since he cannot eliminate it completely, he aims at boring it, at piercing it (in contrast to Joyce who thought himself able to master it): "Bore a hole after the other in [language], until that which hides behind, whether it be something or nothing, begins to leak out—I cannot imagine a higher purpose for the writer today."[11] Beckett's conclusion in relation to our times follows very logically from this anasemic breakthrough in language: "Haunting obsession and, at the same time, the refusal of meagerness—it is, perhaps, at this point that we will one day conclude by acknowledging our dear good old times. That meagerness from which one rushes forth, like the worst of curses, toward the glamour of all and nothing" (*DIS*, 147).

Beckett's historical perception of our moment as that of the "ghost" would tend to assert that our present postmodernity is spectral. This can be understood in two senses, either that history is haunted by a specter that resists any rational reduction, or any modernity or postmodernity will be in themselves "spectral," endlessly generating ghosts ready to haunt an unwitting future, sweeping beneath a stream of virtual images everything that will be conceived of as rationality. The first case would simply be rehashing a psychoanalytic truism affirming that no movement intent upon abolishing the past can avoid the return of a particular historical repressed (in the same way as the construction of a united Europe must put up with the return of the most commonplace sorts of nationalism and religious fanaticism). In the second sense, this meta-historical haunting suggests in less conventional fashion that modernity is the effect of a retroactive projection, of a "future perfect" that plays with its fictions and ghosts as much as with prospective hypotheses and wagers. A haunted modernity will have been (always already) an anterior future tense deploying the spectrum of rival readings and rereadings, of incompatible and proliferating virtualities dubbed "postmodernity."

The spectral position would then appear at the junction between the distress of a difficult birth and the complete indifference fostered by the multiplication of images that neutralize one another in the society of spectacle and cultural zapping. Samuel Beckett can again provide some emblematic figures. One exemplary figure appears through all of his early texts, from *More Pricks than Kicks* to the Trilogy, and is alluded to in *Murphy*: the chosen hero known as Belacqua. The slowness of Belacqua's movements brings a smile to Dante's very lips. But the indolence of the string-instrument maker, among which are lutes (we may hope with Mallarmé), is such that he scoffs at Dante's efforts to continue his path toward paradise. "Go then up above, you, the valiant!" he rails at Dante who labors on the trail and then adds:

O brother, what's the use of climbing? God's angel, he who guards the gate,
would not let me pass through to meet my punishment.

    Outside that gate the skies must circle round as many times as they did
when I lived—since I delayed good sighs until the end—[12]

Indifferent to salvation, the tired and melancholic Belacqua chooses to remain
among the dead, an almost comical ghost with an abrasive sense of humor but
also a dreamer lost in an endless wait. Stuck in this indefinite interregnum, he
cannot be reborn—just as he cannot die—into eternal life. This will provide
Murphy with an adequate model in his state of purgatorial arrest.

    This indefinite arrest or foreclosure, in the Lacanian sense of rejecting a
signifier outside of the symbolic code, occurs in such a way that the guiding
name only survives as the ghost discussed by Abraham and Torok: a phantom-
father who forbids his son from gaining access to the domain of paternity, a
phantom-child who forbids his parents from performing their duties of mourning according to ritual. By contrast, the idealized ataraxia of Belacqua—now
turned into the "hero" of *More Pricks than Kicks*—indirectly highlights the
residual grief that can be uncovered in the simple act of eating a lobster that
must be thrown into boiling water: live scalding lobsters, ectoplasms contorted
with pain in our imaginary, opaque signifiers that migrate from one unconscious to another; ghosts of the interregnum, between mourning and melancholy, vivid projections of a remnant of grief to be cleared away. These spectrographs of grief reverberate in multiple hallucinations, ramifications, verbal
iridescences from Mallarmé to Beckett.

    If we cannot inquire what are ghosts, or know anything definitive about
their sex and gender, can we at least pose the question of their color? On this
point, Freud provides some clarification when he offers from a distance a diagnosis of the curious hallucinations disturbing Arnold Zweig, his novelist friend.
Zweig explains how a liquid bubble floating in his retina makes him see grimacing faces against a background of gray-yellow light:

These faces change more or less according to the rhythm of my pulse beats;
they take on different shapes, but they are always some variation on the face
of a man with a moustache. During the first few months they were Jewish
faces. My eye conjured up every type of Jewish face for me. Then later they
were mainly faces of recumbent men, seen from the chin upwards, their
eyes shut, and so the faces of dead men. Some days they changed into de-
composing, disintegrating faces, then again into death's heads.[13]

Zweig adds that these visions of the faces of dead Jews, probably aroused by his feelings of guilt toward the members of his family, were transformed into those of a Chinese man's grimacing face about which he hallucinated after having been struck by a reading of the *Conquerors* by André Malraux.

Freud explains this incident by asserting that sensorial imprecision fosters projection and aids the fantasizing of the imagination through a phenomenon similar to the "crystal gazing" analyzed by Silberer, a phenomenon that also consisted of the emergence of curious images of old Jews.[14] Freud refers to the techniques devised by Silberer to endoscopically observe hallucinatory phenomena and refers the dread experienced by Zweig back to the dread affecting the dreamer who witnesses how the dead come back to life. In both cases, it is a question of the dreamer's own fear of death. To see a ghost, to hallucinate about a Jewish or Chinese man's death amounts to warding off the fear that one has become a ghost:

> Your experience with the Chinese faces is certainly a decisive proof and your suspicion about the old men in your family is highly probable. It may be assumed one's own personal expectations of death provide the driving force. The whole phenomenon will probably disappear one day, and were it not so tormenting it would provide an excellent opportunity for self-analysis. Through the gap in the retina one could see deep into the unconscious.[15]

This gap is certainly real in the case of Arnold Zweig's vision problems, but it is also to this gap that Freud chose to attach himself, at somewhat of a distance from a passing succession of nightmarish images similar to those accompanying Murphy on the occasion of his flight toward death.

It is again this breach of the ego that Beckett wishes to expand and, like Freud, the Irish writer points out the way by suggesting an ethic that plunges us into mourning but that should not be confused with the Protestant ethics of debt. This work of mourning in progress constitutes a memory and a language against which the subject's survival will be measured, overwhelming it with a duty to survive, when death seems to offer, after all, an easy solution. The duty to not die is expanded as is the duty to speak—even if this is impossible because there is nothing to say and because the means to articulate the lack are missing, as is emphasized by Beckett's famous formula that states the incapacity of expression linked to the absolute obligation of expression.

The wish, then, is to plunge the world into mourning, as if to darken its colors, so that a flash of light will be allowed to burst forth here and there. This is exactly what produces in Beckett's texts the dark hilarity, that cosmic com-

edy that aims, above all, at combatting the return of the Platonism of the beautiful form.

If Belacqua's languid leave-taking has to be relayed to us through his former
friend, Dante, always ready to play the guide for him and all the others, at least
Malone, whose death is surely drawn out a bit, will not deprive us of his diary,
of this never to be fully written account of survival, which alludes ironically to
Chateaubriand's memoirs from beyond the grave, his *Mémoires d'outre-tombe:*

> The truth is, if I did not feel myself dying, I could well believe myself dead,
> expiating my sins, or in one of heaven's mansions. But I feel at last that the
> sands are running out, which would not be the case if I were in heaven, or in
> hell. Beyond the grave, the sensation of being beyond the grave [*de l'outre-
> tombe* in the French original version] was stronger with me six months ago.
> . . . When I have completed my inventory, if my death is not ready for me
> then, I shall write my memoirs. That's funny, I have made a joke.[16]

Preface

1. Jean-Michel Rabaté, *La Pénultième est morte: Spectrographies de la modernité* (Seyssel: Champ Vallon, 1993). This book expands the main issues broached in a collection of essays on Lacanian perspective, focusing on beauty and mourning, *La Beauté amère: Fragments d'esthétiques* (Seyssel: Champ Vallon, 1989). I wish to thank Jonathan Barnett, who has worked with me on the English version of the present book. He prepared a first version of three chapters, subsequently modified, and revised my own translations and rewriting throughout.

2. Jacques Derrida, "Structure, Sign, and Play in the Discourse of the Human Sciences," translated by Alan Bass, in *Writing and Difference* (Chicago: University of Chicago Press, 1967).

3. For a good summary of Kojève's theories and influence, see Vincent Descombes, *Modern French Philosophy*, translated by L. Scott-Fox and J. M. Harding (Cambridge: Cambridge University Press, 1980), 27–48. In summary, we might say that for Hegel the subject of absolute knowledge is always "the man who *knew* too much," a Hitchcockian phrase that is revealing through its compulsory use of the past tense.

4. Roland Barthes, "The Death of the Author," translated by Stephen Heath, in *Image-Music-Text* (Glasgow: Fontana, 1977), 142–48.

5. T. S. Eliot, "Tradition and the Individual Talent," in *The Sacred Wood* (London: Methuen, 1972), 49. Hereafter abbreviated as *SW*.

6. See Friedrich Nietzsche, "On the Uses and Disadvantages of History for Life," translated by R. J. Hollindale, in *Untimely Meditations* (Cambridge: Cambridge University Press, 1983), 59–123. I shall return to this discussion in chapter 9.

7. Paul de Man, "Literary History and Literary Modernity," in *Blindness and Insight*, 2d ed. (London: Routledge, 1989), 142–65.

8. Harold Bloom, *The Anxiety of Influence: A Theory of Poetry* (London: Oxford University Press, 1973), 15–16, 139–55. Hereafter abbreviated as *AI*.

9. Annette Kolodny, "A Map for Rereading: Gender and the Interpretation of Literary Texts," *New Literary History* 11 (1980), reprinted in *The Critical Tradition*, edited by D. H. Richter (New York: St. Martin's Press, 1989), 1126–37.

10. Jorge Luis Borges, "Pierre Menard, autor del Quijote," in *Obras completas (1923–1972)* (Buenos Aires: Emecé, 1974), 444–50.

11. Eliot, "Gerontion," in *The Complete Poems and Plays* (London: Faber, 1985), 38. Hereafter abbreviated as *CPP*.

12. Eliot, *The Family Reunion*, *CPP*, 334–35. The *Family Reunion* contains a crucial statement about the connection of modernism with Greek tragedy in that it presents a "theory of ghosts" in dramatic form. These apparitions can be divided into "specters" (*CPP*, 289), which seems to be the generic term reserved for the "return of the re-

pressed" in general, "phantasms" (*CPP*, 335) calling up "imaginary" visions more private than public, "phantoms" when the symbolic determination by the family in its legacy of guilt is stressed (*CPP*, 334), and finally simply "ghosts" when the Eumenides appear in the real of the stage (*CPP*, 310–11). The three main Lacanian categories are useful here, as always when it is important to distinguish between types of visual illusions in a network that blends notions of symbolic debt and the dramatic acting out of its effects.

13. Ezra Pound, *Personae*, edited by L. Baechler and A. W. Litz (New York: New Directions, 1990), 251.

14. Pound, "Early Translators of Homer," in *Literary Essays*, edited by T. S. Eliot (London: Faber, 1964), 260. Hereafter abbreviated as *LE*.

15. Pound, *The Cantos* (London: Faber, 1968), canto 1, p. 8. I have developed this analysis of Elpenor as a Derridean image of doubling, secondarity, and supplement in my *Language, Sexuality, and Ideology in Ezra Pound's Cantos* (London: Macmillan, 1986), 67–70.

16. Pound, *Selected Letters, 1907–1941*, edited by D. D. Paige (New York: New Directions, 1971), 210.

17. See Daniel Tiffany, *Radio Corpse: Ezra Pound and the Cryptic Image of Modernism* (Cambridge, Mass.: Harvard University Press, 1995).

18. Sigmund Freud, "Thoughts for the Times on War and Death," *The Standard Edition of the Complete Psychological Works of Sigmund Freud* (London: Hogarth, 1953), 14:293. Hereafter abbreviated as *SE*. I also refer here to the German text, "Zeitgemässes über Krieg und Tod," in Freud, *Fragen der Gesellschaft: Ursprünge der Religion* (Francfort: Fischer Studien-Ausgabe, 1974), 54.

19. Freud, "Zeitgemässes über Krieg und Tod," 60.

20. Eliot, *Four Quartets*, *CPP*, 193.

21. Nicolas Abraham, "Notes on the Phantom: A Complement to Freud's Metapsychology," in Nicolas Abraham and Maria Torok, *The Shell and the Kernel*, translated by N. T. Rand (Chicago: University of Chicago Press, 1994), 172.

22. See Nicolas Abraham's extraordinary addition to Shakespeare's play in "The Phantom of *Hamlet*, or the Sixth Act," in Abraham and Torok, *Shell and the Kernel*, 191–205. Hereafter abbreviated as *SK*.

23. Jürgen Habermas, *The Philosophical Discourse of Modernity*, translated by F. G. Lawrence (Cambridge, Mass.: MIT Press, 1991).

24. Immanuel Kant, *Träume eines Geistersehers* (Hamburg: Felix Meiner Verlag, 1975). Kant writes, "I do not understand at all what the word 'Spirit' [Geist] means" (6).

25. Kant, "Ekstatische Reise eines Schwärmers durch die Geisterwelt," subtitle of the second half of *Träume eines Geistersehers*, 50.

26. Arthur Schopenhauer, "Essay on Spirit Seeing and Everything Connected Therewith," in *Parerga and Paralipomena: Short Philosophical Essays*, translated by E. F. J. Payne (Oxford: Clarendon Press, 1974), 237. Hereafter abbreviated as *ESS*.

27. Schopenhauer, *ESS*, translated as "dreaming of reality" (240) and as "dreaming of what is real" (247). See also his *Parerga und Paralipomena*, vol. 1 (Zürich: Haffman, 1991), same pagination as in the English edition.

28. Derrida, *Specters of Marx*, translated by P. Kamuf (New York: Routledge, 1994). A footnote (p. 192) acknowledges the coincidence of a similar reading of Marx's critique of Stirner in *La Pénultième est morte* and *Spectres de Marx*.

29. Derrida, *Of Spirit: Heidegger and the Question*, translated by G. Bennington and R. Bowlby (Chicago: University of Chicago Press, 1989).

30. Walter Benjamin, "The Work of Art in the Age of Mechanical Reproduction," in *Illuminations*, translated by H. Zohn (New York: Schocken, 1969), 217–51. A footnote insists on the idea that "aura" implies "unapproachability": the auratic object remains "distant, however close it may be" (243n. 5).

31. John Hollander, "Yellow," in *Spectral Emanations* (New York: Atheneum, 1978), 15.

Introduction: "The Penultimate . . . is dead"

1. Roland Barthes, *Incidents* (Paris: Seuil, 1987), 80.

2. In the author's preface to his *Memoirs*, written when he was 78. See the *Memoirs of François René Vicomte de Chateaubriand*, vol. 1, translated by A. T. de M. (New York: Putnam's Sons, 1942), xxx. Hereafter abbreviated as *Memoirs*.

3. See the excellent study of Baudelaire's concept of *modernité* by Gérald Froidevaux, *Baudelaire: Représentation et Modernité* (Paris: Corti, 1989), 31. Froidevaux quotes this passage of the *Memoirs*, adding that it is the first occurrence of the term, albeit in a derogatory sense. This has also been noticed by Matei Calinescu in "The Idea of Modernity," in *Five Faces of Modernity* (Durham, N.C.: Duke University Press, 1987), 42–43. The most comprehensive investigation of the term "modern" is in Hans Ulrich Gumbrecht, "A History of the Concept 'Modern,'" in *Making Sense in Life and Literature* (Minneapolis: University of Minnesota Press, 1992), 79–110.

4. See, among many other books, Anthony J. Cascardi, *The Subject of Modernity* (Cambridge: Cambridge University Press, 1992). See also Jean-François Lyotard, *The Postmodern Condition*, translated by G. Bennington and B. Massumi (Minneapolis: University of Minnesota Press, 1984); Jürgen Habermas, *The Philosophical Discourse of Modernity*, translated by F. G. Lawrence (Cambridge, Mass.: MIT Press, 1987); and Gianni Vattimo, *The End of Modernity*, translated by J. R. Snyder (Baltimore, Md.: Johns Hopkins University Press, 1988).

5. I am alluding to the famous last line of "L'Azur" (*"Je suis hanté. L'Azur! l'Azur! l'Azur! l'Azur!"*), which provides the key to the whole collection of early poems. See Stéphane Mallarmé, *Oeuvres complètes*, edited by H. Mondor (Paris: Gallimard, 1945), 38. Hereafter *OC* followed by page number.

6. See Jacques Scherer's edition of Mallarmé's notes for his never completed project in *Le "Livre" de Mallarmé* (Paris: Gallimard, 1957).

7. Lyotard explains how the notion of postmodernism is itself a paradox, since *modo* (just now, a while ago) and *post* combine to suggest an anterior future, in turn suggesting that postmodernity may well have anticipated modernity. See Lyotard, *Le Postmoderne expliqué aux enfants* (Paris: Galilée, 1986), 30–31, translated by Régis Durand as "Answering the Question: What is Postmodernism?" in *The Postmodern Condition* (Minneapolis: University of Minnesota Press), 79–81.

8. Stéphane Mallarmé, "Autobiography," in *Selected Prose, Poems, Essays, and Letters*, translated by B. Cook (Baltimore, Md.: Johns Hopkins University Press, 1956), 15.

9. Ibid., 16.

10. I develop this in *Joyce Upon the Void* (London: Macmillan, 1991), 195–97.

11. I use Robert Greer Cohn's translation in his *Mallarmé's Prose Poems* (Cambridge: Cambridge University Press, 1987), 6–7. Hereafter *MPP* followed by page number.

12. See Edgar Allan Poe, "The Philosophy of Composition," in his *Great Short Works* (New York: Harper and Row, 1970), 529–36.

13. Wallace Stevens, "The Emperor of Ice-Cream," in *Collected Poems* (New York: Random House, 1982), 64.

14. James Joyce, *Ulysses: The Corrected Text*, edited by H. W. Gabler (London: Penguin, 1986), 601.

15. The coupling of the hysterical and obsessional structures as typical of the female subject for the first, of the male subject for the second, runs through all of Lacan's works. See for instance, Jacques Lacan, "Function and Field of Speech and Language" in *Écrits: A Selection*, translated by Alan Sheridan (New York: Norton, 1977), 89–90. See also "La Psychanalyse et son Enseignement," in *Écrits* (Paris: Seuil, 1966), 452–53.

16. See David Hayman's pioneering study, *Joyce et Mallarmé* (Paris: Minard, 1956).

17. Jacques Aubert has been the first to show how Joyce's references to Aquinas were in fact meditated by his reading of Bosanquet's neo-Hegelian aesthetics. See Aubert, *Introduction à l'esthétique de James Joyce* (Paris: Didier, 1973), translated as *The Aesthetics of James Joyce* (Baltimore, Md.: Johns Hopkins University Press, 1992), 8–10. I have developed this insight in *James Joyce, Authorized Reader* (Baltimore, Md.: Johns Hopkins University Press, 1991), 150–92.

18. I have already alluded to Vincent Descombes's brilliant analysis in *Modern French Philosophy*, 27–48. Descombes interestingly connects Hegel and Mallarmé in the context of the Kojèvian critique of a "pure" thought, implying the disappearance of the speaking subject (45). For Croce's criticism, see his *What Is Living and What Is Dead in the Philosophy of Hegel*, translated by D. Ainslie (London: Macmillan, 1915).

19. Charles Baudelaire, "The Seven Old Men," in *The Flowers of Evil*, translated by Roy Campbell (New York: New Directions, 1963), 111.

20. See Arthur Power, *Conversations with James Joyce* (London: Millington, 1978), 74.

21. Marcel Proust, *Remembrances of Things Past*, vol. 3, *Time Regained*, translated by A. Mayor (New York: Random House, 1981), 804. Hereafter abbreviated as *TR*.

22. Dante Alighieri, *The Divine Comedy: Inferno*, translated by A. Mandelbaum (New York: Bantam, 1980), 281.

23. See Derrida, *Given Time, I: Counterfeit Money*, translated by Peggy Kamuf (Chicago: University of Chicago Press, 1992).

Chapter One: The Master of Colors That Know

1. Joyce, *Ulysses*, 31. Hereafter abbreviated as *U*.

2. Dante, *Inferno*, canto 4, 130–31.

3. Aristotle, *De Anima*, translated by W. D. Ross, in *The Works of Aristotle* (Oxford:

Clarendon Press, 1931), 3:418 a. 7. Joyce read Aristotle systematically during his first Paris stay; he used the 1846 French translation of J. Barthelemy Saint Hilaire, *Psychologie d'Aristote*, which translates "transparent" as "diaphane."

4. Aristotle, *De Sensu*, in *Works*, 3:439 a.

5. Pierre Vitoux, "Aristotle, Berkeley and Newman in 'Proteus' and in *Finnegans Wake*," *James Joyce Quarterly* 18, no. 2 (1981): 161–75.

6. George Berkeley, *An Essay Towards a New Theory of Vision* (London: Dent, 1969), 73. Hereafter abbreviated as *NTV*.

7. From the early *Portrait of the Artist*, which begins with the idea that "features of infancy" are reproduced in the adolescent portrait and in the adult person, Joyce always linked his aesthetic theory not only with the act of apprehension but with the genesis of all the categories (perceptual and linguistic) that allow for such an apprehension. In *Stephen Hero*, a typical statement made by Stephen ("If you were an esthetic philosopher you would take note of all my vagaries because here you have the spectacle of the esthetic instinct in action. The philosophic college should spare a detective for me") anticipates the program of a Joyce who will later bequeath all his notebooks and drafts to future researchers. See *Stephen Hero* (London: Jonathan Cape, 1975), 191.

8. See William T. Noon, *Joyce and Aquinas* (New Haven, Conn.: Yale University Press, 1963), chap. 6.

9. See Stephen's exposition of his evolutionary aesthetic in *Portrait of the Artist*, edited by Chester Anderson (Harmondsworth: Penguin, 1968), 212–15.

10. Freud, *Leonardo da Vinci and a Memory of His Childhood* (1910), in *SE*, 11:76. Hereafter abbreviated as *LVMC*.

11. Malcom Bowie, *Freud, Proust, Lacan: Theory as Fiction* (Cambridge: Cambridge University Press, 1987). See also Jean Kimball, "Freud, Leonardo, and Joyce: The Dimensions of a Childhood Memory," *James Joyce Quarterly*, 17 no. 2 (1980): 165–82.

12. Freud, *The Moses of Michelangelo* (1914), in *SE*, 13:212.

13. Da Vinci, *The Notebooks of Leonardo da Vinci*, edited by E. MacCurdy (New York: George Brailler, 1955), 873–74. Hereafter abbreviated as *Notebooks*.

14. For the Italian original, see *Notebooks of Leonardo da Vinci*, vol. 1, edited by Jean-Paul Richter (New York: Dover, 1970), 254.

15. Meyer Schapiro, "Leonardo and Freud: An Art-Historical Study" (1954), in *Renaissance Essays*, edited by P. O. Kristeller and P. P. Wiener (New York: Harper and Row, 1968), 303–36.

16. Ibid., 330.

17. Ibid., 331.

18. K. R. Eissler, *Leonardo da Vinci: Psychoanalytic Notes on the Enigma* (New York: International Universities Press, 1961). Hereafter abbreviated as *LV*. Eissler's book immediately acknowledges the importance of Freud's mistake on the *nibbio* and the total lack of relevance of the mythological comparison with Egyptian mythology. Eissler then not only questions Schapiro's historical assumptions but attempts to make a case for a specifically psychoanalytical reading of Leonardo's works. Although his conclusions seem a little hazardous, especially when he documents Leonardo's obsession with sexual control, his critique of Schapiro's arguments is devastating.

19. Schapiro, "Leonardo and Freud," 336.

20. Denis Diderot, *Oeuvres esthétiques* (Paris: Garnier, 1959), 805 (my translation).

21. Roger de Piles, *The Art of Painting and the Lives of the Painters*, translated by J. Nutt (London, 1706), 13.

22. Ibid., 14.

23. Ibid., 124.

24. G. W. F. Hegel, *Aesthetik*, edited by F. Bassenge (Francfort: Europaïsche Verlagsanstalt, 1955), 2:220 (my translation).

25. Diderot, *Oeuvres esthétiques*, 677 (my translation).

26. Ibid., 681.

27. Jacqueline Lichtenstein, *The Eloquence of Color: Rhetoric and Painting in the French Classical Age*, translated by Emily McVarish (Berkeley: University of California Press, 1993).

28. De Piles, *Cours de Peinture par Principes* (Nîmes: Jacqueline Chambon, 1990), 33–34. Hereafter abbreviated as *PP*.

29. See Derrida, *The Truth in Painting*, translated by Geoff Bennington and Ian McLeod (Chicago: University Press of Chicago, 1987).

30. Michel Pastoureau, *Couleurs, images, symboles: Etudes d'histoire et d'anthropologie* (Paris: Le Léopard d'Or, 1989).

31. I owe this insight to Florence de Mèredieu, "L'implosion dans le champ des couleurs," in *Communications* 48, Special Issue on Video (1988): 247–59.

32. Antonin Artaud, *Van Gogh: The Man Suicided by Society* (1947), in *Selected Writings*, translated by Helen Weaver (New York: Farrar, Strauss, and Giroux, 1976), 483. The slashes indicate paragraph breaks.

33. Ibid., 510.

34. See William Gass, *On Being Blue: A Philosophical Inquiry* (Boston: David R. Godine, 1976), 60 (on "green" as obscene), and 67–71 (on spectral colors and Bishop Berkeley's theory of vision).

35. Jorge Luis Borges, quoted in *Borges en la Escuela Freudiana de Buenos Aires* (Buenos Aires: Agalma, 1993), 75.

36. Alain Coulange, "Portrait," in *Gestes de rien, et pour rien* (Paris: Aencrages, 1983) (my translation).

Chapter Two: André Breton's Ghostly Stance

1. Maurice Blanchot, "Réflexions sur le surréalisme" (Reflexions on surrealism), in *La Part du feu* (Paris: Gallimard, 1949), 90.

2. Catalogue of *André Breton et la Beauté convulsive* (Paris: Centre Pompidou, 1991).

3. Breton, *Nadja*, translated by Richard Howard (New York: Grove Press, 1960), 160. Hereafter abbreviated as *N*.

4. Blanchot, "Réflexions," 93.

5. I am summarizing Blanchot's complex argument found in "Tomorrow at Stake," in *The Infinite Conversation*, translated by S. Hanson (Minneapolis: University of Minnesota Press, 1993), 407–21.

6. I translate literally from the French text in the Pléiade edition of Breton, *Oeuvres*

complètes, edited by M. Bonnet, P. Bernier, E.-A. Hubert, and J. Pierre (Paris: Gallimard, 1988), 1:647. Hereafter abbreviated as *OC*.

7. Breton, *Surrealism and Painting*, translated by S. W. Taylor (New York: Harper and Row, 1972), 13. Hereafter abbreviated as *SP*.

8. See *OC*, 1:1525, which refers to Rivière's article in *La Nouvelle revue française*.

9. See *OC*, 1:195. This is the "Confession Dédaigneuse" (Disdainful confession) with which *Les Pas perdus* starts.

10. See Jacques Lacan, "Kant with Sade," translated by James B. Swenson Jr., *October* 51 (Winter 1989): 54–104.

11. Breton, *Les Pas perdus*, *OC*, 1:202.

12. In *La Révolution surréaliste*, July 1925.

13. See Breton, *L'Amour fou*, in *OC*, edited by M. Bonnet (Paris: Gallimard, 1992), 2:687. See also Breton, *Mad Love*, translated by M. A. Caws (Lincoln: University of Nebraska Press, 1987), 19.

14. Breton, "Introduction to the New York Catalogue of Yves Tanguy's Paintings," New York, 1956, from a personal communication of José Pierre.

15. André Breton and Paul Eluard, *The Immaculate Conception*, translated by Jon Graham (London: Atlas Press, 1990). Hereafter abbreviated as *IC*.

16. Benedetto Croce, *Ce qui est vivant et ce qui est mort de la philosophie de Hegel*, translated by H. Buriot, Giard, and Brière (Paris, 1910; rpt. Dubuque: Reprint Library Brown, n.d.), 51–52. The reference is discussed in *OC* 1:1561–62. Croce's text hereafter abbreviated as *CQVM*.

17. Breton, *Mad Love*, 11.

18. Hegel, *La Philosophie de la nature de Hegel*, 2 vols., translated and annotated by A. Véra (Paris: Ladrange, 1863–66) 1:563. Hereafter abbreviated as *PN*.

19. Breton, *SP*, 346. The original French text quotes Hegel's expression in German. I have reproduced it in parentheses. This letter is added (in a footnote) by Véra to his French version and is not in the German or English texts.

20. *Hegel's Philosophy of Nature*, edited by and translated by M. J. Petry (London: Allen and Unwin, 1970), 2:139. Hereafter abbreviated as *HPH*. I have often used Petry's excellent annotations.

21. Hegel, *The Phenomenology of Mind*, translated by J. B. Baillie (New York: Harper and Row, 1967), 105. I have modified the translation (from 1910 originally).

22. Benedetto Croce, *Aesthetic*, translated by Douglas Ainslie (New York: Farrar, Strauss, and Giroux, 1969), 302–3.

23. I have already alluded to Descombes's summary in his *Modern French Philosophy*, 27–48.

24. Breton, *OC*, 1:807–8. See also 1:1611, the note which identifies Jacques Prévert as the dissident voice and coauthor of *Un Cadavre*, the pamphlet that attacked Breton.

25. Breton, *Earthlight*, translated by B. Zavatsky and Z. Rogow (Los Angeles: Sun and Moon Press, 1993), 102.

26. Ibid., 62. I have modified the translation.

Chapter Three: Roland Barthes, Ghostwriter of Modernity

1. Roland Barthes's "The Death of the Author" was published in 1968. I use Stephen Heath's translation in *Image-Music-Text* (Glasgow: Fontana, 1977), 142–48. The term of "biographeme" is used rather systematically in the 1971 introduction to *Sade, Fourier, Loyola*, translated by Richard Miller (Berkeley: University of California Press, 1989), 9. See page 8 where Barthes has announced "the amicable return of the author."

2. Paul Valéry, *Discours pour le centenaire de la photographie* (Paris: Institut de France, 1939).

3. Lacan, *The Four Fundamental Concepts of Psychoanalysis*, translated by Alan Sheridan (New York: Norton, 1978), 50–64. This passage is explicitly quoted by Barthes in *Camera Lucida* (4), in an allusion to the Aristotelian concept of "tuché."

4. Barthes, "Deliberation" (1979), in *The Rustle of Language*, translated by Richard Howard (Berkeley: University of California Press, 1989), 372. Hereafter abbreviated as *RL*.

5. See *Incidents*, translated by Richard Howard (Berkeley: University of California Press, 1992), 51–52, for a similar evocation of Paris.

6. Barthes, *Camera Lucida*, translated by Richard Howard (New York: Noonday Press, 1981), 9. Hereafter abbreviated as *CL*.

7. Alain Robbe-Grillet, *Le Miroir qui revient* (Paris: Minuit, 1984), 62–63.

8. In *Critique* (1954, 1955). Republished in *Essais critiques* (1964). See the recent edition of Barthes's *Oeuvres complètes*, edited by E. Marty (Paris: Seuil, 1993), 1:1185–93, 1:1212–17.

9. 1963 preface to Bruce Morissette, ed., *Les romans de Robbe-Grillet*, in *Oeuvres complètes*, 1:1317–22.

10. Robbe-Grillet, "Pourquoi j'aime Barthes," in *Prétexte: Roland Barthes*, edited by A. Compagnon (Paris: UGE, 10/18, 1978), 257.

11. A point made by Guy Scarpetta and quoted by D. A. Miller in *Bringing Out Roland Barthes* (Berkeley: University of California Press, 1992), 26–27.

12. "From *Roland Barthes by Roland Barthes*," in *A Barthes Reader*, edited by Susan Sontag (New York: Noonday Press, 1982), 420.

13. Barthes speaks of his ethical recoil in front of the remotivation of form upon which mythologies are founded, in *Mythologies*, translated by Annette Lavers (New York: Noonday Press, 1972), 126.

14. Denis Roche, "Un discours affectif sur l'image," *Magazine littéraire: Special issue Roland Barthes* no. 314 (Oct. 1993): 67.

15. I have been guilty of that simplification in *La Beauté amère*, in a chapter devoted to Barthes and photography.

16. Barthes, *Mythologies* (Paris: Seuil, 1957), 120 (my translation). Hereafter abbreviated as *M*.

17. Barthes, "The Third Meaning: Research Notes on Some Eisenstein Stills," in *Image-Music-Text*, 52–68.

18. See my discussion of Freud, "The Moses of Michelangelo," in chapter 1, about telling details enabling a good analyst to discover the mystery hidden in great works of art.

19. I am referring to the family album provided in *Roland Barthes par Roland Barthes* (Paris: Seuil, 1975), 7. The same photograph is discussed by D. A. Miller in *Bringing Out Roland Barthes*, 34.

20. The slightly different concept of the photograph as a "message without a code" can be found in Barthes, "The Photographic Message," in *Image-Music-Text*, 17.

21. Georges Didi-Huberman, "The Index of the Absent Wound (Monograph on a Stain)," in *October: The First Decade, 1978–1986*, edited by A. Michelson, R. Krauss, D. Crimp, and J. Copjec (Cambridge, Mass.: MIT Press, 1987), 39–57.

22. Pierre Madaule, *Véronique et les chastes* (Dijon: Ulysse- fin-de-siècle, 1988).

23. Ibid., 65.

Chapter Four: Mallarmé's Crypts

1. Freud, "Formulations on the Two Principles of Mental Functioning," *SE*, 12:225.

2. I quote Paul Auster's translation of *Pour un tombeau d'Anatole*, edited by Jean-Pierre Richard (Paris: Seuil, 1961) as *A Tomb for Anatole* (San Francisco: North Point Press, 1983). Quotations in this chapter are from *Tomb for Anatole*, unless otherwise noted.

My page references are to Mallarmé's *feuillets*, which are the same in the French and English versions. I use one slash in order to indicate line breaks and two slashes to indicate a new page. Some words are almost impossible to decipher (followed by question marks), while others are crossed out (in parentheses).

3. Ibid., 103. I modify Auster's translation of "il a creusé notre / tombe / en mourant / concession"; the text plays on the literal meaning of "plot" and on the rhetorical figure I describe, which is lost in his choice of "has granted it."

4. Ibid., 36. I quote the original French text, which is very ambiguous: "sans qu'il en / *sache* rien / —à mon tour / à la jouer, par / cela même qu'enfant / ignore."

5. Ibid., 153, modified. The French phrasing implies that the betrayal consists of the fact that death is "ignorée," both unknown and ignored.

6. Jules Laforgue, who was to have such an influence on T. S. Eliot's decision to become a poet and who claimed to have a deep affinity with Mallarmé, attempted to found his poetic system on the notion of the unconscious. For instance, he wrote a "Propitiatory Complaint to the Inconscient (*sic*)." See *Poems of Jules Laforgue*, translated by Peter Dale (London: Anvil Press, 1986), 35–37. For Laforgue, the unconscious was synonymous with "health" ("You must learn that the Unconscious never knows disease"). This comes from an essay on aesthetics in which he states that he "bows down in front of the Unconscious" ("Notes d'Esthétique," *La Revue blanche* 11 [1896]; rpt. in Laforgue, *Textes de critique d'art* [Lille: Presses Universitaires de Lille, 1988], 158).

7. Serge Leclaire, *On tue un enfant: Essai sur le narcissisme primaire et la pulsion de mort* (Paris: Seuil, 1975).

8. Mallarmé, *Poems*, translated by Roger Fry (New York: Oxford University Press, 1937), 245–47. Another (more literal) version is given in Leo Bersani, *The Death of*

Stéphane Mallarmé (Cambridge: Cambridge University Press, 1982), 95–96: "Does all Pride turn to smoke in the evening [Does all pride of the evening turn to smoke], / A torch snuffed out by a shake / Without the immortal puff of smoke / Being able to delay the desertion! // The old chamber of the heir / Or many a rich but fallen trophy / Would not even be heated / Were he to come through the hall. // Necessary agonies of the past / Gripping as if with claws / Disavowal's sepulchre, // Under the heavy marble it isolates / No other fire is lit / Than the flashing console."

9. Mauron discusses the last verse in this way: "The marble slab evokes on the one hand the chimney-piece of the empty fireplace, on the other the sepulchral slab, a sign of the inevitability of decadence" (*Poems*, 250–51). A systematic interpretation of Mallarmé's last sonnets as keyed to the death of Anatole has been given by André Vial in *Mallarmé: Tétralogie pour un enfant mort* (Paris: Corti, 1976).

10. Fry's translation of Mallarmé's *Poems*, 223.

11. Bersani, *Death of Mallarmé*, viii. Indeed, the vocabulary of the sublime is recurrent in Mallarmé's letters and aesthetic pronouncements. One of his most famous statements occurs in a letter to Cazalis dated from 1866: "Yes, *I know*, we are merely empty forms of matter, but we are indeed sublime in having invented God and our soul. So sublime, my friend, that I want to gaze upon matter, fully conscious that it exists, and yet launching itself madly into Dream, despite the knowledge that Dream has no existence, extolling the Soul and all the divine impressions of that kind which we have collected within us from the beginning of time and proclaiming, in the face of the Void which is truth, these glorious lies!"

One can observe the same logic whereby the act of *knowing* the truth of matter does not preclude the assertion of a necessary sublime lie. The "I know . . . but" functions here as the classical Freudian negation (*Verneinung*) and only needs to be connected with the dialectics of mourning and concession to apply in Anatole's case. I quote the *Selected Letters of Stéphane Mallarmé*, edited by and translated by Rosemary Lloyd (Chicago: University of Chicago Press, 1988), 60.

12. During the crisis of 1867, Mallarmé reached a state of utter annihilation:

I've just spent a terrifying year: my Thought has thought itself and reached a pure Concept. All that my being has suffered as a result during that long death cannot be told, but, fortunately, I am utterly dead, and the least pure region where my Spirit can venture is Eternity. My Spirit, that recluse accustomed to dwelling in its own Purity, is no longer darkened even by the reflection of Time. . . .

That will let you know that I am now impersonal and no longer the Stéphane that you knew, — but a capacity possessed by the spiritual Universe to see itself and develop itself, through what was once me. (*Selected Letters*, 74)

*Chapter Five: Verlaine and Mallarmé between the Angels
and the Ghosts of Languages*

1. Stéphane Mallarmé, *Oeuvres complètes*, edited by H. Mondor and G. Jean-Aubry (Paris: Gallimard, 1961), 363–64. Hereafter abbreviated as *OC*. All translations mine.

2. Paul Valéry, "Stéphane Mallarmé," in *Oeuvres complètes*, vol. 1, edited by J. Hytier (Paris: Gallimard, 1965), 631 (my translations). Hereafter abbreviated as *O*.

3. See the very useful preface, "Les traductions d'Edgar Poe par Mallarmé," by Léon Lemonnier, in *Poèmes d'Edgar Poe*, edited by Lemmonier (Paris: José Corti, 1949), 9–12.

4. Paul Verlaine, *Oeuvres poétiques complètes*, vol. 1, edited by Y. G. Le Dantec (Paris: Gallimard, Pléiade, 1938), 135. Hereafter abbreviated as *OP*. This translation is from *Paul Verlaine: Selected Poems*, translated by C. F. MacIntyre (Berkeley: University of California Press, 1948), 135. All other translations are mine.

5. In 1867 Mallarmé describes his "terrible struggle with that old and cruel plumage, fortunately struck down, God." See his *Correspondence, 1862–1871*, edited by H. Mondor (Paris: Gallimard, 1959), 241.

6. Ibid., 53.

7. Mallarmé, *OC*, 872. In this same response to an inquiry about literary evolution, Mallarmé makes Verlaine the "true father of all youth" because he fought against the influence of Parnasse.

8. See Julia Kristeva, *Revolution in Poetic Language*, translated by Margaret Waller (New York: Columbia University Press, 1984), 195. Unhappily, the English version is extremely abridged and does not translate the chapters devoted to Mallarmé in the French text of 1974.

9. Scherer, *Le "Livre" de Mallarmé*, 11 (A).

10. See Lemonnier, *Poèmes d'Edgar Poe*, 9–12.

11. Mallarmé to Eugène Lefébure, May 17, 1867, translated by Bradford Cook, in Mallarmé, *Selected Poetry and Prose*, edited by Mary Ann Caws (New York: New Directions, 1982), 88.

12. Walter Benjamin, "Theses on the Philosophy of History," in *Illuminations*, translated by Harry Zohn (New York: Schocken Books, 1969), 257–58.

Chapter Six: Broch's Modernity as Crime, or the Sleepwalking of Theory

1. Roger Dragonetti, *Un fantôme dans le kiosque: Mallarmé et l'esthétique du quotidien* (Paris: Seuil, 1992).

2. The important question of the role of the crowd in Mallarmé's work has been excellently treated by Peter Dayan, in his chapter entitled "La Foule," in *Mallarmé's Divine Transposition: Real and Apparent Sources of Literary Value* (Oxford: Clarendon Press, 1986), 47–94.

3. See Zeev Sternhell, *Neither Right nor Left: Fascist Ideology in France*, translated by D. Maisel (Berkeley: University of California Press, 1986), and Sternhell with M. Sznajder and M. Asheri, *The Birth of Fascist Ideology: From Cultural Rebellion to Political Revolution*, translated by D. Maisel (Princeton, N.J.: Princeton University Press, 1994).

4. Hermann Broch, *The Sleepwalkers*, translated by W. and E. Muir (New York: Universal Library, 1964). Hereafter abbreviated as *S*.

5. The best introduction to Broch in English is still Ernestine Schlant, *Hermann Broch* (Boston: Twayne, 1978). Peter Gay's perceptive comments on German modern-

ism can provide a useful background; see particularly his chapter "Encounter with Modernism: German Jews in Wilhelminian Culture," in *Freud, Jews and Other Germans: Masters and Victims in Modernist Culture* (Oxford: Oxford University Press, 1978).

6. Broch, *Briefe, 1929–1959*, in *Gesammelte Werke* (Zürich: Rhein Verlag, 1957), 8:149.

7. See Breon Mitchell, *James Joyce and the German Novel, 1922–1933* (Athens: Ohio University Press, 1976), 151–74. See also my article, "Joyce and Broch, or Who Was the Crocodile?" in *Comparative Literature Series* 19 no. 2 (1982): 121–33.

8. See "Kultur 1908/1909" in Broch, *Philosophische Schriften*, edited by Paul Michael Lützeler (Francfort: Suhrkamp, 1977), 1:11–30. The essay on Loos, "Ornaments (The Case Loos)" is in the same volume, 32–33. A good discussion of Broch's concept of "ecstasy" in all its cultural and political ramifications is in Hubertus Venzlaff, *Hermann Broch: Ekstase und Masse. Untersuchungen und Assoziationen zur politischen Mystik des 20. Jahrhunderts* (Bonn: Bouvier, 1981).

9. Adolph Loos, "Ornament und Verbrechen," in *Sämtliche Schriften*, edited by F. Gluck (Wien: Herold, 1962), 1:276–88.

10. Broch, "Notizen zu einer systematischen Ästhetik" (1912), in *Schriften zur Literatur*, edited by Paul Michael Lützeler (Francfort: Suhrkamp, 1975), 2:11–30.

11. Wilhelm Worringer, *Abstraktion und Einfühlung* (Munich, 1907), translated by M. Bullock as *Abstraction and Empathy* (Cleveland: Meridian Books, 1967).

12. I use Claudia Brodsky's literal translation of the original German text from her fascinating essay, "Writing and Building," in *Hermann Broch: Literature, Philosophy, Politics. The Yale Broch Symposium 1986*, edited by S. Dowden (Columbia: Camden House, 1988), 260. While totally in agreement with Brodsky's argument, which also underlines the discussion of postmodernity in architecture, I differ with her interpretation when she attributes the theses of the "Degradation of Values" unambiguously to Broch (260n. 1).

13. Ernst Bloch, *Geist der Utopie* (Francfort: Suhrkamp, 1973).

14. Ibid., 241.

15. Walter Benjamin, "Karl Kraus," in *Reflections*, translated by E. Jephcott (New York: Schocken Books, 1978), 272–73.

16. Broch first proposed his theory of kitsch in a 1933 lecture, which he later revised and read in English at Yale University in 1950. See "Notes on the Problem of Kitsch," in *Kitsch: The World of Bad Taste*, edited by Gillo Dorfles (New York: Bell, 1969), 49–67. See also Clement Greenberg's famous 1939 essay, "Avant-Garde and Kitsch," in *Art and Culture: Critical Essays* (Boston: Beacon Press, 1961), 3–21. Matei Calinescu has more recently confirmed Broch's idea of a link between kitsch and romanticism, in *Faces of Modernity: Avant-Garde, Decadence, Kitsch* (Bloomington: Indiana University Press, 1977), 240.

17. This notion is developed in Eco's recent essays on semiotics. See for example, *Limits of Interpretation* (Bloomington: Indiana University Press, 1990), 148–49.

18. Broch, *Briefe, 1929–1951*, 18. Also quoted in Schlant, *Hermann Broch*, 61.

19. It is mainly in his essay on Joyce (elaborated between 1931 and 1936) that Broch develops his conviction that one cannot describe any object without introducing the observing subject, which he called "the narrator as idea." This function, as well as the

language through which the object is represented, must be part of the "means of representation." See Broch, *Dichten und Erkennen, Essays, Band I, Gesammelte Werke*, (Zurich: Rhein Verlag, 1955), 6:197.

Chapter Seven: Beckett and the Ghosts of Departed Quantities

1. Wilfred R. Bion, *A Memoir of the Future* (London: Karnac Books, 1991), 95. Hereafter abbreviated as *MF*.

2. Flann O'Brien, *At Swim-Two-Birds* (1939; rpt. New York: Penguin, 1976). The novel, another Irish post-Joycean extravaganza, depicts at one point the revolt of fictional characters against their master and creator.

3. Berkeley, quoted in Bion, *Transformations: Change from Learning to Growth* (New York: Basic Books, 1965), 157. The book is a sort of metadiscourse that translates two other books, *Learning from Experience* and *Elements of Psycho-analysis*, into the set of concepts (all symbolized by letters and organized in a "grid" of functions) that Bion had invented.

4. Deidre Bair, *Samuel Beckett* (New York: Harcourt Brace Jovanovich, 1978). The link between Beckett and Bion has been explored by Didier Anzieu in "Beckett et Bion," *Revue de Psychothérapie* 5–6 (1986): 21–30, and more recently in his novelistic treatment of Beckett in *Beckett et le Psychanalyste* (Paris: Mentha, 1992). In the novel, for instance, Anzieu recreates their parallel diaries and imagines how Beckett and Bion vent their frustrations at each other (34–67). I had also developed the theoretical implications of the meeting between Beckett and Bion in "Beckett et le deuil de la forme," in *Beckett avant Beckett* (Paris: Presses de l'Ecole Normale Supérieure, 1984), 135–51.

5. The first trilogy (*Molloy* [1950], *Malone Dies* [1951], and *The Unnamable* [1952] — the dates are those of the French original version) has been published as one volume (London: Picador, 1979). I refer to this edition as the Trilogy. The second trilogy (*Company* [1980], *Ill Seen Ill Said* [1981], and *Worstward Ho* [1983]) has been published under the general title of *Nohow On* (New York: Calder, 1992).

6. Beckett, *Molloy*, in the Trilogy, 126. Hereafter abbreviated as *MO*.

7. Sighle Kennedy has a very interesting development on Morphe as the god of sleep and as form in *Murphy's Bed: A Study of Real Sources and Sur-Real Associations in Samuel Beckett's First Novel* (Lewisburg: Bucknell University Press, 1971), 62–64.

8. Joyce, *Dubliners* (New York: Viking Critical Library, 1976), 26.

9. Beckett, *Murphy* (1938; rpt. London: Picador, 1973), 6. Hereafter abbreviated as *MU*.

10. Published in Beckett, *Disjecta* (London: Calder, 1983), 55–57 (my translations). Hereafter abbreviated as *DIS*.

11. See Bair, *Beckett*, 174, 197–98.

12. David H. Hesla has brilliantly demonstrated the importance of Gueulincx's occasionalism in Beckett's early works. See his *Shape of Chaos* (Minneapolis: University of Minnesota Press, 1971).

13. The information about Mahony is derived from Vivian Mercier, *The Irish Comic Tradition* (Oxford: Oxford University Press, 1962), 223–24.

14. Gardner Murphy, *An Historical Introduction to Modern Psychology*, with a supplement by Heinrich Klürer (London: Kegan and Paul, 1929).

15. See Bair, *Beckett*, 240–50, for an almost surrealist evocation of Beckett's travels through Nazi Germany.

16. Murphy, *Historical Introduction*, 237–38.

17. Bion, "A Theory of Thinking," in *Second Thoughts: Selected Papers on Psycho-Analysis* (Northvale: Jason Aronson, 1993), 115.

18. Ibid., 18.

19. See J. S. Grotstein, preface to Bion, *Second Thoughts*. He writes: "Bion is often compared with Lacan, not only in terms of the complexity of their contributions, but also in terms of their similar journeys into the origins and nature of *meaning*. They both seem to distrust that truth can emerge from linear prose and therefore appear to induce or radiate meaning by a style that could be called *poetics* [*sic*]" (xi).

20. Bion, *Second Thoughts*, 165.

21. Wolfgang Köhler, in *Gestaltpsychology* (New York: Liveright, 1929), takes the term "isomorphism" as the conceptual basis for his system. Beckett seems to have also used Kurt Koffka's book, *Principles of Gestalt Psychology* (New York: Harcourt and Brace, 1935), 62–67, as well as the general discussion on the intelligence of apes in Köhler's *Mentality of Apes* (New York: Harcourt and Brace, 1925) for his novel. The chess-playing chimpanzees had fascinated him at the time of the writing of *Murphy*.

22. Koffka, *Principles of Gestalt Psychology*, 25–28, 55–61.

23. Ibid., 559ff, for a description of the Würzburg school and a critique of their theses in the name of monism and isomorphism.

24. Ibid., 208.

25. See Beckett, *Film* (New York: Grove Press, 1969), 11. I shall develop this in the next chapter.

26. Blanchot, *Thomas the Obscure*, translated by Robert Lamberton (New York: Station Hill Press, 1988), 14–15.

27. Bair, *Beckett*, 208–9.

28. Ibid., 208.

29. Blanchot, *Thomas the Obscure*, 15.

30. See Bion, *Transformations*, 158–59.

31. Ibid., 148.

32. Quoted in Bion, *Two Papers: The Grid and Caesura* (London: Karnac Books, 1989), 38. Bion used the passage in numerous talks and seminars.

33. Letter quoted in Bair, *Beckett*, 228.

Chapter Eight: Shades of the Color Gray

1. See Katharine Worth, "Beckett's Ghosts," in *Beckett in Dublin*, edited by S. E. Wilmer (Dublin: Lilliput Press, 1992), 62–74; Anjela Moorjani, "Beckett's Devious Deitics," in *Rethinking Beckett* (London: Macmillan, 1990), 20–30. In a very interesting way, Moorjani links the paradoxes of the utterance of a "Not-I" with the return of a cryptic voice of an entombed Other and refers to Abraham and Torok's concept of

"cryptonymia." Worth's essay describes as "ghost plays" the last television or theater plays from *Eh Joe* to *What Where*, collected in Beckett, *The Complete Dramatic Works* (London: Faber, 1990), 359–476. Hereafter abbreviated as *CDW*.

2. Gilles Deleuze, "L'épuisé," postface, in Beckett, *Quad et autres pièces pour la télévision* (Paris: Editions de Minuit, 1992), 86–88.

3. Ibid., 78.

4. From an interview in *Les Nouvelles Littéraires* in February 1961, translated in Lawrence Graver and Raymond Federman, eds., *Samuel Beckett: The Critical Heritage* (Boston: Routledge and Kegan Paul, 1979), 216.

5. Carla Locatelli, *Unwording the Word: Samuel Beckett's Prose Works after the Nobel Prize* (Philadelphia: University of Pennsylvania Press, 1990), 2–3.

6. Beckett, *Stories and Texts for Nothing* (New York: Grove Press, 1967). Hereafter abbreviated as *TN*.

7. The term "enunciation" is used here in the meaning given to it by Emile Benveniste in his *Problems of General Linguistics*. See Moorjani's article for a useful application of the term. More and more Beckettians feel obliged to use these notions in their approaches; above all, see the excellent unpublished thesis of Daniel Katz, "Summing Up: Subjectivity and Consciousness in the Prose of Samuel Beckett" (Ph.D. diss., Stanford University, 1993).

8. Alain Badiou, "L'écriture du générique: Samuel Beckett," in *Conditions* (Paris: Seuil, 1992), 329–66 (especially 340).

9. Eliot, *The Waste Land*, in *Collected Poems, 1909–1962* (London: Faber, 1963), 77. Eliot's note only refers to an account of an expedition to the Antarctic, when the explorers think there is one person too many, but does not point to the obvious allusion to Christ's return at Emmaus. The famous lines 411–14:

> *Dayadhvam*: I have heard the key
> Turn in the door once and turn once only
> We think of the key, each in his prison
> Thinking of the key, each confirms a prison

are glossed in the notes by reference to Bradley's account of solipsism.

10. Badiou, *Conditions*, 338–39.

11. Beckett, *Film*, with complete scenario, illustrations, production shots, and Alan Schneider's essay, "On Directing *Film*" (New York: Grove Press, 1969). Hereafter abbreviated as *F*.

12. Beckett, *Ill Seen Ill Said*, in *Nohow On* (New York: Calder, 1992), 58–60. I have numbered the paragraphs and indicated the numbers in brackets. Hereafter abbreviated as *ISIS*.

13. Monique Nagem, "Know Happiness: Irony in *Ill Seen Ill Said*," in *"Make Sense Who May": Essays on Samuel Beckett's Later Works*, edited by R. J. Davis and L. St. J. Butler (Gerrads Cross: Colin Smythe, 1988), 77–90.

14. Beckett had probably written the French version first. Its title, *Mal Vu Mal Dit*, could have been translated into "Misseen Missaid," as two passages of *Worstward Ho* suggest: "Say for be said. Missaid. From now say for be missaid," and "See for be seen.

Misseen. From now see for be misseen" (in *Nohow On*, 101, 104). Thus the English title can be considered as meaningful, even in these paragrammatic plays with initials. As most commentators have pointed out, the fate of Beckett's bilingual *oeuvre* is to create two intertextual networks that do not overlap completely.

15. Sir James George Frazer, *Adonis, Attis, Osiris* (1914; rpt. New York: St. Martin's Press, 1966), 2:119.

16. Eliot, *The Four Quartets*, in *Collected Poems, 1909–1962*, 211–12.

17. In his "German Letter" of 1937, in which he defines his new poetic of the "unword," Beckett seems to praise Gertrude Stein above Joyce: "Perhaps the logographs of Gertrude Stein are nearer to what I have in mind. At least the texture of language has become porous, if only, alas, quite by chance, as consequence of a technique similar to that of Feininger. . . . On the way to this literature of the unword, which is so desirable to me, some form of Nominalist irony might be a necessary stage" (translated from German by Ruby Cohn, *Disjecta*, 172–73).

18. Worth, "Beckett's Ghosts," 66.

Chapter Nine: Uncoupling Modernism

1. I have preferred Collins's 1910 translation to more recent versions, for historical reasons and also for his better sense of rhythm: Friedrich Nietzsche, "The Use and Abuse of History," from *Thoughts Out of Season*, in *The Complete Works of Friedrich Nietzsche*, 18 vols., edited by O. Levy, translated by A. Collins (Edinburgh and London: T. N. Foulis, 1909–13), 5:33, 5:55. See also Nietzsche, "On the Use and Disadvantages of History for Life," in *Untimely Meditations*, translated by R. J. Hollindale (Cambridge: Cambridge University Press, 1983), 79. Paul de Man has aptly summarized the entire argument. See his "Literary History and Literary Modernity," in *Blindness and Insight*, rev. ed. (London: Routledge, 1983), 142–65.

2. See Astradur Eysteinsson, *The Concept of Modernism* (Ithaca, N.Y.: Cornell University Press, 1990); Michael Levenson, *A Genealogy of Modernism* (Cambridge: Cambridge University Press, 1984); Andrew Ross, *The Failure of Modernism* (New York: Columbia University Press, 1986). One of the most symptomatic discussions can be found in Hugh Kenner's seminal essay "The Making of the Modernist Canon," in *Mazes* (San Francisco: North Point Press, 1989), 28–42. Hugh Kenner meditates very lucidly on the limits of a canon he himself helped to define, and he accounts for some of the more debatable "exclusions" such as Stevens and Woolf. See also the challenging theses (mainly drawn from Adorno) of Peter Bürger, *The Decline of Modernism* (University Park: Pennsylvania State University Press, 1992).

3. Wayne Koestenbaum, *Double Talk: The Erotics of Male Literary Collaboration* (New York: Routledge, 1989). Hereafter abbreviated as *DT*. I shall refer systematically to the chapter on *"The Waste Land:* T. S. Eliot's and Ezra Pound's Collaboration on Hysteria" (112–39).

4. See Richard Sieburth's study of Remy de Gourmont's influence on Pound, *Instigations: Pound and Remy de Gourmont* (Cambridge, Mass.: Harvard University Press, 1978), 68–93.

5. Edward Said, *Beginnings*, rev. ed. (New York: Columbia University Press, 1985), xiii.

6. Pound to René Taupin (in French), May 1928, in *Selected Letters, 1907–1941*, edited by D. D. Paige (New York: New Directions, 1950), 218. Hereafter abbreviated as *SL*.

7. I have already alluded to Gérard Froidevaux's rich study of Baudelaire's theory of modernity in *Baudelaire: Représentation et Modernité*.

8. I have developed this point in my *James Joyce* (Paris: Hachette, 1993), 9–23.

9. Arthur Rimbaud to Paul Demeny, May 15, 1871, in *Collected Poems*, translated by Oliver Bernard (London: Penguin, 1986), 16. Hereafter abbreviated as *CP*.

10. I use the translation provided by E. M. Lang in his version of Edmond Lepelletier's biography, *Paul Verlaine: His Life—His Work* (1909; rpt. New York: AMS Press, 1970), 256. I have modified it to remain closer to the original.

11. Kristeva, *Revolution in Poetic Language*.

12. I quote C. F. MacIntyre's translation in Verlaine's *Selected Poems* (Berkeley: University of California Press, 1948), 103.

13. Wyndham Lewis, *Blasting and Bombardiering* (London: Calder and Boyars, 1937), 32. The chapter is entitled "Mr. W. L. as Leader of the 'Great London Vortex.'" Lewis adds: "Life was one big bloodless brawl, prior to the Great Bloodletting" (35).

14. See Forrest Read, *Pound/Joyce* (London: Faber, 1968).

15. Eliot, *Letters of T. S. Eliot*, edited by Valerie Eliot (London: Faber, 1988), 1:497–99.

16. Ibid., 499.

17. I have developed this analysis in *Language, Sexuality and Ideology in Ezra Pound's Cantos* (London: Macmillan, 1986), 213–23.

18. Eliot, *The Waste Land: A Facsimile and Transcript of the Original Drafts Including the Annotations of Ezra Pound*, edited by Valerie Eliot (London: Faber, 1971), 47.

19. Ibid., 97.

20. Empedocles said: "For I have already become a boy and a girl / And a bush and a bird and a fiery fish from the sea" (*The Poems of Empedocles*, translated by Brad Inwood [Toronto: University of Toronto Press, 1992], 153).

21. This is what Flaubert writes when he describes the pleasure he takes in creating the world of *Madame Bovary*: "Today, for instance, man and woman, lover and beloved, I rode in a forest on an autumn afternoon under the yellow leaves and I was also the horse, the leaves, the wind, the words my people spoke, even the red sun that made them half-shut their love-drowned eyes." Flaubert, *Selected Letters*, translated by F. Steegmuller (New York: Random House, 1957), 163.

22. Eliot, *Letters*, 1:318.

23. Emile Benveniste, "Deux modèles linguistiques de la cité," in *Problèmes de linguistique générale* (Paris: Gallimard, 1974), 2:272–80.

24. *The Modernist: A Monthly Magazine of Modern Art and Letters* (New York, 1919). For the historical context, see John Unterecker, *Voyager: A Life of Hart Crane* (New York: Farrar, Strauss and Giroux, 1969), 145.

25. See Richard Perceval Graves, *Robert Graves: The Years with Laura Riding* (1926–

1940) (New York and London: Penguin, 1990), 18–25. For a feminist perspective on Laura Riding's stubborn resistance to all types of critical discourses, see K. K. Ruthven, "How to Avoid Being Canonized: Laura Riding," in *New Formations* 9 (Winter 1989): 242–60.

26. Robert Graves and Laura Riding, *A Survey of Modernist Poetry* (London: Heinemann, London, 1927). Hereafter abbreviated as *SMP*.

27. Laura Riding, *Collected Poems* (New York: Random House, 1938), 144. Hereafter abbreviated as *RCP*.

28. Breton, *What Is Surrealism? Selected Writings*, edited by Franklin Rosemont (New York: Monad Press/Pathfinder Press, 1978), 26.

29. Lisa Ruddick, *Reading Gertrude Stein: Body, Text, Gnosis* (Ithaca, N.Y.: Cornell University Press, 1990).

30. Quoted in Diana Souhami, *Gertrude and Alice* (London: Collins, 1991), 126. Hereafter abbreviated as *GA*.

31. Stein, *Selected Writings*, edited by Carl Van Vechten (New York: Random House, 1990), 52–53.

32. I have developed this in "Le modernisme et la peinture: Le cas de Gertrude Stein," *Interfaces* 5 (Spring 1994).

33. Stein, *Everybody's Autobiography* (London: Heineman, 1938), 70.

34. See *GA*, 157–58; and William Gass, "Gertrude Stein and the Geography of the Sentence," in *The World Within the Word* (Boston: Godine, 1979), 63–123.

35. Stein, *Everybody's Autobiography*, 67.

36. Stein, *Painted Lace* (New Haven, Conn.: Yale University Press, 1955), 43.

37. See Leo Steinberg, *Other Criteria* (New York: Oxford University Press, 1972), 55–91. Clement Greenberg's influential essay, "Modernist Painting," first published in 1965, was reprinted in *The New Art*, edited by G. Battcock (New York: Harper and Row, 1966).

38. Stein, *Geography and Plays* (Madison: University of Wisconsin Press, 1993), 8.

39. Alice Toklas added a few sentences to *Ada*, which remained in Gertrude's style: "Trembling was all living, living was loving, some one was then the other one. Certainly this one was loving this Ada then. And certainly Ada all her living then was happier in living than any one else who ever could, who was, who ever will be living." Quoted in *GA*, 137.

40. As for the famous additions of a few lines to the *Waste Land* that are clearly in Vivien Eliot's hand in the manuscript, they indeed testify to a collaboration, but suggest also the reasons for its failure. The famous line: "What you / get married for / if you don't / want to have / children" (*Waste Land: Facsimile*, 21), added by Vivien to the pub dialogue—bringing in a theme that looms so large in the recent play and film adaptation *Tom and Viv*—suggests how female hysteria could generate male hysteria as a response. This, in turn, may have led to the purely male collaboration with Pound. Although Pound never appears in the play and film, it is nevertheless interesting to see how they depict the way Vivien's brother, Maurice Haigh-Wood, becomes another "male collaborator" who works with "Tom" toward the exclusion, disenfranchisement, and final incarceration of "Viv."

41. Stein, *Geography and Plays*, 418–19.

42. Stein, *Selected Writings*, 610, 612.

Conclusion: The "Moderns" and Their Ghosts

1. Baruch Spinoza, "Correspondence," in *On the Improvement of the Understanding: The Ethics. Correspondence*, translated by R. H. M. Elwes (New York: Dover, 1955), 376. I shall refer to the Correspondence in this volume by *SCO* and to the Ethics in the same volume by *SET*.

2. Max Stirner, *The Ego and His Own*, translated by Steven T. Byington (New York: Benjamin R. Tucker, 1907), 33–34. Hereafter abbreviated as *EO*.

3. Karl Marx and Friedrich Engels, *The German Ideology*, in *Collected Works*, vol. 5 (New York: International Publishers, 1976), 152. Hereafter abbreviated as *GI*.

4. I use the revised but incomplete translation of Stirner's *Ego and His Own*, by John Carroll (London: Jonathan Cape, 1971), 261, and have changed "affair" into "cause" (*Sache*).

5. Jacques Schérer, *Le "Livre" de Mallarmé* (Paris: Gallimard, 1957).

6. I translate from "Deux feuillets inédits," by Stéphane Mallarmé in *fig*. 4 (Dec. 1990), 32.

7. I develop this point in the last chapter and conclusion of my *James Joyce*.

8. Ella Freeman Sharpe, "The Impatience of Hamlet," in *Collected Papers on Psychoanalysis* (London: Hogarth Press, 1950), 203–13.

9. See Nicolas Abraham, "Notes on the Phantom," in *SK*, 173.

10. Maria Torok, "Story of Fear," in *SK*, 177–86. See also Abraham and Torok, *The Wolf Man's Magic Word: A Cryptonomy* (Minneapolis: University of Minnesota Press, 1986).

11. Beckett's letter was originally written in German: "Ein Loch nach dem andern in ihr [der Sprache] zu bohren, bis das Dahinterkauende, sei es etwas oder nichts, durchzusickern anfängt—ich kann mir für den heutigen Schriftsteller kein höheres Ziel vorstellen" (*DIS*, 52).

12. Dante, *Purgatorio*, canto 4, l.127–31, in *The Divine Comedy*, translated by A. Mandelbaum (Berkeley: University of California Press, 1982), 37.

13. *The Letters of Arnold Zweig and Sigmund Freud*, edited by Ernst L. Freud, translated by E. and W. Robson-Scott (New York: Harcourt, Brace, and World, 1970), 11.

14. Ibid., 14.

15. Ibid.

16. *Malone Dies*, in the Trilogy, 169.

Index

romanticism, xix, 9–10, 12, 106, 124, 131, 141, 143, 146, 195–96, 222–3
Rosmini, A., 63
Ross, A., 189
Roujon, H., 110–11
Rothko, M., 213
Rubens, P. P., 33
Ruddick, L., 211
Rushdie, S., 81
Russell, B., 182

Sabellius, 20
Sade, D. A. F. de, 53, 228
Said, E., 191
Salomé, L.-A., 169
Sappho, xiii
Sartre, J.-P., 67, 80
Schapiro, M., 29–31
Scheerbart, P., 132
Schelling, F. W., 136
Schinkel, K. F., 133
Schneider, A., 177–79
Schopenhauer, A., xviii–xx, 14, 129–30
Schubert, F., 1
Schumann, R., 1
Seneca, 95
Shakespeare, W., xviii, 15, 18, 21, 207–8, 228–29
Sharpe, E., 228–29
Shelley, P. B., 195
shroud (sudarium), 29, 82
Silberer, H., 232
Sinclair, P., 157
sleepwalking, xix–xx, 14, 49, 122–47
Socrates, 16
Sollers, P., 1, 67
Solmi, E., 22
Soupault, P., 61, 189
Spinoza, B., xx, 4, 217–23, 228
Stalin, J., 57, 64
Stein, G., 141, 184, 188–89, 190, 205, 209, 210–215
Stein, L., 211–12
Steinberg, L., 213
Stella, F., 213
Sternhell, Z., 123
Stevens, W., xiii, 7
Stirner, M., xxi, 72–73, 222–28
Suetonius, 218

surrealism, xiv, 4, 12, 30, 42–46, 49–50, 57, 60–62, 64–65, 67–68, 81, 211, 216
Swedenborg, E., xviii–xix

Talbot, W. 77, 82
Tanguy, Y., 54, 65
Tate, A., 204
Tennyson, A., 197
Thiers, A., 53
Thomas, D., 208
Thyraeus, 218
Tiresias, xiv–xv, 191, 200
Toklas, A., 190, 205, 210–15
Tolstoy, L., x
Tommè, L. di, 31
Torok, M., xvii–xviii, 13, 171, 229, 231
transparency, 16–18, 52, 56, 63, 171–72
Trotsky, L., 57
Tzara, T., 77

Valéry, P., 12, 68, 102–3, 106, 107, 110–11
Van der Zee, J., 77
Van de Velde, H., 128
Van Gogh, V., 38–39
Vasari, G., 33
Vauvenargues, L. de, 53
Véra, A., 56–58
Verlaine, P., 5, 100, 100–107, 115, 189–90, 192–96, 200, 215
Veronica, 82
Vico, G., 9, 11, 63–64, 102
Villiers de l'Isle-Adam, M., 109
Virgil, 13–14, 147, 202
Virgin (Mary), 26–31, 37, 40, 184, 219
Virilio, P., 43
Vitoux, P., 19–20

Wagner, R., 108, 116–17, 119, 123
Warhol, A., 77, 213
Warren, R. P., 204
Watt, W., 158–59
Weininger, O., 130
Wessing, K., 75
Whitehead, A. N., 212
Wilde, O., 36
Williams, W. C., xiii, 203, 206, 212
Wilson, R., 78
Witt, J. and C., 221